Charles Dowding's
No dig gardening
Course 1
FROM WEEDS TO VEGETABLES EASILY AND QUICKLY

Charles has published ten books, alongside annual calendars and diaries of sowing dates.

He features in numerous gardening publications and
regularly teaches at his home in Somerset, South West England.

He is followed on YouTube and Instagram by over half a million people worldwide.

This book, published in 2020, and exclusive online videos, comprise his first online course,
originally released in February 2019.

© Charles Dowding 2020
Published by No Dig Garden 2020
Imprint of Charles Dowding Ltd

Edited by Anna Maskell
Copy edited by Elisabeth Ingles
Indexed by Helen Iddles
Designed by Lucy or Robert
Printed by Cambrian Press

Acknowledgements

The no dig adventure continues to amaze and delight a rapidly growing number of gardeners and farmers. Special thanks to Stephanie Hafferty for help at Homeacres, to Edward my son and David Adams for recording it on film, and to my many helpers who all bring something interesting to share while gardening. Most notably Felix Hofmann, Finn McAleer, Josh Rogers and Jasper Shaw; also James Blair who helped to formulate the quizzes while not digging at Homeacres. As for this book, Anna is a most thorough editor, and Lucy or Robert have laid it out beautifully.

PHOTOS & ILLUSTRATIONS

Heather Edwards front cover
Stephanie Hafferty p.7 top, p.8 middle, p.9 top, p.10 top, p.26 top, p.47 top two, p.48 top, p.49 top right, p.55, p.57 bottom, p.74 first, p.79 first, p.87 bottom right, p.89 left middle & top right, p.92 bottom, p.98, p.119 bottom left, p.122 left side top three, p.124 top left, p.128 top right, p.141 top, p.159 top left, p.166 top left, p.181 top right, p.188 mid left, p.203 bottom right, p.204
My mother Ruth Dowding p.13 top
Jonathan Buckley p.18
Susie Dowding p.20
Hannah Robinson cartoon p.24
Robin Baxter p.30 first
Ann Swithinbank p.39 right
Tenley Newton p.40 both photos on right
Karen Drexler p.43 bottom 3 photos
Finn McAleer p.48 second, p.88 top right
Sandy Marks p.48 bottom
Robbie Labanowski p.51 top left, p.52 third, p.68 third p.90 bottom left, p.207 right second
Katelyn Solbakk p.53
Nicholas Maskell illustrations pp.61, 97, 187, 200
Laurence Jarrett Kerr p.69
Edward Dowding p.81, p.134 bottom right, p.150 bottom right
Josh Rogers p.82 top left, p.203 top right
Rosie Stott p.82 top right
Sue Catlow p.88 left side, p.95 top left
Richard Collett-White p.95 top right
Nino Sostaric p.119 left third
Sophie Wildman-Gurung p.132 left third
Felix Hofmann p.137 left both
James Blair p.142, p.162 mid right
Nicola Smith p.151
Sheila Day p.194 third
Ceri Thomas p.207 top left
Jason Ingram p.207 right third
All others by Charles Dowding

Planting plan on p.206 courtesy of Ceri Thomas, Editor, *Which? Gardening* magazine whose 2020 issue featured the Small Garden at Homeacres. To subscribe contact 029 2267 0005 or visit https://try.which.co.uk/gardening-membership

Left Homeacres' fie[ld]
arrived, and after th[e]
had been mown by a

Bottom, from left Th[e]
view ten months later – [no]
soil has been disturbed, just
mulches laid to kill weeds and
make beds

The same view again, five years
later – intensive cropping and
no weeds: the main work is
sowing, planting, and picking

How to use this course

The course is about stimulation, more than instruction. Its 19 lessons are grouped into 7 modules of different subject matter. Each lesson has text to read and many photos to illustrate what I teach. There is much to absorb, so take your time.

There is a multiple choice quiz for you to complete at the end of each lesson. Don't worry, these aren't designed to catch you out! They are to reinforce your understanding, and to help you to digest your own learning. There's a final quiz too, designed to bring it all together. Do look to enjoy the quizzes as a way to clarify things.

Here is an overview of all the modules and lessons. There is a chronology to the lessons, and I'd recommend working your way through from the beginning. However, you can dive into any lesson at any time, it's totally up to you.

Above The Three-strip trial in July 2015 – first and second plantings

Below The Three-strip trial in October 2015 – new compost and plantings

My sourdough rye bread is 'no knead' – quicker, easier, and with great structure

MODULE 1
INTRODUCING NO DIG

The history of no dig, always successful, makes one wonder why it has not caught on before in a bigger way. I explain the benefits to soil and gardener.

Lesson 1
The advantages and recent history of no dig
We start with an overview of the advantages of no dig, and why it's such an effective method. To help you understand more about it, I've put together a history of no dig practice. It will give you more of an idea of where we are now, and reminds us that there is nothing new under the sun.

Lesson 2
Simple, time-saving, productive
An overview of the no dig method, and how it enables comprehensive weed clearance at the same time as successional plantings throughout the season. I explain the simplicity and the time-saving benefits, while showing you the results.

MODULE 2
TOP RESULTS FOR LESS TIME NEEDED

In this module we explore the results of no dig on different soils, and also how it compares to growth in dug soil. We look at results from the side-by-side trials I run, including the dig / no dig comparison beds which I have cropped every year since 2007. I give you my perspectives on the results.

No dig has, until recently, been frowned on by traditional gardeners and institutions. However this is now changing. The process of change shows how it can be good to question accepted beliefs. I encourage you to develop your hunches in order to understand gardening more fully.

Lesson 3
No dig on different soil types
Whether your soil is clay, stony or sandy, no dig is the best method for being time-efficient, holding fertility, and giving fine harvests. I show you my first market garden from 1982, which was on stony limestone soil, then two market gardens on clay, before the silt of Homeacres. Plus we look at clay in Kent and sand in Florida.

Lesson 4
Comparing dig and no dig for 13 years – what the differences reveal

I add my interpretations to the sometimes dramatic differences you see. These beds reveal a lot about both dig and no dig, with comparisons that are always fascinating, including when differences are small.

Lesson 5
A Three-strip trial and continuous cropping

This wide-ranging trial compares growth when using different composts, and when soil is loosened by forking. In addition, there is a 'no rotation' element, and you see the results of growing leeks and cabbage for four years consecutively in the same soil.

Lesson 6
Myths – what you don't need to do

One of my favourite topics is gardening myths! They are so numerous and so obvious when you analyse them, and it's fun to realise how much time we can save. Understanding how they came about also helps us to understand more about how soil and plants are often explained, and how we can spot more mistakes.

MODULE 3
LAYING OUT BEDS AND PATHS

I explain how you might set up a garden, including the benefits and importance of well-maintained paths. You see examples from different parts of Homeacres and from my previous garden at Lower Farm.

Lesson 7
Bed width and orientation, sides or not

You can have beds of any width, and align them in whichever way works best for you in the context of your site. I explain the value of sides to beds in some situations, and the many reasons you may not want them.

Above January 2013 – starting a new garden with beds and paths

Below The view in mid-March – weeds dying under mulches

The same view two months later – with new cardboard on many paths

Lesson 8
Paths – how they feed your plants and how to look after them
How to clear paths of weeds and keep them weed-free, and why this is worthwhile. I explain reasons for having paths of different widths, and how narrow paths without bed sides can increase your cropping.

MODULE 4
WEEDS

This is a huge topic and second only to soil, particularly if you have a weedy site when starting out. Appropriate mulching in year one leads you to experience the joy of weed-free soil. Not 100% weed-free for sure, but highly manageable, and I show you how.

- Identify your main weeds to know better how to mulch, what types of mulch to use, and how to stay weed-free all the time.
- Learn the important differences between annual and perennial weeds.

Lesson 9
Know your weeds – the two types
It helps to name and understand each weed, so you have an idea of how to mulch or remove the mix you may find. In particular, I explain the characteristics and differences of annual and perennial weeds, and how their growth tendencies affect what you need to do, in order to achieve clean soil for easy growing.

Lesson 10
Organic mulches
Eliminating perennial weeds is possible with no dig, and here is the how-to, using mulches of organic matter only. When digging out perennial weeds there are always a few roots that regrow; with no dig, 100% elimination is possible.

Lesson 11
Non-organic mulches
Non-organic mulches – plastic of various kinds – do not look nice but sometimes have a use in year one, mainly for reducing and eliminating perennial weeds. You can also reuse the same plastic, several times if needed.

I show how to use them in conjunction with organic matter, to improve soil at the same time as clearing weeds and growing a harvest.

Lesson 12
Staying weed-free – 'little and often'
You always need to be aware of how weeds can recolonise soil, and react to them when seen, yet no dig takes all the pressure out of this. I explain how weeding can be enjoyable because there is little of it to do. I share tips on how to stay weed-free in this lovely scenario.

From top
December 2012 – new garden at Homeacres, Charles spreading old cow manure for a bed to plant raspberry canes

February 2013 – the first mulches in the greenhouse before its erection

Paths in June – new cardboard along the edges

From top
Charles with August harvests at Homeacres, 2019

View to the house on 20 December – mulched beds with compost and old wood chip on the paths

FERTILITY, COMPOST AND SOIL

These three words have a usage and meaning that varies with context. I give you the definitions that matter for no dig, simpler than often explained.

Soil and compost behave so differently. We look at composts you can buy or source for free, and how to make compost at home.

Lesson 13
Make your own compost
Homemade compost has abundant life, and I show how to increase the microbes and organisms. Everybody's heaps and additions are different; once you have a grasp of the principles, you can create a process that works in your space.

Lesson 14
What compost offers, when to apply, and amounts needed
Fertility is often equated to nutrients feeding plants, yet true and long-term fertility is about so much more than this. I explain how easy it is to grow great plants when you know surprisingly little about nutrient supply and uptake. Green fingers and a biological approach, rather than calculations and spreadsheets!

Lesson 15
Understanding soil, and comparing it with compost
I had a fun comment on Instagram, a 'professional horticulturist' who declared that soil and compost are the same thing! I show you how they are not, why they are not and how it helps your gardening when you understand the differences.

Lesson 16
Types of compost
The one word 'compost' covers so many products and possibilities. Enjoy the tour of different types in this lesson, and the results of growth comparisons from using four of them.

MODULE 6
CROPPING SMALLER SPACES

How to create a bed with compost on weeds – you can plant it straight away then see how everything grows. I explain the cropping plans for this bed through a few seasons, and the harvests too.

I use my Small Garden of 25 m² / 269 ft² to show you how, in no dig, plantings can succeed each other through the course of one year. You will learn some vegetable choices and planting methods.

Lesson 17
A new bed – plantings and harvests over five years

This is a story of one bed: how we made it in a morning then planted and sowed in the afternoon, and its subsequent growth over the following years. Year five shows possibilities for interplanting. Plus I have used the bed to trial unusual vegetables, so you have a peek at which may be worthwhile and which may not be.

Lesson 18
Growing abundance – two years of planting and cropping in the Small Garden

The Small Garden is 25 m² / 269 ft²; I take you through the details of soil preparation (very little!), spring sowing, planting, edging and harvesting. Then you see the new plantings in summer, meaning that every part of the garden has grown two, or even three vegetables in one year.

MODULE 7
A SUMMARY AND THE FINAL QUIZ

Lesson 19
No dig distilled

I summarise the main aspects of no dig. These salient and simple points give you a core of understanding, the keys to your productive garden.

From top
With David, the video maker, after planting the new bed

A May harvest from the Small Garden –
2.08 kg / 4.6 lb of leaves, radish and turnip

Starlight peas in June

troduction

Welcome to a course which will save you time, give you pleasure in gardening, and health-giving food to eat. All this is achievable and much easier, once you understand how to care for and nourish soil.

No dig is a straightforward, time-efficient way of enhancing soil quality and fertility. We don't work or see the soil, and you don't need soil tests to understand it. Evidence is given by plants, and I demonstrate this throughout the course.

My teaching is based on experience and results, from 38 years of growing. The methods I explain and illustrate are sometimes different from commonly held beliefs, and in every case I explain why. These differences are what enable you to save time and achieve more reliable results.

The photos are mostly of the garden at Homeacres where I live now, in South West England. Our latitude is 51°N, with eight hours between sunrise and sunset in midwinter, rising to 16 and more in midsummer. The climate is temperate oceanic, warmed by the North Atlantic Drift, also called the Gulf Stream.

WILL THESE UNDERSTANDINGS APPLY IN DIFFERENT CLIMATES?

... ...h so. The growing amount of feedback from all around the world illustrates
... ...eds whether your climate is hot, cold, dry or wet:

...omoting your no dig method here in our country, the Philippines. It really
... can see amazing results. Finally we found the best farming method that can be
easily done by anyone.
Agri-nihan, comment on *Growing Success* video, 23.1.20

Even though we are in Zone 3a with one planting a year, I am having success with
intensive no dig beds. I use less garden space and did less weeding, wonderful!
Switching to this method has made great soil and saved me time and energy, thank you
from northern B.C. Canada.
Tall Cedars, YouTube, 30.10.19

My new no dig flower garden is doing great in comparison to my neighbour's gardens.
We have had a very hot June this year here again but there was no such thing as a drought
in my new garden at all. Everybody around's been complaining about drought but me!
Beata Wypych from Poland, email, 22.8.19

Hello Mr. Dowding, I am in Northern California, a mile east of the ocean. From your videos
I attempted my first no dig garden at the end of 2018. Even through winter storms it
started producing, and by the time spring arrived, I had an abundant, healthy, thriving
garden, with my nearest neighbours taking notice, and swearing they must take up the
method themselves.
Linda Schneider, email, 15.6.19

I wholeheartedly agree with the no dig method of growing . . . even through the most
challenging lack of rain and disturbed weather patterns here in South East Queensland,
my gardens have continued to produce whereas most other gardeners in the area have
given up on their production.
Russell from Queensland, The Free Radicals on YouTube, 01.05.19

Our climates couldn't be more different – I'm in south Louisiana, USA, about 30 miles
inland from the gulf of Mexico. Yet I find your gardening methods work well for the
vegetables and herbs that will tolerate our heat and wildly inconsistent rain patterns
here in Acadiana.
Sidney J Barras Jr, Charles' Facebook page, 15.5.18

MY BACKGROUND

I became keen on gardening in 1979, when my mother needed help to plant some trees.
Something about handling plants and soil made me feel really good. Soon after, I became
interested in food and nutrition while still at university. I read Peter Stringer's book, *Animal
Rights*, and became vegetarian, possibly the first one at my college – the kitchen staff
found it amusing.

I joined the Soil Association shortly after, a subscription-based organisation of 4,000 people.
They were founded in 1946, with a mission to promote and know more about soil health in
farming and gardening. They ran a trial in Suffolk to investigate any links between soil, plant
and human health.

I had been working on the family farm since learning to drive a tractor at age 14, but was not positively engaged. It was a big farm for those times, with grass and cereals covering 400 hectares / 988 acres, and 300 dairy cows in five herds.

Despite living on a farm, I felt separate from it, and the only farm produce in our house was milk. Of more interest to me were the vegetables and raspberries from the garden. I still remember the eureka moment of discovering delicious broad beans at age 15.

In 1981 I worked for a year at the Argyll Hotel, on the small island of Iona off western Scotland, as a 'maintenance man'. While there, I became interested in their vegetable garden and did some jobs to help out, then grew keen to get home and start gardening.

In early 1982 I made a mound, the original style of *hugelbeet*, with a base of sticks rather than logs. It ran east to west, and its south side enabled me to harvest carrots as early as May, which impressed my parents. I practised by working in their garden, and I visited and worked on organic market gardens. They were rare in those days because organic was 'leading edge' and highly unprofitable.

In August 1982, I used the farm tractor to rotavate 0.66 hectares / 1.6 acres of old pasture. The soil was Cotswold Brash, stony and loamy with over 7% organic matter, thanks to being permanent pasture for the cows.

During September and October, my next step was using a spade to shape raised beds. I shovelled soil from 60 cm / 2 ft wide paths to 1.5 m / 5 ft wide beds. I then spread old hay on some of the beds and old straw in all of the paths, to prevent weeds from growing.

This mulching – covering – with undecomposed materials resulted in a lot of slugs and damage to new plantings in particular. This led to my using compost mulch instead.

The fact that my market garden was no dig, as well as organic, slipped under the radar (*see Lesson 3*). I was not proclaiming it, but no dig felt right. By 1987 I had almost 3 hectares / 7 acres of no dig beds, although I always rotavated in the first autumn of converting land from pasture to soil. At the time it was the only way I knew how to achieve this.

NATIONAL TELEVISION

In 1988 the BBC appeared, to film a whole episode on organic gardening with Geoff Hamilton. He had become iconic and had warm communication skills.

From top By 1988 my methods were being noticed, and I hosted the BBC's *Gardeners' World* TV show for two days; Geoff Hamilton is second left

August 2016 – *Gardeners' World* filmed at Homeacres, and interviewed me about no dig again

Geoff was amazed at my results from using only compost and no synthetic fertilisers or pesticides. What we didn't discuss, and he did not comment on, was the no dig part.

The extract below is from the archive of BBC footage of the 1988 programme, and starts with Geoff's question: 'Charles – the crops are looking really good, what type of fertiliser are you using on them?'

I answered: 'I'm not using any Geoff, it's good soil and we're putting on quite heavy dressings of manure and compost and that's enough.' Geoff replied: 'No chemicals at all, that's really quite remarkable!'

Footnotes to the above are:

- In the 1980s most gardeners relied on artificial fertiliser and pesticides, more than they do now.

- Because there was such a low use of composts in gardens generally, I described my dressings as 'heavy', whereas now I would call them normal, or even light – about 1.2 cm / 0.5 in of compost per year. Plus I was adding straw to paths.

- The soil was of average fertility, Grade 3, and very stony. I remember that I had wanted Geoff to look less wrong for thinking he had to use fertilisers!

- Subsequently, in 2016, the BBC came to Homeacres and filmed for *Gardeners' World* once again. This time it was exclusively about no dig and my successes with the method.

I have also appeared on three other BBC programmes: Charlie Dymmock's *Garden Rescue* in 2017; *Escape to the Country*, also in 2017; and *Gardeners' World* in 2008, with Sarah Raven.

EARLY DIFFICULTIES AT HOMEACRES

I started making the garden at Homeacres in November 2012, trying many different methods for mulching very strong weed growth. Almost everything had succeeded by summer 2013.

However, when researching my documents for this course, I came across a diary entry I had forgotten called 'Stirrings'. I had filed it away on 4 June 2013, and could scarcely believe what I was reading! I have not edited anything.

> 'I am feeling overwhelmed by the amount of time needed for this new garden. Have I taken on too much? The continual, persistent growth of couch grass, especially where I have experimented with thinner or briefer mulches, is getting me down. So is the aloneness of it – but that is exactly what I wanted, to be more in my own space, not behaving according to other people's rules.'

(It continues in a similar vein, less relevant to gardening.)

I include this to encourage you not to be overwhelmed! And in case starting your garden feels like a big commitment of time and effort, for an uncertain benefit. Take it from me, the rewards – year after every subsequent year – justify it, and my experience demonstrates it.

Enjoy the course.

Module 1
Introducing no dig

The advantages and recent history of no dig

It is instructive, and also fascinating, to discover where no dig has come from and how it has developed. And to consider why it did not become popular, even though its practitioners enjoyed such success.

No dig copies nature's way of caring for soil, and the soil responds by caring for plants, hence the great results. Sounds too easy? Not exactly, but knowing the details is what makes it work.

Vegetables need plentiful moisture and fertility, hence my emphasis on being generous with your mulches when growing them. No dig also works with thinner mulches, but crops will be less abundant and weeds may be more numerous.

I recommend maintaining a cover or mulch of organic matter, so the soil underneath is mostly invisible. One application a year can achieve this. Organisms in the soil keep eating the surface material and mixing it with soil materials, to create an open structure for the growth of plant roots.

SOIL STRUCTURE, THE NATURAL AND EASY WAY

Most soil already has a good structure for plant roots to grow, and is full of growth-enabling organisms. Millions of fungal threads, nematodes, millipedes and earthworms, to name a few of soil's inhabitants, are being helpful right under our feet and out of sight.

You have already started no dig without knowing! Since the last time you dug, tilled or forked your soil, it has been healing itself: growing networks of mycelia, breeding health-bringing organisms, and recreating a stable structure. No dig facilitates this work, and nutrients stay available without the complexities of soil tests.

View of the west side of Homeacres in September 2018 – the main work is sowing, planting, and picking

Further viewing
YouTube video – *No dig explained in 3 minutes*

SIGNIFICANT ADVANTAGES OF NO DIG, FOR SOIL AND FOR US

If anyone asks you what is good about no dig, here are the main answers. We will explore these further throughout the course.

1 You can start at any time of the year, even before you have finished this course! Have a go using just one bed, and learn as you grow.

2 There is no need to dig or weed first, except for woody plants – just cover with a mulch.

3 With compost mulches, you can plant beds on the same day as you make them.

4 You enjoy gardening more, because weeds germinate less.

5 Mycorrhizal fungi stay intact, so they can help plant roots to find more food and moisture because they are smaller than roots, and can reach into tiny crevices.

6 Moisture is retained – and available to a considerable depth – because there is no 'shatter zone' of different densities, which is created after cultivations. Water struggles to move either up or down across a boundary of materials with different densities. Hence it is now not recommended to place crocks or stones at the bottom of pots under the compost, supposedly to improve drainage but, in reality, making it worse.

7 Mud does not stick to your boots in wet weather, because drainage is good, and the soil's structure has not been broken by tools or machinery. Soil particles stay clustered in aggregates, enabling excess water to rub through, so you can garden when you need to.

8 You can quickly resow or replant at any time of year, with no soil preparation needed. Clear preceding plants by simply twisting them out, to leave most of the roots in the soil.

9 Warmth is retained by soil in winter, because deep-level warmth can rise, unhindered by damage from cultivations.

10 Carbon stays in the soil, instead of being converted to CO_2 by oxidation after cultivations.

11 You need less compost than if you were digging the soil, *see overleaf*.

Charles with September produce

A RECENT HISTORY OF NO DIG

It would be fascinating to know the full human history of not working the soil. Below are a few of the no dig pioneers from recent times, who enjoyed amazing results but were on the fringes of mainstream gardening and farming.

Arthur Guest

In the 1940s, gardeners practising no dig in the UK included Arthur Guest, a miner from Yorkshire, in his sixties by then. His results were so good that he kept winning prizes at horticultural shows. Then he wrote a book, which sold worldwide, and later in life became a BBC presenter, espousing what he called 'natural gardening' and not being a 'slave to the spade'.

Guest used to dig in a 'traditional' way. After adopting no dig, he wrote that he used 40% less compost, thanks to soil organisms being healthier and compost being used to 'maximum advantage' on the surface.

Guest's small book has been reprinted by the UK seed firm Marshalls, and it's a great read if you ever find a copy. As well as compost from his own garden and some horse manure, he used a fair amount of sawdust mulch. One amazing statement reads, 'I had club root fairly badly, but compost treatment cured this in two years.'

F.C. King

King was the head gardener at Levens Hall in Cumbria, UK, for three decades. He visited many gardens and had the resources to trial no dig in the 1940s. His books are full of good ideas, they include: *Gardening with Compost*[1] and *The Weed Problem, a New Approach*[2]. The quotes below are from the latter:

'These, and many similar results which I have witnessed, confirm my opinion that less digging means fewer pests and diseases.' (p.83)

'At the approach of spring, the difference between my dug and undug plots is truly remarkable . . . the undug portions of the garden are always infinitely drier and in better condition for planting or sowing than are the plots that have been dug [which] often resemble a quagmire.' (p.85)

'The general conclusions I have drawn after many years of patient investigation of the value of no digging are:

1 This system offers many advantages over regular digging in the control of weeds.

2 Contrary to popular belief, such land is well-drained and capable of producing excellent crops, showing signs neither of asphyxiation nor of chlorotic conditions.

3 The soil is appreciably warmer in winter and spring.

4 The earthworm population is increased, judging by the number of casts found on the surface.

5 Less labour is required in the preparation of better seed-beds.

6 A well-defined zone of dark rich soil is formed, which absorbs rather than reflects sunshine.

7 Good control is maintained over sucking insects, aphids chiefly.' (p. 90)

Like Guest, King answers the question that I am often asked, about the supposed 'extra compost needed for no dig':

> 'Garden soils are more often over-cultivated than under-cultivated. Even in the palmiest days of horticulture this was true, and the credit for the abundant production of days gone by should rightly be given to the large quantity of organic matter that most gardens received. Regular cultivation, without an adequate supply of organic matter, is likely to upset the natural balance between mineral and organic matter because cultivation must increase the rate of decomposition of the organic matter in soil while affecting the mineral content very little. [Therefore] the less we dig, the longer will our supply of humus last.' (pp.76–7)

Shewell Cooper

A contemporary of King was William Shewell Cooper, described by Val Bourne in the *Oxford Times* of 18 November 2010:

> 'My gardening guru of the 1960s was Shewell Cooper (1900–1982) who wrote at least 30 books, including a gardening encyclopedia. Shewell Cooper was famous for pioneering no dig gardening in Britain.
>
> 'He founded the Good Gardeners Association (4,000 members in the 1950s) and was a founding member of the Soil Association in 1946. His garden, at Arkley Manor near Barnet, attracted 10,000 visitors a year and he travelled the world explaining organic gardening. Recently I came across his son Ramsay while in conversation with a modern exponent of no dig gardening – Charles Dowding. Ramsay still practises no dig gardening and he has a demonstration plot at Capel Manor College in Enfield. The picture shows them both.
>
> 'Modern gardeners could do with more of this practical wisdom, instead of the celebrity-led television that seems to impart little.'

Arkley Manor had to be sold to pay taxes when Shewell Cooper died. The GGA continued, but declined and then died in 2015, perhaps from confusion over what it stood for. For some reason Shewell Cooper did not use the phrase 'no dig' to describe his association, perhaps showing what an 'unsexy' phrase it was at that time, with little interest in soil apart from as a 'bank for nutrients'.

I enjoyed conversing with Ramsay, still gardening at 80 years old. This photo was taken just six years before he died in 2016.

With Ramsay Shewell Cooper, at an RHS show in London, October 2010

Gerard N. Smith

Smith, a horticultural consultant, wrote books on growing dahlias, chrysanthemums, and one called *Organic Surface Cultivation: Its Theory and Practice*[3].

He gave his background in the Soil Association's *Mother Earth* magazine of Winter 1950:

> 'I have been gardening for more than 45 years and cannot really say when I changed to organic methods. It was a trial-and-error process taking five years or more, and three books decided that the methods were on the right lines. These were *The Living Soil*[4], *Ploughman's Folly*[5], and F.C. King's *The Weed Problem*[2].
>
> 'My present state of mind is that the "non-digging" of King is an inescapable corollary to fertility-building with compost in the garden. If you dig your compost into the soil, you will lose, or at least postpone, the valuable effects. That is the Buried Fertility method and the initials are significant.'

Masanobu Fukuoka

In Japan, in 1938, Masanobu Fukuoka started pioneering work on his farm. He called his method Natural Farming, 'a Buddhist way of farming that originates in the philosophy of "Mu" or nothingness, and returns to a "do-nothing" nature' (p.23, *The Natural Way of Farming*[6]).

His method was to scatter seeds, wrapped in clay, into a ripening grain crop such as barley, which had also been undersown with clover. The clay was to protect the seeds, while they germinated on the surface of ground that was never tilled.

Fukuoka's system is precise and needs timely interventions, including a flooding of the young rice to weaken the clover. In his subtropical climate he could grow two grain crops every year, also using some chicken manure, but no artificial fertiliser or pesticides. The straw that remained, after each crop had been harvested, became mulch for the next one.

Ruth Stout

Ruth Stout, in 1950s–80s USA, became a gardening pioneer by accident. In 1944, while waiting for the ploughman to till her vegetable garden, she lost patience and thought to sow seeds in the soil as it was, after pulling any weeds.

Her husband kept animals on their small farm and gave her spoiled hay. She simply laid it on her vegetable garden and did not bother with the tillage part. It worked like a dream, and she made her method popular with magazine articles and in her book, *No Work Gardening*[7].

I came across this book in 1982 and applied hay mulches in Somerset, UK. The result: slugs! However, in the book there is little mention of slugs. Ruth Stout did not suffer them because of Connecticut's cold winters and dry summers. In fact, I don't think she realised the link between hay and slugs.

In the book, Ruth Stout advised gardeners to lay beer traps if slugs were a problem. Beer traps are effective – indeed she mentions how one man caught 1,000 in three days. This is fine, except she makes little of the time (and beer) needed. My approach for pests is to minimise the time needed in dealing with them, by preventing them rather than reacting to them. After my experience with slugs in 1983, I abandoned hay and developed the method of compost mulching.

A WORD ON SOIL TESTS

I have had a few soil tests done over the years and am not a fan. By all means, if you are comfortable doing or paying for a test, carry on. However, I recommend it only if growth on your property or in your area is poor. This may be because of acid soil, which fortunately is rare, and lime is the remedy.

Tests are snapshots in time and can cause unnecessary worries. They can easily, but erroneously, pick out apparent anomalies which may not actually matter. This prevents gardeners simply looking at existing growth for reassurance. When you improve soil life, nutrients become more available to plants, soil structure improves, and growth balances out.

Every book says you need to check pH to know about acidity or alkalinity, but what should you do with that knowledge? Perhaps read another book to find out and become immersed in complexities!

Most of us do not need to test. Almost all soil tests are geared towards using fertilisers and amendments, and just a few are able to interpret soil biology. Even those have issues, which I discovered in 2010 when a test highlighted 'poor fungal life' in soil that was growing superb crops.

The ones I would recommend, and they are not cheap, are biological tests along the lines of work by Dr Elaine Ingham. She has pioneered soil microbiology research and knowledge, since graduating in 1977 with an MSc in Microbiology. In 1996 she founded Soil Food Web Inc.[8], and currently works at Oregon State University.

- The complexity of soil testing is illustrated by a comment from the director of a company that makes potting compost. He said that their best method of testing for quality is to give the compost to some growers and then to receive feedback on growth. He finds this to be more reliable than lab test results showing nutrient content.

SOIL TYPES

Descriptions of soil type are usually based on density, from clay being the densest, through silt and loam, to sand the coarsest. Most soils have some or all of these types, with a variable amount of stones and organic matter.

No dig means you see little of the soil and instead enjoy its results, without worrying about its detailed qualities or needing to know a lot about it. The no dig method works on clay, silt, loam, stone and sand. I received this message by email from Ann de Baldo, who subsequently took this course online:

I live in Florida, USA. I have adapted no dig principles to our sandy soil and it works like a charm.

1   *Gardening with Compost*, F.C. King, Faber & Faber, 1951
2   *The Weed Problem, a New Approach*, F.C. King, Faber & Faber, 1951
3   *Organic Soil Cultivation: its Theory and Practice*, Gerard Smith, 1950
4   *The Living Soil*, Eve Balfour, Faber & Faber, 1943. Balfour founded the Soil Association in 1946
5   *Ploughman's Folly*, Edward H. Faulkner, Michael Joseph, 1945. Also by Faulkner *Ploughing in Prejudices*, Michael Joseph, 1948
6   *The Natural Way of Farming*, Masanobu Fukuoka, Japan Publications Inc., 1985
7   *The Ruth Stout No Work Garden Book*, Bantam Books / Rodale Press, 1971
8   *Teaming with Microbes, a gardener's guide to the Soil Food Web*, Jeff Lowenfels and Wayne Lewis, Timber Press, 2006

Quiz Lesson 1

	Question	Multiple choice
1	The no dig approach requires more compost than if you dig, for the same result.	True or false?
2	Based on the observations of F.C. King, what effect does no dig have on the amount of pests and diseases?	A No dig results in fewer pests and diseases. B No dig results in the same incidence of pest and disease as when digging. C No dig slightly increases pest and disease, compared to digging.
3	In damp climates, which pests are encouraged by the use of hay mulches?	A Slugs. B Earwigs. C Rabbits.
4	Do I recommend gardeners to undertake a soil test before starting on a new site or garden?	A I recommend you test soil every year, in order to know what is in there. B Soil tests enable you to add the correct fertilisers. C In almost all cases, I don't see the benefit of soil tests for gardeners.
5	At what point does the no dig process slowly begin, in terms of soil building, or rebuilding, its life processes?	A Straight after you stop forking / digging / tilling. B Only after you apply cardboard. C After you do a soil test, and add the correct minerals.
6	After soil, what do I suggest is the second most important part of good gardening practice?	A Mulching and managing weeds, so as to have very few. B Regular watering of vegetables. C A strict four-year rotation. D Laying cardboard every year.
7	'Green fingers instead of spreadsheets' – what am I referring to?	A Soil fertility, as more than measuring nutrients. B Sheet mulching of weeds. C Gardening being better for your health than office work. D Analysis of moisture levels.
8	How do I describe gardening myths?	A Old and interesting folklore. B Ancient beliefs of great value. C Non-scientific methods. D Jobs you don't need to do.
9	Spreading compost and mulching with organic matter were common practice in the 1980s.	True or false?

Lesson 2
Simple, time-saving, productive

I notice that gardening has been made to seem very complicated, even by people who really should know better. A key part of this course is learning how to to use the simplest, cheapest and, above all, quickest method.

People have been led to believe that it's more difficult and harder work than it needs to be. This is illustrated by the questions I am repeatedly asked, such as this one:

We have a few raised beds, made three years ago, and want to do your no dig instead, how could I convert these beds? Would I have to dig out, put the cardboard etc down, and put same soil / compost over it? Or put new compost over it? Or place cardboard etc over all the existing compost now, then place new compost etc straight on top of cardboard? Just seems a lot more work if I have to re-dig, but I do think it would be worth it in the long run! Or do you have another suggestion?

To which the answer is shorter than the question! Level with a rake and spread 3–5 cm / 1–2 in of compost on top of the soil, which I imagine is in a state of reasonable fertility. If there are many weeds, lay cardboard first and then the compost on top of this.

- Cardboard is a weeding timesaver, when weeds are large and numerous. You don't need to use it otherwise.

No dig, right from day one, is less about what we do to 'fix' soil and more about how we enhance its natural liveliness. Compost / organic matter on the surface encourages organisms in the soil to travel upwards and feed, which improves aeration and structure. Their excretions contain feed for other organisms and / or plants, so the cycle of life is enabled and magnified.

The next simple step is to sow and plant into the surface compost, when it's the right season for each different vegetable.

Drills for carrots in mid-March – different varieties sown in surface compost

Carrots growing in late May, covered by mesh; broad beans to the right

Harvest from the end of July of final and larger roots – Purple Haze and Rainbow varieties; notice the length of fine roots, which had been growing into clay

You've completely changed my methods from overly complicated to simple and effective.
Sarah Olney, on Instagram, December 2018

BIG HARVESTS, AND HEALTHY TOO

Carrots illustrate the falseness of the 'organic' teaching I was brought up with in the 1980s. They were (and still often are) called 'light feeders', and the soil was *left unfed*, with no compost in the winter before sowing.

I was also told that spreading compost before sowing carrots 'made them fork', and resulted in 'lush leaves and less root growth'.

This is how I interpret these comments, from the results of my no dig growing:

- Terms such as 'light feeders' come from the fertiliser manufacturers' lexicon, and ignore life processes in the soil.

- Forking roots happen because of the soil cultivation, which was being practised, but not mentioned, because it was seen as normal. Forking is not caused by applications of compost applied to the surface.

- Lush leaves happen if gardeners spread nitrogenous fertilisers, which are like junk food to plant roots: abundant and unbalanced. Whereas feeding soil life with mulches of organic matter results in strong, healthy and balanced growth of all plants.

Hence the wonderful growth one sees in no dig, and the big harvests.

The photos to the left, and those on p.26, illustrate another massive misunderstanding – until recently believed by most gardeners – that 'soil needs to be loosened for roots to go down.'

DO YOU NEED TO LOOSEN SOIL BEFORE STARTING NO DIG?

The answer is absolutely not, because it's better to preserve the existing structure and soil life, and to simply apply surface mulches of organic matter. These feed soil organisms, whose activity creates a good structure for growth.

It's a terrible and arrogant assumption that only man or woman can create soil suitable to grow plants. Just look at the wonders of growth in untended nature and copy what happens there – leave soil undisturbed, and encourage soil inhabitants to feed at the surface.

The first step in no dig is to mulch, only that, and with as high a quality food as you can. Compost comes top, and this includes old animal manure, leaf mould and composts you can buy. Undecomposed mulches like hay work too, but add fertility more slowly and encourage slugs in damp climates.

- An *exception* to commencing without soil disturbance is if you start with a plot of uneven ground, whether a 'lunar landscape' or just hollows that feel awkward to walk on. I recommend using a sharp spade to slice off the peaks, and then place that soil in the hollows until you have a level surface. Then mulch.

- Level does not mean no slope (*see Lesson 7 for more on laying out beds on slopes*).

I had this question on YouTube:

I am making a garden on the west coast of Canada from land that has only been a forest. It has been logged and tortured by heavy machinery, and is mostly sand and gravel with a great many rocks. Before I found you, I was digging six inch trenches and filling them back up with sifted soil and manure, removing a great many rocks in the process. How does no dig work with such rocky land?

My answer is to remove only protruding rocks and stumps, then mulch. For example earthworms (*Lumbricus terrestris*, different to compost or red wiggler worms *Eisinia fetida*) are surface feeders, yet often live quite deep in the soil and therefore travel up and down to feed on mulches. This movement maintains and increases their network of channels, which endure many years longer than any temporary 'aeration' after digging or forking. Loosening of soils through using tools creates only a short-lived tilth, which collapses after a few months and then needs remaking every year or more. Diggers are on a treadmill.

By comparison, with no dig – and a surface mulch of organic matter – soil structure continually improves. (*Refer to the Glossary for a definition of the term 'compacted soil', which is fortunately rare.*)

There are exceptionally few instances where any mechanical loosening would improve soil structure. If you have doubts about your soil condition, I still suggest to leave it well alone and simply to mulch the surface.

With carrots from the two trial beds – no dig on the left, dig on the right (*see Lesson 4 for more on this*)

Homeacres' clay soil shows on the lower end of this parsnip, which had been levered out with a spade

The empty area on the left is planted with garlic, then I spread this compost on top (year one in the Small Garden)

After 72 mm / 2.8 in rain in 43 hours, the paths are free of water – only the unmulched edge has water lying on the surface

After the heavy rainfall, this is the only part of Homeacres' cropped area with any surface water – and only for an hour or two

Every year my trial results show how plants are rooting more successfully into undisturbed soil. No dig carrots are a graphic example – mostly longer, fatter and with more colour. Carrots from the dig bed tend to be paler, and their leaves less glossy.

Rooting downwards is clearly easy for plants when soil is left undisturbed. The parsnip in the photo, left, shows us the different qualities of soil at deeper levels – it has rooted through unloosened clay at depth.

NO DIG IS BRILLIANT FOR HEAVY SOILS

Clay is dense, but also structured thanks to soil life, and results are best when this structure is left alone. Soil texture changes only gradually as one descends into undisturbed soils, without the sharp variations caused by cultivations. Water drains evenly downwards after rain, while moisture can also travel upwards in dry conditions.

I observe how good the drainage is at Homeacres, and this was illustrated by a storm which produced 72 mm / 2.8 in of rain over 43 hours, between 19–21 November, 2016. Then again by another 52 mm / 2 in of rain in four hours on 11th August, 2019.

The first storm was on saturated soil and the second on dry soil, both of which can cause problems. Homeacres has a dense silt soil, and the photos, left, taken after the 2016 storm show water lying on grass edges but not in the main garden at all, even on paths where I had been pushing heavy wheelbarrows. The only area of water on paths was near to an old greenhouse where there may be some concrete deeper down. However growth is good there, and it's not worth digging a hole to attempt any remedy.

NUTRIENTS ARE HELD IN THE SOIL'S ORGANIC MATTER

Any rainwater not used by plants just drains through, and sometimes people worry that nutrients are being 'leached' (carried and lost) downwards, especially in winter. However this is just not true; if it were, Homeacres would not crop as it does – throughout a whole year and after just one application of compost.

- The key understanding is that nutrients in compost, and nutrients in soil which have been processed / excreted by soil organisms, are not water soluble.

Compost is not fertiliser and I urge you not to think of it in those terms (*see Lesson 14*).

A related question that I am sometimes asked is:

Do I need to cover soil in winter with cardboard or polythene?

My answer is: it depends on which weeds are growing. If there are more weeds than you can remove by hand, cover with cardboard or polythene, depending partly on the size of the area. If laying polythene to kill weeds, spread any organic matter on the weedy ground first.

- Then worms and other soil life can feed on this while enjoying the safe darkness under a cover, meaning your soil will be in better condition when the polythene comes off.

When weeds are removable by hand, do this before covering the soil surface with 3–5 cm / 1–2 in of compost of any kind, whether old manure, your own homemade compost or purchased compost.

- Soil organisms stay active in any mild weather and appreciate this food at the surface, which is their preferred place to forage and eat.

- Polythene mulches need removing at some point, while cardboard does not because it decomposes and is eaten by soil organisms.

Compost protects soil from weather, and results in fewer slugs than where covers are laid. Nutrients in compost are not washed away by rain and become available when roots are needing them, when warmth and soil fungi combine. Simply spread compost once a year in early winter, for sustained growth over 12 months, and apply no feeds at any time, just 3–5 cm / 1–2 in of compost once a year – though a larger amount of compost is needed in year one, say 7–15 cm / 3–6 in.

The sequence of photos, right, shows a year of growth, after making new beds in late autumn.

November 2017 – mulching a new area with compost on cardboard over weeds, and using temporary wooden sides

2 March 2018 – after the winter's first snow; there are now new beds on this whole area

17 May – the beds to the left are three months old; those to the right are six months old

5 July – cabbage are now followed by broad / fava beans, and herbs are followed by beetroot (next to greenhouse)

7 October – chervil and spring onions just planted after the French beans had finished; to the left is chard, planted after mixed crops

5 December – the beds are now one year old and have cropped a huge amount with almost no weeding needed, and no feeding at any point during the growing season

NEW BEDS, NO NEED TO WAIT

There is a misunderstanding about newly made beds, that you need to 'wait to plant'. In fact you can sow or plant on the same day that you cover weeds with compost, as long as it's the correct time of year for each planting.

When I started at Homeacres it was midwinter, so too cold for planting, and the first beds were empty for two to three months until spring arrived. I was still making new beds in the spring, and planted some of them straight away.

By May, even though beds still had weeds dying underneath, the garden was almost full of vegetables and flowers.

There were residual pests such as slugs, which had been living and eating in the thick grass and weeds. Two other differences between year one and subsequent years were:

- I laid cardboard in pathways, because perennial weeds such as couch grass and dandelions were still trying to grow.
- Many beds had temporary wooden sides, mostly old fence posts laid on the ground to hold new compost in place, and to give a precise, weed-free edge.

We'll cover more on this throughout the course.

One caveat is if you have bought compost which is still hot when delivered – if possible, leave it to mature in a heap for two months before using. *(Lesson 14 shows how, in spring 2013, vegetable growth was not good in such compost, but was then excellent for summer plantings three to four months later.)*

The view of Homeacres soon after I arrived in November 2012 – the main field was growing pasture and weeds; you can see a delivery of 5 tonnes of old cow manure (top left)

Six months later, and weeds are dead or dying under mulches – mostly compost for the beds, and cardboard for the paths

By 30 June there is abundant growth of vegetables, and we laid new cardboard on any paths where weeds had grown through

September 2013 – the first summer at Homeacres, and these are second crops; all perennial weeds are now dead, except for bindweed

Jump five years to February 2018 – no cardboard needed, and the only wooden sides are those on the trial beds

Early May – spring plantings have been made and a few are even cropping, after being fleeced over in April

Mid-June – the garden is full of growth, and we will soon start to empty some beds after harvests

Early September – most vegetables are second plantings; none of the beds have received compost or other amendments since the winter

Early December – we spread compost on all the beds which become empty after clearing the final harvests; some beds also have compost spread under the plant

BED SIDES AND PATHS

I suggest you leave new beds' temporary sides in place for three to six months, sometimes less. Here, when we lift and remove them, there are clusters of slugs hiding underneath in the moist environment they need.

Beds without sides result in fewer ants as well as slugs, and their sloping sides can be also be planted into so that space is maximised.

The sequence of photos on p.31 shows beds without sides, except for my two trial beds whose wooden boards are mostly oak. This decomposes very slowly compared to most softwoods, which results in fewer slugs.

Speed of planting and replanting

A transformative feature of no dig is the ease of second cropping, throughout a growing season. There is no bed preparation needed, and nothing to add in terms of fertility – just clear and plant. Weeds are few, which is another timesaver.

The serenity and rapidity of summer's second plantings means you rarely grow green manures (*see p.35 for more information on this*). There is no need for them, and it's easy-to-grow food instead. This means you need a smaller area to grow the same amount of harvests.

May

August

December

RAISING PLANTS

Second cropping, or succeeding with succession, is helped by skilling up on propagation, especially in the summer. The photos below show sowings I made in August 2018, and how rapidly they become ready to plant.

Many of these vegetables could be sown direct rather than raised as seedlings to plant, but I find it easier, quicker and more productive to raise transplants. My second course covers this in more detail.

10 August 2018 – sowings from this day, and recent days, include spinach, salad rocket, mustards and chervil

Just three days later – notice the new growth

Another six days later – the seedlings are almost ready to plant, in cleared beds or as interplants

SECOND PLANTINGS FOR HEALTHY SOIL

The photos on p.34 show the rapid growth of summer plantings. They help to keep beds full of vegetables until the end of our main growing season, in about early November. After that, some beds continue to crop winter leaves and roots.

Timings for summer plantings will vary according to your climate. Homeacres is Zone 8, usually with the first frost by late October. My website: charlesdowding.co.uk shows the weather at Homeacres, so you can to compare it with yours. *(Look at 'Weather Now' under the 'Learn' tab.)*

- In my experience, I have found that it's better for soil to be growing plants during the growing season (which, in this climate, means not in winter) rather than beds being empty. The roots of growing plants are food for microbes, and help to keep the network of soil life busy and nourished.

- Winter in many climates sees the soil and most plants dormant, or growing very slowly. Microbes are fed and protected by the mulch of compost, which keeps soil ready for planting any time from late winter onwards.

5 August – onions have been pulled, spring broccoli has been planted after broad beans, and chicories have been planted after peas, onions and calabrese

11 August – see the change after only six days of summer

5 September – the garden is fully clothed for autumn

16 September – first harvests of spinach can be seen on the left, having been planted just 22 days earlier

GREEN MANURES?

If you don't want to grow a second planting, you could sow a green manure. But that suggests you are cropping a larger area than is needed for food. I find there are many misunderstandings about green manures for gardening. It's a method taken from farming, and with too little consideration for the differences in growing vegetables.

- It's quicker and more successful to make new plantings in compost-mulched beds. By comparison, having to mulch an overwintered green manure loses time in spring and often increases slugs.

- With the second cropping system I recommend, there is not enough growing time in autumn for green manures to establish. They can be grown only if you forgo the second / summer planting of vegetables.

- No dig soil is not 'bare' in winter. It is covered by a mulch and soil life is preserved beneath, undisturbed.

Further viewing
YouTube video – *Propagation: germinate, grow and plant seedlings for a long season of bigger harvests*

Quiz Lesson 2

	Question	Multiple choice
1	When starting a new no dig bed, when would you lay cardboard before mulching with compost?	A Always – it's essential to encourage the soil to regenerate. B Sometimes – if the soil is particularly hard. C Never – just mulch with compost. D Sometimes – if there are many weeds and they are growing strongly.
2	Which is more important?	A To feed soil life with mulches, whatever you plan to grow. B To know about 'light' and 'heavy' feeding vegetables. C To feed plants so that they grow with large, soft leaves.
3	Firm, mulched soil is better for plant growth than fluffy soil which has been loosened by tools.	True or false?
4	No dig beds need the soil to be loosened after a few years to improve drainage.	True or false?
5	How water-soluble are nutrients found in soil and compost?	A All nutrients in soil and compost are water-soluble. B They are all water-soluble in soil. C They are all water-soluble in compost. D Most nutrients in compost, and nutrients processed by organisms in soil, are not water-soluble.
6	How long must you wait before planting into the compost of a new no dig bed?	A Three to six months, to make sure the weeds have died. B Two weeks, to give time for worms and other organisms to aerate the bed. C You can plant on the same day as you mulch the bed, when it's the correct season and the compost is mature.
7	Are permanent wooden sides essential for a no dig bed?	A No – it's better not to have them, as they provide a haven for slugs and other pests. B Yes – they must be used to keep beds clearly marked, and to stop people walking on them. C Always – and it's a drain on the budget.
8	How often must you sow green manures with no dig?	A Once a year, every year. B Every four years on rotation. C It's entirely your choice, mostly it works well to keep cropping vegetables.
9	If starting with a non-level site, uncomfortable to walk on say, with lots of uneven surface, what might be good to do before starting? Choose the answer which covers the most possibilities.	A Use a sharp spade to scrape soil (and any weeds) off the high bits, to place in the low bits or hollows, until more or less level. B Buy a soil / compost mix to fill the holes and hollows. C Both of these can be a starting point.
10	Is it obligatory to add more compost before transplanting succession vegetables in summer?	A Absolutely not – perhaps only if you have spread very little compost in the preceding winter. B I advise spreading compost every time, before you sow or transplant. C Use compost like fertiliser – add it several times a year.

Module 2
Top results for less time needed

No dig on different soil types

A lovely aspect of no dig is that soils that are usually considered difficult – clay or stony for example – become easy to garden. Soils that are 'difficult to work' are usually perfectly fertile, and with no dig we enhance that fertility, while sowing and planting in a soft surface of organic matter. This surface is easier for weeding too.

The no dig methodology in this course applies to all soils. The only variation I suggest is to use more compost on sandy and chalky soils, whose fertility and moisture retention are poor.

One more consideration is liability to flooding, which is a site and climate issue, and nothing to do with soil management. Raised beds and no dig will help, but you may need to undertake drainage work too.

(*See Lesson 15 for more on soil, and how it compares to compost.*)

I can illustrate the flexibility of no dig, using the gardens I have made as examples of working with soils of very different quality.

STONY SOIL

My first market garden, which I commenced in autumn 1982, was a brash soil full of limestone. I reckon these stones contribute to growth as they slowly turn to soil over millennia, and they can hold some moisture too. Growth was strong and healthy, but my parsnips and carrots were not often straight.

My first market garden, which was on brash soil, covered 1.8 hectares by 1985; I put thin mulches of compost on raised beds, with straw on the paths

Incidentally, this soil had a pH in the upper 7s, even 8.5 in places. Crops were all good except for asparagus, which I should be curious to try there again using extra compost – I was using less compost in the 1980s. The other difficulty was scab on potatoes, a result of the high pH, and again this would have been reduced by using more compost.

This garden was 10 km / 6 mi from Homeacres, with a similar climate.

During the 1980s I was no dig, but without mentioning it, because an even more standout approach at that time was being organic, still considered to be almost revolutionary – I was registered organic with the Soil Association. My approach wasn't no dig from the beginning because I used a tractor and rotavator to 'break the pasture' when starting a new piece of ground. I used strings to mark out 1.5 m / 5 ft beds and 60 cm / 24 in paths and shovelled soil from paths to beds, which thus became raised.

- Now I do not raise beds like this because I have worked out that there is a bit of mythology about 'raised beds', and growth is as good – if not better – on beds that are only a little higher than paths. The only time a high bed could be worthwhile is in areas that are prone to flooding. (Raised beds also put less strain on your back, though in gardening there is always some bending required.)

Another change is that I now make paths narrower, at 40 cm / 16 in wide, but in those days I had access to a lot of free straw and was not short of space. However, in mild winters the paths did need hand weeding, of grass growing from seeds in the straw after the annual mulch of straw had decomposed.

We spread the path straw in spring, rather than winter, to reduce the time it was down before sowing and planting, and in order to keep slug numbers reasonable. Nonetheless I suffered more slug damage than I do now, and also the straw kept soil temperature lower in the paths – not an advantage in spring. This is a reason not to mulch with straw in cool climates, because its light colour means that sunlight is partly reflected and the soil below is slow to warm.

I mulched paths with straw because my main worry when beginning was that weeds would grow more than my crops. I was cropping an area of 6,000 m² / 1.5 acres on my own. During 1982 I had done some homework on the methods and results of other organic growers. Most of them were struggling to keep on top of weeds.

In 1983 my crops were good, and initially this was thanks to the soil being fertile and healthy after several years in pasture and from being grazed by cows. I maintained fertility with 1–2 cm / 0.4–0.8 in of compost each autumn or winter (less than I use now), but I was double cropping much less as well, and yields were lower than at Homeacres.

My first crop for sale was butterhead lettuce, sold as hearts, in May 1983

By 1987 I was experimenting with fleece, having previously spent a lot of time using cloches

Cabbage, kale and flowers in 1988 – the sixth year of cropping these no dig beds

Another result of the thin amount of compost mulch was more germination of weed seeds on all the beds. We did a fair amount of hoeing and were often hitting stones, making it hard work.

WHITE CLAY IN SOUTH WEST FRANCE

Tanger, my no dig garden in France from 1992 to 1997, was on the densest white clay (called *Boulbène*) that I could imagine. It was not liked by neighbouring farmers who had the same soil.

Back in 1992, I did not appreciate that Boulbène soil was so dense in winter that it was prone to being waterlogged; then in summer it dried very hard. Yet growth was excellent in the garden when I left it undisturbed and spread compost mulch. In the farm fields I knew only to plough, and struggled!

My vegetables were admired at market, including by farmers who knew the soil I was growing in. I grew organically too, and at first they were sceptical of a 'bio' (organic) approach, especially the no fertiliser part. However, several of them switched to it later when they noticed how many customers wanted that level of quality and would pay more for it.

At first in France I was worried about weed growth and moisture retention, having seen the amount of weeds growing when we viewed the farm in September. I mulched with hay for a couple of years, before noticing a fair number of slugs and weeds growing from seeds in the hay.

Above Tanger's top garden is white clay and pebbles, and was full of bindweed when I arrived

Below The farm buildings from below – most fields were on a slope

Above Sorting haricot beans after having shelled them, by walking on the dry pods

Below 1996 – in a garden I made below the farm, growing vegetables for the local market

Digging in a no dig bed – dark humus on top and crumbly clay below; 11 years before this soil was smelly and airless – sticky in winter, rock hard in summer

The no dig clay at 40 cm / 16 in – many earthworm holes are visible at the bottom, great for drainage and aeration

In that same year, these parsnips grew in the clay

We also dug a hole in the same clay soil in my brother's ploughed field, which had not received any organic matter for six years – his clay is on the left, mine is on the right

One result of ploughing clay is slow drainage between the ploughed and undisturbed soil

Again I switched to compost, making it easier to control weeds and retain moisture at the same time.

YELLOW CLAY IN SOMERSET WITH A LOAMY SURFACE

After France I made a market garden at Lower Farm in Shepton Montague, Somerset, the village where I grew up and had my first market garden. It was one mile away and at the other end of the village, but on completely different soil!

In November 1999 I took over a third of an acre of wet soil, which had been compacted in wet weather by heavy machines – it was the bottom triangle of a steep corner, awkward for large tractors. In some places I would find putrefying lumps of grey and airless soil, whose surface was sticky in winter and hard in summer.

It was a challenge, and growth in year one was barely even average. This was partly because I had spread no more than a 3–4 cm / 1.5 in cover of old horse manure on the beds, after clearing the weeds by pulling them – a sticky job. If I had known then what I know now I would have started with a thicker mulch, and in some places would have used cardboard.

Gradually my compost mulches changed the soil and gave it structure as it returned to life. Soil organisms multiplied and restored air, improving drainage and plant growth without any cultivations or forking. During the second year there was good growth; for example parsnips grew deep and long into the dense soil, which was also being aerated in dry summer conditions by some cracking.

I could have had faster results and fewer weeds by applying, say, 10 cm / 4 in of old manure or bought compost. However, at the time I did not need

41

high yields – sales were slow, before I discovered salad bags – and I was doing some building work.

Gradually I was learning, by observation, how soil can improve without physical intervention. In the first two years I spent a lot of time hoeing the hard surface until it became softer on top, thanks to mulching.

The photo at the foot of p.41 shows an unintended effect of cultivations in general, in this case of ploughing the field above my vegetable beds. The photo is from October, after 10 mm / 0.4 in of rain had fallen in 30 minutes, and water is running out of the cultivated area, down along my paths. (*See Lesson 7 for more on paths and their orientation – there are good reasons why these paths run up and down, rather than across the slope.*) Every autumn I spread another 3–4 cm / 1.5 in of compost: any of my own, old horse manure, green waste compost, or cow manure which I had bought. From year three onwards my vegetables were abundant. Furthermore weeds were few, and easy to pull or hoe in a surface which stayed soft in dry weather and was not sticky in winter.

My conclusion is that when you feed earthworms and other soil organisms from above, it allows soil to recover damaged structure over time. A rare exception is with soils where a true pan has developed, such that growth and drainage are awful. In this case a dig or forking is worthwhile, but only once. Incidentally, what is sometimes referred to as 'compaction' is just soil's natural firmness, which is good.

Crops in 2011, in the corner of the field where the soil had been compacted 11 years earlier

Carrots pulled in early June – they were grown under mesh in the same field corner

Another field corner at Lower Farm, where I intercropped apple trees with vegetables

Also at Lower Farm – soil in the old kitchen garden was dark and soft, probably from centuries of 'night soil' (human waste from drop-down loos)

Sissinghurst no dig market garden in May 2013 – it was a very cold spring

The same garden in March 2018 – mostly green waste compost on the beds, and wood chips on the paths

Sandy soil in Karen Drexler's garden, Florida

Homeacres soil profile under the drive, during building work, May 2013

Karen's garden in autumn – compost applied a year before, the sandy soil been washed by more than a metre (several feet) of rain since compost was applied

CLAY IN KENT

In 2012 I was asked, through Sarah Raven, to advise the National Trust about their uneconomic market garden at Sissinghurst in Kent, South East England. The soil is yellow clay with not much loam on top, and it had been damaged by two years of machine cultivations, on about four acres of land. Harvests were small and weeds were plentiful. The land was certified organic, and they were being advised by the UK's Soil Association.

I saw immediately that for the amount of harvests they needed the land area was too large. I recommended five things in particular:

1 To sell all the machinery, of which there was a lot.

2 To concentrate on high value crops, rather than growing field crops such as potatoes.

3 To grow everything in the 3,000 m^2 / 0.74 acre area which already had beds. These were being dug and were weedy, with not much compost used.

4 To concentrate all the compost for use on the beds in this smaller area and make it no dig. Also to buy some green waste compost.

5 To reduce the number of staff (many were volunteers) and to give them better support, such as a greenhouse for propagation.

The Trust implemented these changes and, within two years, the garden was needing much less input of time for a similar value of crops and from an area a quarter of the size.

SANDY SOIL

A final observation about soil types is from a friend who gardens on sand in Florida. Sand is hungry for food and moisture, but, since switching to no dig with compost mulches, she has found that her harvests are large and continue for longer.

The climate is hot and wet, and drainage is better now with no dig. Rainfall is 1300 mm / 51 in per year, with two thirds falling in the summer months when it is intense.

WHY ADDING COMPOST DOES NOT RAISE THE WHOLE GARDEN

I am often asked the question:
Won't I need a stepladder to get into my garden after years of repeatedly adding compost?

The answer is no for sure, and these are the reasons:

- Compost is of low density and settles to a reduced volume within a few months (though it may look a lot when you first apply it). This is also why I recommend walking on compost when making new beds, except if it is soggy.

- Compost is food for soil organisms, whose excretions are much denser than what they eat – notice the solidity of worm casts.

- The plants you grow and harvest take nutrition and carbon out of the soil.

An initial higher dose of compost is an investment in your growing for several years ahead. After year one, and in every succeeding year, you apply less.

Per weight of harvests taken you need less compost for no dig than for dig. When set against the reduction in time needed to manage a bed or garden over several years, the amount of compost is small.

Small Garden year eight, showing how its level
has not risen above the surrounding grass edge

Quiz Lesson 3

	Question	Multiple choice
1	The methods and materials you need for no dig change according to your soil type.	True or false?
2	When might it be an advantage to raise beds, with soil from paths or elsewhere? Choose two answers.	A On a site which lies very wet, from drainage being slow in that area. B On sandy soil. C To reduce the amount of bending down (though there is always some bending required).
3	What are the advantages of beds that are just a little raised, compared to path level? Choose the answer that describes the most possibilities.	A Plants on bed edges can easily access paths for moisture and food. B Less mulch falls from bed to path, because sides are not steep. C All of these. D There is better conservation of moisture in beds.
4	What effect does a mulch of cereal straw have on soil temperature?	A It slows the rise of the temperature in spring, and generally keeps soil cooler. B It makes no difference to soil temperature. C It increases soil temperature in bright sunshine.
5	What effect does a mulch of cereal straw have on moisture in soil?	A It holds more moisture in spring, but can prevent rain. reaching the soil in dry conditions, unless the rain is heavy. B It adds moisture to soil all the time. C It makes no difference.
6	How did I improve the compacted clay soil at Lower Farm?	A By mulching the surface with compost. B With thorough broadforking. C By digging a drainage ditch.
7	To have more harvests you always need more land, and perhaps machinery too.	True or false?

Comparing dig and no dig for 13 years – what the differences reveal

Every year, since 2007, I have grown vegetables and recorded the harvests from dig and no dig beds, each with a surface area of 7.5 m² / 81 ft².

Yields over 13 years, from 2007 to 2019, totalled:

- 1035 kg / 2282 lb from the dig beds.
- 1135 kg / 2502 lb from the same area of no dig beds.

These weights are of trimmed vegetables, and from the same plantings on both beds (at Lower Farm and then at Homeacres), with the same amount of compost added to each bed.

- Compost is spread on top of the no dig bed.
- Compost is incorporated into the dig bed, as in traditional gardening practice.

(*See Lesson 5 for a trial where compost is on top for both.*)

TWO IDENTICAL TRIAL BEDS

I ran this trial at Lower Farm for six years, and have run a very similar one at Homeacres for another seven so far, including in 2019. The Lower Farm trial consisted of four smaller beds, each measuring 1.5 × 2.5 m / 5 × 8 ft. When I moved to Homeacres, I simplified it to one bed of each, but with the same total area.

When I began the comparison in 2007, I had no idea whatsoever how growth would differ between dig and no dig, because I did not dig as part of annual soil preparation.

The harvest totals for Lower Farm (2007–12) were:

- 376 kg / 829 lb from the dig bed.
- 400 kg / 882 lb from the no dig bed.

As well as higher yields from no dig, I observed other notable differences. The soil was much easier to weed and water on the no dig beds at Lower Farm, and I noticed that parsnips rooted more deeply! The results at Homeacres have been broadly similar. Soil at Lower Farm was clay, and at Homeacres is silt over clay.

Yields from the two Homeacres' beds, in the seven years between 2013 and 2019, totalled:

- 656 kg / 1446 lb from the dig bed.
- 728 kg / 1605 lb from the no dig bed.

(*See also the bar chart, right*)

Over the two sites, and in 11 years out of 13, the no dig bed was higher yielding.

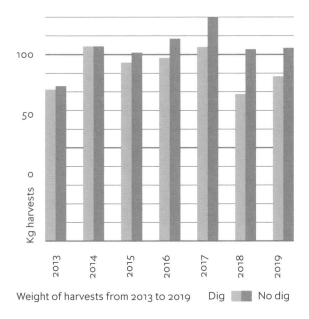

Kg harvests

Weight of harvests from 2013 to 2019   Dig   No dig

Mostly there is not a huge difference between the beds, but a common variation is *stronger growth in early spring* in the no dig bed. In the cold spring of 2018 this was especially marked – seedlings started strongly in surface compost, compared to loosened soil into which the compost was incorporated while digging.

To a gardener who habitually digs, the dig bed's soil would appear absolutely brilliant – soft and friable. Until you see the difference in growth. I suspect that, among other things, there is damage to fungal networks (*see Lesson 14*).

In spring 2018 there was more slug and wireworm damage on the dig bed, which contradicted the common assertion that 'digging allows birds to eat pests'.

Above Charles digging in December 2012, when the Homeacres trial began

Below On the same day – filling the no dig bed with the same amount of compost that we had added to the dig bed's trenches

Above Tipping compost (old cow manure) into the trench, after each one had been dug out

Below Two months later – I laid cardboard on the weedy paths, and some wood shavings on top of the card

What this statement should mention is how digging allows birds to eat worms, and other beneficial inhabitants of the soil. This disrupts the natural and fragile balance of pest and predator, for example ground beetles (*Carabus violaceus*) that eat slugs. Other beetle species climb plants to feed on aphids and caterpillars.

There is still plenty to be discovered about how soil organisms interact, and I reckon most of it will highlight the value of no dig / no till. My trial results point to that, as do these photos.

GROWTH DIFFERENCES – 2018

The growth differences revealed by this trial have now been consistent for 12 years, and lead me to question a lot of things, such as why the method of digging is so promoted and respected, even though it requires more time and results in inferior growth, less moisture retention, more weeds, more pests and worse drainage. Not to mention muddy boots and roots.

I suspect the answer is psychological, a desire to 'fit in' and be like other people. Also religious – the need for hard work, and to have dominion over nature.

Thankfully there are now enough 'no diggers' for these reasons to count for less. Have a look at the Facebook group 'No Dig Gardening – Undug', for example. It started in 2013 after a weekend course at Homeacres, where a few of us were lamenting the predominance in 'no dig social media' (such as it was) of permaculture using hay and straw mulches. The group keeps on growing – it now has, at the time of writing, 19,146 members, and two of the moderators were on that 2013 course: Stephanie Hafferty and Jan Wilmot.

The harvests of 19 June can be seen in the table on p.51.

December 2017 – after digging, I dropped compost in each subsequent trench

The trial beds are ready – the dig bed is on the left; the no dig bed has been compost mulched, and Finn is stabilising the sides

We made the first plantings and sowings on 31 March, then covered the beds with fleece; this is 15 days later

3 May – the final removal of fleece, after mostly cold and dull weather in April; some strong differences already, especially at the further end

21 May – the no dig bed is closest, with (left to right) onions, kohlrabi, potatoes, cabbage, lettuce, carrots, beetroot, spinach, and peas

Late June – harvesting Casablanca potatoes, a first / second early variety

27 May – end view, with the dig bed on the left and the no dig on the right; onions, kohlrabi, and potatoes are in the foreground

28 June – I have planted Cavolo Nero kale between carrots, which are soon to finish

By early June there is a new planting of celeriac next to the peas, while the spinach has only one more week of picking before it flowers

15 July – by now the beds have mostly new plantings; of the first plantings, only the onions are still left to pick

Harvests of 19 June – from the dig bed on the left and the no dig on the right

24 July – the dig bed in front and the no dig behind; these are second plantings after summer harvests – leeks, celeriac, celery, frizzy endive, kale, carrots, red beetroot, French beans, Golden beetroot, cucumber, and onions drying

These beds are a microcosm of the garden, with so many different vegetables in a relatively small area. They illustrate two important and often misunderstood aspects of vegetable growing:

- Many vegetables grow in half a season and, after clearing them in early to mid-summer, there is time to grow another harvest for autumn, winter and spring. See the 2018 and 2019 results tables below for ideas of first and second plantings.

- A four-year rotation is not necessary, unless your soil has been abused over decades (or longer), by digging and careless growing. For example on some allotments there are soil diseases, such as clubroot of brassicas and white rot of onions. Most soils do not have these long-lasting problems and need less attention given to rotation – especially when the soil is healthy no dig.

WATERING TEST

I put a video about this on YouTube: *Comparing water infiltration on dug soil with compost under, and no dig soil with compost on top*. The captions to the photos, right, explain what we did. I was shocked by the difference, when imagining the effects of heavy rain on cultivated fields.

HARVESTS – 2018

Towards the end of summer, growth usually looks more even than in spring and early summer. Harvests are another matter however, for example the red beetroot and leeks that we pulled in autumn, which looked similar when growing but weighed 15–50% more from the no dig bed. The results of 2018 show the widest difference that I had ever recorded – around 30% more harvests from no dig throughout the season. Perhaps it's to do with a stronger response to the dry conditions, although we water both beds the same amount.

The dig bed: watering between carrots with 2 × 12 l / 3.2 gal half-empty cans

The dig bed: after 30 seconds of watering

The no dig bed: watering between carrots with 2 × 12 l / 3.2 gal half-empty cans

The no dig bed: after 30 seconds of watering

HARVESTS OF 19 JUNE 2018		
Crop	Dig g	No Dig g
Peas Delikata	80	710
Beetroot Avonearly	170	630
Carrots Nantes	40	380
Lettuce leaves	1350	1550
Potatoes Cas.	1710	1530
TOTAL	**3.35 kg** **7.39 lb**	**4.80 kg** **10.58 lb**

2018 – FIRST AND SECOND PLANTINGS				
First – Second planting First planting: spring and summer Second planting: summer and autumn	First Dig kg	First No Dig kg	Second Dig kg	Second No Dig kg
Peas – (dill) Leeks	0.80	3.32	2.46	3.87
Spinach – Celeriac	0.03	2.42	4.23	3.78
Beetroot – Celery	1.21	2.86	1.90	7.04
Carrots – Endive	0.26	0.92	3.66	4.13
Carrots – Kale	0.26	0.92	3.38	4.51
Lettuce – Carrots	9.62	12.75	3.91	6.37
Cabbage – Beetroot	0.16	0.93	8.80	10.28
Potatoes – French beans	7.90	6.82	3.34	3.40
Potato – Beetroot	7.90	6.82	6.27	6.99
Kohlrabi – Cucumber	0.06	0.61	1.75	3.45
Onion – Lettuce	5.18	4.82	5.03	5.24
Kaibroc, third after cucumber	–	–	1.59	1.88
TOTAL	**33.38 kg** **73.59 lb**	**43.19 kg** **95.22 lb**	**46.32 kg** **102.11 lb**	**60.94 kg** **134.35 lb**
TOTAL HARVEST	**Dig Bed** **79.7 kg / 175.7 lb**		**No Dig Bed** **104.1 kg / 229.5 lb**	

15 September
All second plantings made in the summer (dig bed on the left, no dig on the right)

Harvests from 20 September – 0.41 kg / 0.9 lb of carrots from the dig bed and 0.75 kg / 1.7 lb from the no dig bed; plus 2.19 kg / 4.8 lb of beetroot from the dig bed and 3.15 kg / 6.9 lb from the no dig bed – each bed had the same number of roots

9 October
(Dig bed on the left)
lettuce are cropping where onions had been, plus Kaibroc broccoli has followed cucumber

14 October
Final harvest of June-sown Nantes carrots: left 1.07 kg / 2.4 lb from the dig bed; and right 2.51 kg / 5.5 lb from the no dig bed, 132 days since sowing

HARVESTS – 2019

For the seventh time I dug the dig bed in December, and incorporated two large barrows of compost. On top of the no dig bed I simply spread the same amount, which settled to a layer of 2.5 cm / 1 in. I also spread 25% of homemade compost and 25% of mushroom compost, not mixed together but each batch scattered evenly on top.

Spring growth of the dig bed's potatoes was fine, but its spinach and beetroot were desperately slow, as in 2018.

Frost on 6 May – fleece over the potatoes; dig bed on the left

June – no dig bed closest

September – dig bed on the left

October – no dig bed closest

2019 – FIRST AND SECOND PLANTINGS				
First – Second planting First planting: spring and summer Second planting: summer and autumn	First Dig kg	First No Dig kg	Second Dig kg	Second No Dig kg
Beetroot – Beetroot	1.59	4.58	7.18	6.71
Cabbage – Carrot	2.36	2.57	4.72	5.02
Carrot – Celeriac	0.88	0.50	2.65	3.27
Lettuce – Celery	12.95	15.85	2.33	4.64
Onion – Cucumber	6.80	7.50	8.08	9.19
Peas (pods) – Endive	3.50	5.89	4.43	5.61
Potatoes – Fennel	15.29	14.21	0.72	0.93
Radish – French beans	0.43	0.94	4.05	4.93
Spinach – Kale	0.0	2.07	5.03	2.72
Turnip – Leeks	0.22	1.54	6.71	7.07
– Lettuce			1.54	2.24
TOTAL	44.02 kg 97.05 lb	55.65 kg 122.69 lb	47.44 kg 104.59 lb	52.33 kg 115.37 lb
TOTAL HARVEST	Dig Bed 91.46 kg / 201.63 lb		No Dig Bed 107.98 kg / 238.06 lb	

MEASURING THE SOIL DIFFERENCES – OCTOBER 2019

I sent samples of soil from each bed, taken at a depth of 15 cm / 6 in, to a microbiologist in Norway – Katelyn Solbakk. The results of her study resulted in a paper, which included the table below.

Solbakk's paper illustrates and explains the differences she saw in a microscope analysis of each bed's soil, and can be summarised as follows:

'There was a very noticeable difference in the physical condition between the dig and no dig samples. All samples did appear to be rich in organic matter, but the no dig samples were exceptionally clean and well aggregated. The structure was significantly weaker in the dug soil, with more loose, unbound debris and fewer large aggregates. The no dig samples had a very clean appearance with large, strong aggregates and very little unbound material.'

One hears little about protozoa, but here is what Katelyn has to say about them on her website – mikroliv.no.

'Protozoa are important but often under-appreciated members of the soil food web. The main ecological role of soil protozoa, as it is currently understood from our perspective, is to free up nutrients that have been immobilized by bacteria, completing what is known as the "microbial loop". Different species of protozoa are known to selectively hunt particular types of bacteria, so if there are many types of protozoa, it could be a sign that there are many types of bacteria as well. Protozoa have also been found to provide benefits to plants that extend beyond the release of nutrients, such as improved growth and disease resistance.'

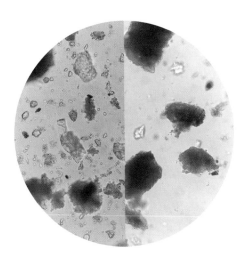

Katelyn's microscope analysis of soil – from the dig bed (left), and the no dig bed (right) – shows the aggregation of the no dig soil creating better resistance to erosion, with less unbound material

The evaluation of protozoa in each bed, from Katelyn Solbakk's report

SINGLE CELLED EUKARYOTES	DIG	NO DIG	FULL GARDEN
Testate amoebas	12	216	48
Round testate amoebas	0	24	0
Flagellates	144	444	1104
Ciliates	0	24	24
Cysts	144	288	240
Diatoms	156	252	228
Naked amoebas	12	84	72
Heliozoa	0	12	0
Types of flagellates	4	9	12
No. of groups	6	9	7
Biodiversity rating	1.5	1.8	1.3
TOTAL EVALUATION OF PROTOZOA	**1.8**	**2.2**	**1.8**

Of the samples taken from each bed, Katelyn wrote:

'In these samples, there was a considerable improvement in protozoa abundance and diversity in both the no dig trial bed and the full garden sample, compared to the dug bed.'

TIME AND WEED DIFFERENCES

The dig beds need more time than no dig:

- Around two and a half hours for digging.
- An extra half hour through the season for weeding.

Disturbing soil causes weed seeds to germinate (*see Lesson 9 and the photos from Lower Farm in 2010, right*). The classic reason given for this is that cultivation exposes some weed seeds to the light, triggering their germination. I think another reason is that disturbed soil *needs to heal*, and weeds are part of the healing process. We see an example of this with chickweed, which grows so fast after the passage of a rotavator – I know this from experience!

The photo of surface conditions between the parsnips (in July 2010) is after four weeks with just 27 mm / 1.1 in of rain, and afternoon temperatures of 21–24°C / 70–75°F. No water was given, and the dug clay is cracking along the lines where my spade had entered, allowing a lot of moisture to escape.

TRIALS AND UPTAKE ELSEWHERE

Following my work to promote no dig, I am heartened to see its uptake by official bodies, who, until recently, were following well established but old-fashioned Victorian methods. For example, the current gardens manager at RHS Wisley heard me lecture on no dig at Kew Gardens in 2011 and decided to give it a try on her allotment. The results were so consistently good that she has introduced the method to students at Wisley in Surrey, and to apprentices studying there. Wisley's edibles garden is now no dig.

Kew Gardens in London give each of their students a bed, to grow vegetables and then be examined on. Since 2018, these beds have been no dig. Many National Trust gardens are now no dig too.

Another significant trial started in 2016, at Beechgrove garden in north east Scotland, near Aberdeen. The garden is run entirely for the BBC television series *The Beechgrove Garden*. They set up two areas side by side – one dig, and the other no dig – and initially were sceptical of how the no dig plants would grow. Each year the no dig vegetables have grown strongly, to the point when, in November 2018, they decided to convert all of their vegetable growing to no dig.

You are in good company!

Above The dig bed in April with spinach, beetroot, and weed seedlings growing

Below The no dig bed on the same day, with the same crops and clean compost

Above The dig bed in a dry July – the parsnip bed was dug in winter and compost dug in; now it is cracking

Below The no dig parsnip bed was not dug in winter and it is not cracking

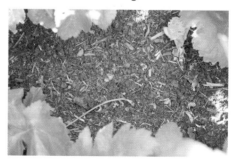

Further reading & viewing
More details on the dig / no dig trials from 2013–2018 can be found on my website: charlesdowding.co.uk

Two YouTube videos of my no dig bed at Homeacres in 2017 show you exactly how I managed to grow over 120 kg on 7.5 m² / 265 lb on 81 ft² —

First plantings of half season veg before seconds in summer, 120 kg / 264 lb veg in a year

Increase harvests with second plantings in same year

At Wisley in Surrey, the RHS give each student (or apprentice) a plot which is half dig and half no dig

With Jim McColl at the BBC's Beechgrove Garden in Scotland, where their 2016–18 trial of dig and no dig beds has recorded stronger harvests from no dig; Jim was sceptical at first, but now loves no dig

Quiz Lesson 4

	Question	Multiple choice
1	Which of these are common differences between the dig and no dig beds in my trials? Choose the answer which covers the most aspects.	A All of these. B There are more weeds on the dig beds, all year long. C Water soaks into the mulched surface of the no dig bed, more easily than the dig bed with soil on top. D Growth in spring is faster on the no dig bed.
2	Roughly how much extra time is needed at Homeacres each year to maintain the dig bed, compared to the no dig bed?	A Three hours. B There is no difference in the time needed. C Two and a half hours.
3	Name two aspects of vegetable growing that are highlighted by the way I run this trial.	A Most vegetables grow in half a year, in climates with this level of warmth. B Vegetables all need the same amount of water. C A four-year rotation is less important than usually thought. D Weeds are less common in dug soil.
4	When BBC Scotland started their trial at Beechgrove Garden, they were enthusiastic about no dig.	True or false?

The Three-strip trial and continuous cropping

COMPARING FORKING / NO DIG, DIFFERENT COMPOSTS AND NO ROTATION

A trial I have run since 2013 looks to understand the effects on plant growth of soil cultivation, compost use, and no rotation. Or I should say minimal rotation, as you see below.

The trial came about after meeting some Japanese growers near Avebury. They followed the Shumei teachings of Mochiki Okada (1882–1955), who advocated cultivating gratitude to soil for health in mind and body:

- No compost or manure is added to soil, as this can prevent it from achieving its 'natural composition of complexity and balance'.

- No rotation, so continuous cropping of the same plants in the same place every year, to 'encourage growth of specific soil organisms beneficial to each one'.

- Seed is saved, so that all seeds contain the genetic information they require to grow best in the location and soil they 'know'.

- Weeds are tolerated and so is cultivation. At Avebury they even use a rotavator – I observed this frequently during the time I was working with them.

I like some of their approach, except for one thing in particular: I feel no dig and surface mulching both express maximum gratitude to soil! The only home-saved seeds I use are climbing and broad / fava beans. All other seeds are from Bingenheimer Saatgut, raised in the broadly similar climate of Germany and organic or biodynamic as well.

THE THREE-STRIP TRIAL

The three strips of this trial each measure 2 × 9 m / 7 × 30 ft. Between each strip is a 40 cm / 16 in path, from the concrete path to the trees.

In 2013 we didn't add any organic matter to Strips 1 or 2, compared to 5 cm / 2 in of old, but rather lumpy cow manure, which was added to Strip 3. Weeds were killed by digging Strip 1, and by mulching the other two strips with polythene. The main growth before this trial was grass, with creeping buttercup and dandelions (*see Lesson 9, which is all about weeds*).

First year summary (2013):

- Strip 1 – dig, no compost, weeds killed by the digging.

- Strip 2 – no dig, no compost, weeds killed by polythene mulch.

- Strip 3 – no dig, 5 cm / 2 in of compost, weeds killed by compost and polythene mulch.

January 2013 – the start of the trial, with Strip 1 being dug by the Japanese growers

April – the polythene has been temporarily rolled back; Strip 3 is being finished with some more old cow manure

I rolled back the polythene on 19 May – most of the grass had died, but some clover and dandelion plants were still alive, just

Strip 2 has been mulched with cardboard and landscape fabric; Strip 1 has all been dug, with the turves turned over

The first plantings on 22 May were beans, squash and celeriac, with the same spacings on each strip

Steph spreading old cow manure on part of what will become Strip 3

The most difficult holes to make were on Strip 2, with no dig and no compost creating sticky soil

12 days later – I laid cardboard over part of Strip 2, where it looked like clover may be regrowing

Covering Strips 2 and 3 with polythene, to exclude light and kill weeds

End of June – the cardboard did not work, so I used a sharp spade to turn over the top 2.5 cm / 1 in of Strip 2

Strip 1 in early July – cabbage, leeks, beetroot, celeriac, squash, and beans

Strip 2 on the same day

Strip 3 on the same day

29 July – you can see the growth differences of Uchiki Kuri squash; Strip 1 is the closest

7 September – Strip 1 is closest

In the first two months after planting, growth was much the slowest in Strip 2. I believe there were two reasons for this:

- No compost meant that new plants were in competition for nutrients, with weed roots that were still decomposing. A milder version of having wood in the soil, which has a similar effect. Hence my recommendation to apply some compost / organic matter on top of decomposing weeds, especially when you want to crop immediately, at the same time as weeds are dying.

- The digging of Strip 1 happened four months before first plantings: time for bacteria to decompose many weed roots and thus have more nutrients available for plant growth. Digging stimulates bacterial activity in the short term – through introducing oxygen at the time of cultivation – but not in a sustainable, long-term way.

By autumn the difference between Strips 1 and 2 was much smaller, such that their final harvests were similar (although skewed by the beetroot, which swelled a lot in autumn).

- The standout result was a 50% higher total harvest from Strip 3, and it was this, along with Steph's urging, that persuaded me to change the trial parameters.

One factor to be considered in my trials is that I am running a market garden, not a research station. I do not have funding for trials, unless I fund them from private income or sale of goods. I did not want the lower yields and lower revenue that resulted from not adding compost to Strips 1 and 2. Also it would have taken more time to keep them weed-free, meant more watering, and would have depressed the bountiful look of Homeacres' garden.

Above Mustard green manure (*Synapsis alba*) in mid-October, between vegetables still to harvest

Below February 2014 – I have dug Strip 1 again, and mulched Strip 3 with another 5 cm / 2 in of old cow manure

Above March – new broad beans have been planted, and leeks are still growing; there is rockdust on half of each strip

Below 10 April – the final harvest of leeks, from Strip 3 on the left and Strip 1 on the right

2013 HARVESTS, THREE-STRIP TRIAL			
Vegetable	Strip 1 Dig	Strip 2 No dig	Strip 3 No dig with cow manure compost
	kg	kg	kg
Beans Czar	0.95	0.83	0.75
Beans Borlotti	0.57	0.23	0.77
Squash Kabocha	4.39 3 plants	2.74 2 plants	7.75 3 plants
Squash Kuri	5.42 7 plants	3.07 4 plants	8.95 9 plants
Celeriac	1.51	1.14	2.82
Beetroot	16.56	20.86	25.96
Leek Zermatt	1.6	1.37	2.48
Leek Bandit 22 per strip	3.03	3.36	5.55
Cabbage Filderkraut	5.5	6.18	6.16
Cabbage Kalibos	1.51	0.85	1.14
TOTAL	41.04 kg 90.48 lb	40.63 kg 89.57 lb	62.33 kg 137.41 lb

Above May 2014 – we reconfigured the trial layout, and added 5 cm / 2 in of green waste compost to the new beds of Strips 1 and 2

Below Early July – growth is stronger than in 2013; beans, squash, beetroot, broad beans and leeks are all in the same areas as they had been the previous year

Above Early October – after many harvests (including squash), and with mustard sown four weeks earlier

Below November – mustard for green manure

CHANGES IN 2014

In May 2014, I used my sharp spade to scrape 4–5 cm / 1.5–2 in of soil from the 30 cm / 12 in width of what became sunken paths, between slightly raised 1.2 m / 4 ft beds. Steph was helping, and together we spread compost on Strips 1 and 2. This raised the beds enough to demarcate them in a clear way, with six beds in each strip.

The lowering of paths and raising of beds is an optional extra in any garden. At Homeacres I mostly have beds 'raised' with compost only, which are not very high – a more accurate term would be mounds. However if your site is wet, say with water lying in winter, I would lower the paths to raise the beds; this does involve some earth-moving.

The other change was to switch from annual digging to forking, from autumn 2014. In February 2014 I had already dug Strip 1, so the effect of forking is from 2015 onwards.

Strip 1 is different to the dig bed of my other trial, because of forking and not digging, and applying compost as a mulch rather than incorporating it.

Summary from 2014 onwards:

- Strip 1 – soil loosened by forking each winter without inversion, then 5 cm / 2 in of green waste / mushroom compost (half of each) on the surface in December (In 2014 it was all green waste).

- Strip 2 – no dig, then the same compost as Strip 1: 5 cm / 2 in of green waste / mushroom compost (half of each) on the surface each December (In 2014 it was all green waste).

- Strip 3 – no dig, then 5 cm / 2 in of composted cow manure on the surface in winter; the paths had a wood chip mulch in March.

Looking at the photo from May 2014, top left, you can see the six beds of each strip and the narrow paths between. I left these paths as old pasture without any mulch; some of the dead grass and weeds were still visible for almost two years.

I numbered the beds, with Bed 1 nearest the concrete path and Bed 6 nearest the apple trees.

2014 HARVESTS, THREE-STRIP TRIAL			
Vegetable	Strip 1 Dig with green waste compost kg	Strip 2 No dig with green waste compost kg	Strip 3 No dig with cow manure compost kg
Beans Czar, dry	1.36	1.45	1.49
Beans Borlotti, dry	1.10	1.10	1.51
Beetroot – 1st	7.09	8.89	1.89 leatherjackets
Beetroot – 2nd	4.54	4.54	5.22
Broad bean	3.77	3.87	4.06
Potato	3.92	3.37	5.25
Lettuce	5.92	8.9	7.97
Endive	11.42	14.98	8.49
Mustard – 2nd	2.49	2.61	2.64
Squash	10.29 6 plants	10.34 4 plants	14.66 10 plants
Leeks – 1st	2.41	3.64	3.78
Leeks – 2nd	1.73	2.64	4.15
Carrot (slugs)	0.25	1.29	0.17
Brussels	2.66	2.02	2.03
Cabbage, red	4.19	4.33	6.24
Kale	0.33	0.62	0.51
TOTAL	65.36 kg 144.09 lb	74.59 kg 164.44 lb	70.06 kg 154.46 lb

THREE STRIP TRIAL

Mustard killed by frost of −6°C / 21°F, just four weeks earlier

Therefore each of the three strips has six beds, as shown above right.

GREEN MANURES OR VEGETABLES?

After the squash harvest in each of the first three years, I sowed mustard as a green manure because I didn't need the space for other vegetables. This mustard is suitable for no dig, because of being killed by frosts of −5°C / 23°F or lower. Some gardeners worry because it's a brassica, but I rotate less than they do, and that is another aspect of this trial.

Since 2016, I have taken to planting brassicas and spinach after the squash harvest and often on the same day, in late August. Kuri squash are brilliant for this because they mature so early, compared to say, butternut.

DIFFERENCES IN PEST DAMAGE

We noticed more pest damage on Strip 3 in 2014 (mostly slugs), thanks to the cow manure being not fully composted and rather lumpy, with some straw still visible. Since 2016 I have been careful to use finer cow manure, making a more even surface with only small lumps.

2014 was a difficult spring for leatherjacket damage. They are larvae of craneflies (*Tipula spp*). Mostly the brown larvae live among grass roots and may be a problem in year one, when you are planting into compost on old pasture where the larvae are already present. It was unusual for them to be such a problem in year two.

The only remedy I know is to hunt with one's fingers in the compost, near to seedling plants which are visibly damaged. You can see holes in base leaves and even plants that have fallen over due to stems being eaten. Steph and I found a fair few leatherjackets, especially among small beetroot and lettuce; most damage is to spring plantings, then the larvae pupate in June.

2015–17

Again in 2015 there was more slug damage on Strip 3, especially to carrot seedlings and even to some parsnips. Strip 2 gave more harvests than Strip 1, for reasons yet to be discovered. I suspect it's because of damage to mycorrhizal fungi.

Left, from top
March – the beds are ready for 2015, with broad beans under fleece

August 2015 – summer abundance; the leeks (under mesh) were planted after potatoes

Six weeks later, and there are only small differences between the strips

Right, from top
Mid-October – Josh forking the soil of Strip 1, loosening not inverting

The same day in October, and new salad plants are where climbing beans had just finished

October harvest of parsnips – Strip 1 on the left, Strip 3 on the right; the total weight was around 3.6 kg / 8 lb

2015 HARVESTS, THREE-STRIP TRIAL				
Bed	Vegetable	Strip 1 Dig with green waste compost kg	Strip 2 No dig with green waste compost kg	Strip 3 No dig with cow manure compost kg
1	Garlic	1.42	1.14	0.92
1	Beans Czar	1.63	1.66	1.49
1	Beans Borlotti	1.30	1.00	1.48
2	Squash Kuri	14.7 9 plants	16.91 10 plants	23.74 17 plants
3	Spinach	3.77	3.87	4.06
3	Beetroot	2.34	2.63	3.39
3	Parsley April	0.12	0.14	0.10
3	Broccoli Sibsey	1.76	2.68	1.42
3	Red cabbage 3 per strip	4.80	4.32	3.61
3	Savoy cabbage 3 per strip	3.34	3.06	3.51
4	Potato Rocket	1.26	1.63	1.35
4	Potato Charlotte	7.76	7.54	7.37
4	Leeks	6.73	8.70	9.87
5	Broad beans Aquadulce	8.47	8.14	9.87
5	Endive, lettuce	15.85	15.05	13.70
6	Carrot Nantes	1.79	2.05	0
6	Parsnips Gladiator	8.99	15.10	9.92
6	Parsnips White Gem	7.61	9.78	10.53
	TOTAL	91.78 kg 202.34 lb	104.31 kg 229.96 lb	104.54 kg 230.47 lb

2016 HARVESTS, THREE-STRIP TRIAL				
Bed	Vegetable	Strip 1 Dig with green waste compost kg	Strip 2 No dig with green waste compost kg	Strip 3 No dig with cow manure compost kg
1	Mustard, Green in the Snow	3.10	3.21	3.71
1	Beans Czar	1.15	1.22	1.27
1	Beans Borlotti	1.04	1.05	1.20
1	Winter salads	0.66	1.24	0.78
2	Squash Kuri	6.05	14.39	8.03
2	Chinese cabbage	12.31	14.06	10.95
3	Broad beans Aquadulce	19.34	14.95	8.58
3	Filderkraut cabbage 6 per bed	12.97	16.67	14.23
4	Potato Marie Rose	7.17	7.54	7.27
4	Potato Charlotte	6.31	7.42	7.92
4	Leeks	10.60	10.37	11.13
5	Lettuce	18.51	20.22	19.16
6	Chicory	6.41	5.49	7.74
6	Carrot Nantes	0.32	0.69	0
6	Radish Poloneza	0.48	0.69	0.55
6	Parsnips Gladiator	9.27	10.98	5.06
6	Parsnips White Gem	5.62	11.02	4.38
	TOTAL	120.30 kg 265.24 lb	143.12 kg 315.53 lb	111.96 kg 246.83 lb

June 2016 – broad beans already harvested, and there are new plants of cabbage

Above March 2017 – the winter salads are still cropping, and the beans are already growing strongly

Below September 2017 – I had to grow beetroot in Beds 2, after gales destroyed the squash plants in June

The forking we do is as gentle as possible; I aim to loosen only, with almost no lifting of soil lumps. The soil always feels pretty loose while forking.

2016 was a year of bountiful harvests, after a warm spring and fine summer, and the totals from each strip continued to rise. This was also due to changes in the vegetables grown, such as lettuce – always high yielding by weight.

Furthermore I had more help and could be more rapid with second plantings, often on the same day after clearing the first crops. For example, on the same morning we might harvest all remaining potatoes and then plant leeks.

Another factor in the higher totals is cabbage. The Filderkraut had time to make heavy hearts, after we had cleared the broad beans. And Chinese cabbage is mostly water! In this climate its best time of growth is autumn, from sowing between 30 July and 7 August. Slugs love Chinese cabbage, and Strip 3 suffered again, as did the carrot seedlings.

In autumn 2016 we spread older (3 years) and finer cow manure compost, and this helped growth on Strip 3 in 2017. Nonetheless there was damage to carrot seedlings again, and in August I filled gaps in Bed 6 of Strip 3 with plants of kohlrabi.

Leek yields in 2017 were the highest ever, growing for the third year in Beds 4, after potatoes. The Filderkraut cabbage heads grew enormous, also their third year in Beds 3.

There was an interruption to 'no rotation' in Beds 2, after high winds on 7 June ripped out the plants. I had some spare beetroot from a sowing in early June and we planted them instead.

Adding the harvests of 2014–17 gives interesting totals. The figures suggest that forking soil is not helping growth, and that finer compost gives best results. Also that continuous cropping (no rotation) is less terrible than one often hears!

I was wondering how this would all go in 2018, and whether the totals from each strip would continue to rise.

Bed	Vegetable	Strip 1 Dig with mushroom compost kg	Strip 2 No dig with mushroom compost kg	Strip 3 No dig with cow manure compost kg
		2017 HARVESTS, THREE-STRIP TRIAL		
1	Winter salads & spinach	4.36	7.58	6.31
1	Beans Czar	1.85	2.34	2.04
1	Beans Borlotti	0.92	1.14	1.28
2	Beetroot Robuschka	26.96	24.64	29.00
3	Broad beans Aquadulce	12.08	11.65	9.75
3	Filderkraut cabbage	19.01	21.05	20.93
3	Leek	0.84	0.51	0.96
4	Potato	9.17	9.77	10.48
4	Leeks	15.32	14.31	16.04
5	Lettuce	22.17	24.83	26.34
5	Chicory	3.52	3.64	4.22
5	Leek	2.68	3.24	3.16
6	Spinach Palco	9.29	10.53	10.81
6	Carrots	14.90	6.17	4.58
6	Kohlrabi	1.62	6.68	11.28
	Total to 11.08 First crops	59.07	64.36	63.67
	TOTAL	144.69 kg 318.97 lb	148.08 kg 326.46 lb	157.18 kg 346.52 lb

Year	Strip 1 Dig forked, bought compost kg	Strip 2 No dig bought compost kg	Strip 3 No dig with cow manure compost kg
	2014–17 TOTAL HARVESTS, THREE-STRIP TRIAL		
2014	67.92	78.55	75.41
2015	90.23	101.71	102.42
2016	120.33	142.14	111.97
2017	144.69	148.08	157.18
4 year TOTAL	423.17 kg 932.93 lb	470.48 kg 1037.23 lb	446.08 kg 983.44 lb

The trial continues, Charles spacing potatoes to plant, April 2020

From top 1 April 2018 – similar results to those of the previous year

August 2018 – some water had been given after a very dry three months

November 2018 – new compost for the coming year had been spread on Bed 5 of Strips 2 and 3; there is cow manure compost on the right

2018

The 2018 results reflect a dry growing season from early May until November, with only 272.2 mm / 11 in of rain in that half of the year. This compares to the average of 474 mm / 19 in for that period, an unusually large anomaly for such a long length of time. Plus it was warmer and often breezy, with high rates of evapotranspiration.

Considering the weather, growth was good. We watered from rain butts when possible and with a hose as well – maintenance rations, except for salads and plants close to harvest. Moisture levels looked similar on all beds, judging by the amount of wilting leaves on hot afternoons in the summer.

Our watering helped the neighbouring apple trees, and by October I was noticing plenty of new growth on trees adjoining the kale of Beds 6, which struggled for moisture as a result! See photos, right. In contrast, the apple trees which are bordered by grass made almost no new growth after their July pruning. Normally they would have added another 10–20 cm / 4–8 in of new wood by October.

The table, right, reveals continuing trends and some new differences, in particular larger second crops from Strip 3. Leeks, cabbage and chicory noticeably grew stronger in this strip in autumn 2018.

Perhaps there is a higher nutrient status in the cow manure, although it was three to four years old by 2018. Furthermore, the cow manure heap had been open to rain washing through for two years, and had grown squash in 2016, then potatoes and kohlrabi in 2017.

For some reason the squash harvest on Bed 2 of Strip 3 continued to disappoint, and I have noticed, when dibbing holes to plant, that the soil is harder there. This bed puzzles me.

Once again, forking has slightly depressed the yields of Strip 1. Sometimes the growth looks similar between Strips 1 and 2, but harvests weigh less, from leaves being less dense. Possibly this is related to damaged soil fungi, resulting in lower availability of nutrients and moisture.

2018 HARVESTS, THREE-STRIP TRIAL			
Vegetable	Strip 1 Dig forked with green waste & mushroom compost	Strip 2 No dig with green waste & mushroom compost	Strip 3 No dig with cow manure compost
	kg	kg	kg
Winter salads & spinach	4.61	5.89	4.50
Beans Czar	1.36	1.35	1.50
Beans Borlotti	0.82	1.06	1.20
Squash Kuri	12.73	16.28	7.56
Spinach	4.18	4.40	4.55
Broad beans Aquadulce	9.35	13.08	10.93
Filderkraut cabbage	9.12	8.42	13.36
Potato	12.82	14.29	14.18
Leeks	8.81	8.97	12.30
Lettuce	17.63	18.46	17.04
Chicory 506TT	13.06	12.67	15.02
Spinach Palco	6.27	6.75	6.85
Leeks	6.73	8.70	9.87
Kale Cavolo Nero	4.00	3.31	2.79
TOTAL	104.76 kg 230.96 lb	114.93 kg 253.38 lb	111.78 kg 246.43 lb

From top 5 September – an Adams Pearmain apple tree in its sixth year, showing new wood at the top that has grown since July, a result of watering the neighbouring kale

On the same day, a nearby Lord Lambourne apple tree, with grass on both sides and showing little new wood after its July pruning

Above Late May 2019 – Strip 3 on the left

Below June 2019 – Strip 1 is nearest

Above September 2019 – Strip 1 is on the left

Below November 2019 – the nearest beds are winter salads, planted on 10 October after beans

2019 SHOWS STRIP 3 CATCHING UP, AND CONTINUOUS CROPPING GOING WELL

Two things were especially notable in 2019:

- There were higher harvests from Strip 3 – though we did use a different cow manure (from a depot rather than a farm), and the straw was chopped.

- There was the highest ever harvest of broad beans, cabbages and potatoes, in the fifth consecutive year of *growing in the same soil*. In case you may wonder, these plants root deep into the soil. I am often asked if the annual application of compost is equivalent to 'new soil'. The answer is no, it's just food for soil organisms, and plants are rooting into the same soil which is well fed.

The 2019 harvests total 363 kg on 65 m^2, including paths. That equates to 56 tonnes per hectare or 22 tonnes per acre of kitchen-ready food (except for the pods of broad beans).

Each of the tables shown contain interesting figures, but they are all a snapshot of one year only. And the trial continues.

Further viewing
YouTube videos –

Rotation: how necessary is it for vegetables?

Three-strip trial: effects (or not) of no rotation, and comparing forked soil & no dig

2019 HARVESTS, THREE-STRIP TRIAL			
Vegetable	Strip 1 Dig forked with green waste & mushroom compost	Strip 2 No dig with green waste & mushroom compost	Strip 3 No dig with cow manure compost
	kg	kg	kg
Winter salads & spinach	6.07	6.99	7.29
Beans Czar	2.46	2.14	2.43
Beans Borlotti	1.37	1.23	1.29
Squash Kuri	5.46	9.29	5.65
Spinach	4.97	4.24	3.74
Broad beans Aquadulce	15.10	15.45	16.95
Filderkraut cabbage	16.07	18.04	21.10
Potato	16.10	16.38	15.70
Leeks	7.70	7.47	10.26
Lettuce	16.26	18.82	20.43
Chicory 506TT	9.83	7.11	9.45
Spinach Palco	6.64	6.72	10.36
Kale Cavolo Nero	4.32	3.99	3.67
TOTAL to 27.08 First crops	112.35 kg 247.69 lb	117.87 kg 259.89 lb	128.32 kg 282.90 lb

THREE-STRIP TRIAL RESULTS, 2014–19
showing some evening out with Strip 2 less ahead, Strip 3 catching up

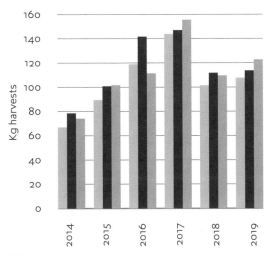

Kg harvests

2014 2015 2016 2017 2018 2019

■ Strip 1 – Forked 50% mushroom compost, 50% green waste
■ Strip 2 – No dig 50% mushroom compost, 50% green waste
■ Strip 3 – No dig composted cow manure

Results from each of the three strips over six years

STRIP 3: 683.52
STRIP 2: 702.16
STRIP 1: 639.26

Quiz Lesson 5

	Question		Multiple choice
1	Which of these statements is not true?	A	In this trial, all compost mulches are applied on the surface.
		B	In Strip 1 of this trial, the soil is loosened with a fork, and not moved or turned.
		C	Two of the three strips are for comparing growth with different composts.
		D	In this trial there is a four-year rotation for each bed.
2	Name the main reason for slower growth on the no dig, unmulched strip in year one (Strip 2).	A	Moisture was retained better in the dug strip.
		B	No compost meant vegetables had to source all their. food from soil, where weed roots were using some of it to decompose.
		C	Weeds grew more in the no dig strip.
3	Why did I change the trial in May 2014, by adding compost mulches to the beds of Strips 1 and 2? Choose three answers.	A	Yields were 50% lower in 2013, from not spreading mulch (compost).
		B	It made digging easier.
		C	I wanted to grow different vegetables.
		D	To have more harvests for the same amount of work.
		E	More time would be needed for weeding if no compost was added.
4	Why did yields from the three strips rise each year until 2017? Choose the answer which covers the most aspects.	A	All of these.
		B	Being more ready with summer transplants, to ensure minimum time lost between clearing and replanting.
		C	Planting vegetables which gave more weight per area.
		D	The beds were full of vegetables for more of the growing season.
5	According to what I write here, which is the best way of expressing gratitude to soil?	A	A no dig approach, leaving soil life undisturbed.
		B	Practising no rotation.
		C	Not adding any mulch.
		D	Regular rotavating.

Drone view of the Three-strip trial in June 2020, and on Midsummer's Day

Myths – what you don't need to do

If you learn just one thing from this lesson, may it be to question things which you feel don't make sense. I call them myths or misunderstandings, and they are common. Worse, they are often perpetrated by people in positions of authority, or those who claim superior knowledge.

Positions of authority do not automatically result in true statements – I am not wishing to be critical of anyone, just saying how it is. I feel that more of us need to ask the questions which our hunches suggest, in order to move forward our understandings and methods.

I received this comment on YouTube from Daniel Foster on 10 February 2019, commenting on my YouTube video – *Garden myths that take our time:*

I have been gardening / growing / advising for nearly forty years and I wholeheartedly endorse what you say. By coincidence, I also grew an excellent crop of parsnips that season (2016) on ground where I had applied a thick mulch of compost and manure. As you say, the tradition of inventing myths, over-complicating things and making lazy assumptions is also true in other aspects of life. It's all about disempowering the public, so the 'experts' can create an easy role (and career) for themselves. Whereas real experts (like you) actually build people's confidence, encourage them to learn from their own observations and trust in their own instincts.

I want to build your confidence through understandings that work. This may at first seem odd, because many misunderstandings are deeply rooted, to the point that you may think 'surely that can't be wrong'.

We need to search a bit for the origins of established beliefs, to understand the confusions and extra work they cause. Digging is the main myth, and many others are related to it – crop rotation for example.

MYTH 1 – CROP ROTATION IN FARMING

Much advice on rotation states that an interval of four years is needed between plants of the same family, to reduce disease and increase cropping. This dates back to the 1730s and the work of Charles 'Turnip' Townshend on his Norfolk farms – not gardens. He copied and developed a method already used in Holland.

Townshend replaced a fallow year, in the traditional three-year rotation, with fertility-building clover, and added turnips to make it a four-year rotation. This increased total output and enabled farm animals to survive winter, without a large slaughter every autumn.

Both the clover and turnips were food for animals, in this case mostly sheep, whose droppings and manure added fertility. This practice was soon widely adopted by farmers, and productivity increased overall.

However, through the last hundred years, the goalposts have moved significantly. The use of synthetic nitrogen fertiliser has diminished that original need for the fertility provided by clover and animal manure.

You could practise a four-year rotation if your garden were large enough to accommodate clover for a year. However, vegetables require greater fertility than field crops, and yields from such a system would be low, in proportion to the time spent preparing ground: planting, weeding, picking and clearing. Townshend's method was for *farming in fields and with animals, not for gardening.*

Above These are all root vegetables, but from many different families

Above April – the fourth consecutive year of broad beans in the same bed, and potatoes have been planted to their right (also the fourth year in the same soil)

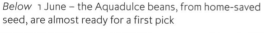

Below 1 June – the Aquadulce beans, from home-saved seed, are almost ready for a first pick

Below October – cabbage have followed beans and leeks have followed potatoes, in the fourth consecutive year

MYTH 2 – CROP ROTATION IN GARDENING

Rotation theory for vegetables emphasises a categorisation of plants into families or groups, to reduce disease and make the most of limited fertility. Families and groups are not the same, and this leads to misunderstandings.

I often read that 'root vegetables' are one group of the four years, but this makes little sense in terms of avoiding disease, which is linked to family characteristics such as late blight of potato and tomato. All of the roots and tubers in the first photo, top left facing page, are from different families, and are not related:

- Carrots are umbellifers, as are parsnips, salsify and scorzonera.

- Kohlrabi is a brassica, along with swede, turnip and radish.

- Beetroot are of the beet family, related to chard and leaf beet.

- Garlic are alliums, like leeks and onions.

- Potatoes are solanums, related to tomatoes and aubergines.

If anyone mentions 'root vegetables' as a category in rotations, take the rest of what they say with a pinch of salt. They may be using that category because root vegetables are sometimes called 'light feeders', which makes little sense for soil's hungry organisms. We feed the soil, not the plants (*see below*).

To finish with a caveat, that if you are unlucky enough to take over a UK allotment whose soil has been abused by over-cultivation, you may inherit soil diseases like clubroot, and need to practise a rotation. No dig and surface feeding will help soil to heal, but it will take years, rather than months, for the problems to reduce as soil life recovers.

MYTH 3 – FEEDING PLANTS

An aspect of rotation advice is the categorisation of plants into 'heavy' and 'light' feeders. This has some traction if you rely on synthetic fertilisers and like making calculations (*see Lesson 14*), but for anyone using a no dig approach – with organic matter to feed soil life – it makes no sense. Soil organisms are alive, and need food and water in the soil. You can turn a blind ear to anyone talking in terms of not giving compost for 'light feeders'.

Compost is not fertiliser in the usual sense of the word, as in nutrients for a particular planting. The nutrients in fertilisers are mostly water-soluble and readily available. In contrast, compost's array of nutrients are held in a water-insoluble state, until plants need to access them. They are also eaten and excreted by soil life, which converts them into a wider range of food options for roots.

This contradicts advice such as 'don't give compost before sowing carrots or you will have more leaf than root'. This statement shows a misunderstanding of what compost is, and assumes it has free nitrogen which will flood the soil (as soluble fertilisers do) and cause leaves to grow more than roots.

As we saw in Lesson 5, there are farmers and gardeners who believe in the opposite of rotation, and call it continuous cropping. They consider it an advantage to soil and plants. My feelings are between the two: that it's good to leave at least half a year between plantings of the same family, but without a need for intervals of two or more years. Especially with healthy, no dig soil.

MYTH 4 – COMPOST 'FERTILITY'

I often read that 'green / garden waste compost has no fertility'. This is such a bald statement. For one thing it's massively vague, and we need to know what is meant by fertility. Nutrient levels are actually often good, although release slowly.

The organic matter is food for soil organisms, which then make nutrients available to plants. In addition they improve structure, another and vital aspect of fertility. A common thread of mythical statements is an isolation of one aspect, without considering the whole picture.

Above Roots like firm conditions, so I tread compost when filling a new bed – this was for onions *(also see Lesson 16)*

Above January 2013 – this soil has been squashed by a dumper truck: what to do?

Below I let it dry, levelled it with a spade, then scattered grass seed and 1 cm / 0.4 in of compost

Below By summer the soil's bed condition is only a memory, with minimal effort needed

From top Tree roots only need a small hole at planting time, no larger than their roots – these are one-year-old maidens

By their second summer there are strong branches, all from the stick-like trunk of 18 months earlier

The mulch, and new growth in their third summer – the apple trees are healthy and cropping

MYTH 5 – ROOTS

There is a common misunderstanding that 'plant roots need loosened soil to root in'. To the point that even some no dig gardeners say you should 'never walk on the beds'. During courses at Homeacres I make a point of walking on a bed while explaining this, so that participants can see how I don't sink in, yet how the surface is springy.

I suspect the manufacturers of rototillers, for pushing the belief in loose soil on gardeners! The strong growth of plants in no dig gardens is strong evidence to the contrary. The structure of no dig soil is firm, yet with a matrix of air and moisture channels, created and maintained by life in the soil.

Even that sea of mud at Homeacres, in winter 2013, did not move me to dig or fork the ground. I did make a hole with a trowel to have a look, and found that the soil was still undamaged below the top layer, 5–6 cm / 2 in, of damaged soil.

It's a heavy soil here, and the dry winds of March initiated cracking, which allowed entry of air. Then, in April, I levelled the surface with a spade, scattered grass seed, and spread 1 cm / 0.4 in of compost.

By June, the combination of worms feeding on the compost near the surface, plus new roots of grass, meant that this soil was on the way to being restored. Far more quickly and easily than if I had tried to aerate the soil myself.

MYTH 6 – TREE PLANTING

Take it from me (and check the photos left for confirmation), your trees will benefit from their roots needing to push into firm soil. This is what they have evolved to do, and the firm soil is an excellent anchor for stabilising trees in wind.

Ignore anybody who says you need to make a larger hole than the roots of your tree. Another time-saver is that these trees have never been staked, including those on M26 rootstock, which often has a stake recommended. The RHS advise permanent staking of trees on M26 rootstock, and five years of staking for MM106.

The only trees I stake are the small ones, on M27 rootstocks, which grow shorter roots and risk falling over when fruit grows heavy. No other Homeacres' apple trees have ever had a stake, and are exposed to the prevailing south west wind. This can blow strong, because there is not much between us and the Atlantic ocean, 50 km / 31 mi to the north west.

Another piece of unhelpful advice I hear is to backfill planting holes with some organic matter, to 'feed the roots'. This goes against how nature works, with roots and soil organisms feeding near the surface and soil fertility building from above. Keep your organic matter for surface mulching, where it also helps to reduce growth of weeds.

MYTH 7 – COMPOST FOR POTTING

I often read expressions of worry over using different composts according to the stage of growth. Even compost manufacturers baulk at seedlings growing in their higher-feed composts – part of the reason for 'seed composts', which have fewer nutrients than potting composts. The other reason for using seed composts is better drainage.

I have sown and pricked out into Levingtons MP3, just to see – it's one of the most nutrient-rich composts available. Seeds and seedlings grew fine, just as they do in cow and horse manure, which is often claimed to 'burn seedlings'.

This might happen if the manure were fresh from the animal, but no sensible gardener would use such a manure. The 'burn seedlings' claim puts a lot of people off using great compost! It even pushes them to use mixes with soil in, which often results in weaker plants, less air in the mix, and more weed growth (*see Lesson 15*). The main time that I make a distinction between composts for sowing vegetable seeds, and those for growing on, is when I use them for basil or lettuce. I find that these germinate best when drainage and air levels are high, so I mix 50% perlite or vermiculite with my normal potting compost, especially for basil.

For propagation, just purchase one batch of potting or multi-purpose compost (called potting soil in the USA), and have some vermiculite or perlite available to add to the compost when sowing lettuce and basil.

MYTH 8 – COMPOST HEAPS

It's often said that compost heaps need slatted sides to 'let the air in'. Yet have you ever wondered how much air can flow into a solid heap?! From what I have seen, very little does, and instead what happens with slatted sides is that you find there is:

- A loss of moisture at the edges.
- Reduced warmth near the edges.
- Some regrowth of weeds, from any roots finding light at the edge.

If your heaps are enclosed by pallets, I would line them with thick cardboard. This will last a few months, long enough to benefit the fermenting heap (*see Lesson 13 for more about this*).

MYTH 9 – THE THREE SISTERS

I am often advised to use this easy method of intercropping. However, in the UK, it's mainly by people who have read about it, not practised it, and who have not understood the reasoning. I had the following comment from Linda Pankhurst, who took this course online:

I want to comment on your statement about how myths proliferate. Years ago I tried the 'Three Sisters' method of growing squash, beans and sweetcorn in the same bed to benefit all three. Apparently the Native Americans in the US did this and the early US settlers copied it with success.

From top You can sow and plant into nutrient-rich compost – the tray on the right is 18-month-old cow manure, the one on the left is multi-purpose potting compost

Beetroot sown on the same day – multi-purpose compost on the left and cow manure on the right

Comparing growth of kale – in double strength compost on the left, and my normal multi-purpose compost on the right

From top Compost heaps can have solid sides!

Homemade compost – three months old, and made in a heap with solid sides

You can add blighted material to compost heaps, and perennial weeds too (*see Lesson 17*)

The theory is that the beans can climb the sweetcorn stems and the squash sprawl about covering the ground, suppressing weeds and keeping the ground cool and moist.

What they don't tell you is that the beans climb up the sweetcorn and wrap themselves around the cobs as they form. When you want to pick the sweetcorn you have to unwrap the yet-to-crop bean stems . . . sacrificing their harvest because the stems always snap. And you can't actually get at any of the crops properly because you can't walk on all the squash growth.

What the gardeners who preach this have failed to think about, is that the Native Americans and early American settlers were using all three crops as winter food, leaving them all to grow to full maturity in situ and taking the whole crop at once in autumn, once the foliage had dried. Squash and beans were to store for winter and the corn was also to harvest when dry, to grind for polenta or to feed the whole cob to chickens.

Those who advocate this method often wouldn't if they had tried it. We don't usually leave corn to go hard, and we like the beans young and fresh.

In the UK I have had success with 'Two Sisters': sweetcorn for fresh cobs between winter squash. Transplant both at the same time, with the squash 1 m / 3 ft apart, and one or two sweetcorn plants between each squash plant. Unfortunately, I can't practise this at Homeacres because badgers eat the corn and make a mess in the process.

MYTH 10 – REVERENCE FOR THE VICTORIANS

In the UK, in particular, confusion arises from the misplaced esteem given to methods of the nineteenth century, especially the fine gardens of wealthy aristocrats. Their methods were and are copied, without appreciating that they were based on a lot of cheap labour and a desire for perfection to please the owners.

- Those much admired hotbed pineapples cost around £5,000 each in modern-day wages, because of all the time needed to keep filling and emptying the pits providing warmth.

- You don't need to wash or even brush pots or trays between use – I don't, and my plants are healthy. This misunderstanding maybe arises from the use of clay pots in older times, and indeed clay does need more cleaning than plastic because plant roots enter the clay if left in there, making the next plant difficult to tap out.

- It is often recommended to support melons on cordon plants with a net. However, I have grown hundreds of melons of decent sizes, without ever supporting them.

MYTH 11 – STORE ROOT VEGETABLES IN SAND

This is another aristocratic leftover, misleading so many and causing unnecessary worry and expense. When packed in sand, root vegetables keep very nicely – but it's not obligatory.

If we have any root vegetables that we don't plan to use within the next two weeks, we place them in crates, boxes or sacks. There is no sand, but a little soil remains on the roots from when they were harvested, and they live in a damp shed.

A root cellar would be necessary in cold climates to prevent the freezing of roots, especially potatoes. Other root vegetables can survive slight freezing, and store well in a temperature range of 1–10°C / 34–50°F.

MYTH 12 – HARDENING SEEDLINGS BEFORE PLANTING

A significant time waster is the advice to harden off all greenhouse-grown plants before setting them in the ground. At Homeacres we plant straight from the greenhouse, even on cold days of say 5°C / 41°F, though I prefer it warmer!

We inherited many myths from the Victorians, such as melons needing support as they swell and ripen

These module trays have been used 5–20 times, without ever having been cleaned – that myth comes from the days of clay pots

An exception is if I need space in the greenhouse and am not quite ready (short of time or space) for a batch of plants, so they live on a table outside for a few days.

Courgette plants need warmth to grow, and once I took some straight from the greenhouse and transplanted them into ground which still had ice on, from a late frost. It was May and warming fast; these plants grew just fine, with fleece laid on them for the first ten days.

Fleece (row cover / reemay) helps a lot, and there is no need to lay it on empty beds before planting, supposedly to 'pre-warm' the soil. All the benefit comes after planting, when protection from wind, and the warmth arising from sunlight, can be used for growth. Fleece is quick to use and can lie directly on plants – my next course, Growing Success, teaches more about this.

From top Vegetables store well in boxes, crates and sacks, with no need for sand

1 May – potatoes harvested in August, from a sack in my shed; the shoots just need rubbing off before washing and cooking

MYTH 13 – FEEDING TOMATOES

It is assumed that tomatoes need regular feeding, and yes, they do when grown in containers. Tomatoes in no dig and mulched soil often don't need extra food, so you save time and money by not feeding them.

If plant leaves look pale, and growth is weak, then this suggests you give a liquid feed; however, this should not happen when soil has a mulch of 5–7 cm / 2–3 in of compost applied before planting. This once-a-year dressing of soil food also serves for cropping different vegetables in winter, without any further amendments during a whole year. You save time and money.

MYTH 14 – COMPOST HOLDS NUTRIENTS

Plenty of gardeners believe that rain washes nutrients out of composts, so you read statements like 'compost should be spread in spring before planting', or 'covered with polythene through winter if spread then'. If this were the case, planet Earth would be way less abundant than it is now, as all the food – held in humus / compost on forest floors and in grassy fields – would be washed out!

Save time by not hardening off – use fleece instead; these plants came straight out of the greenhouse

Fleeced beds are all planted and sown, but during April I keep the fleece on top of seedlings – this was a −3°C / 27°F morning

We removed the fleeces after warmer weather had arrived – this is just 16 days later

Furthermore my gardens would not have worked, because I apply compost as food for soil organisms before the winter. This means beds are ready for planting early in spring, and plant roots love the soft, weathered compost surface. A lot of rain washes through before plants start to grow.

Not covering beds with plastic is a job saved, and money too. The only time you may need a polythene cover is to kill rampant weeds in year one (*see Lesson 1*). In any mild winter there can be weeds germinating from newly spread compost, and a little hand weeding is worthwhile. The weed roots are easy to pull from such a soft surface – so different to the stickiness of soil.

There is no need to feed tomatoes when the soil has been well fed thanks to compost – these plants did not have any feeds

Likewise no feeds given for these plants, except for feeding the soil with 6 cm / 2.5 in of compost in May, before planting

It is important to consider biology as well as chemistry. The no dig method results in high biological activity, which supports and retains high levels of nutrients. These are not soluble in water and therefore don't wash out, just as they do not flood the roots of plants.

One interesting point arising from how nutrients 'hang around' in no dig soil is how this appears to happen less with cultivated soils. Much of the research about nutrient leaching is done on ploughed and tilled soil, yet without specifying this. A stormwater test carried out at Singing Frogs market garden in California found clean water after it had passed through the soil. They are no dig, and apply 5 cm / 2 in of compost per year.

The owner, Paul Kaiser, argues that his circumstances are clearly within bounds, for four reasons. Firstly, he says the extra nitrogen is necessary, because he's farming so many more crops per acre than the average farm. Secondly, he says soil tests show that his nitrogen levels are 'right where they should be for healthy crops.' Thirdly, he says the crops are clearly eating it up: on some, the leaves occasionally turn yellow (usually a sign of nitrogen deficiency). And fourthly, he says that his ponds, which catch the farm's run-off, are visibly clear and full of wildlife. And recent stormwater tests were also clean, even during 2017's heavy rains. If water is polluted with nitrogen or phosphorus, it's normally clogged with algae, which kills fish and other aquatic life by robbing them of oxygen. This problem did plague Kaiser during the first year, after particularly heavy composting, but has pretty much

December – spreading the annual dose of compost, after having cleared celeriac

It's fine to spread compost in autumn and winter, because its nutrients are not soluble in water so remain there when it rains

Good compost is often more brown than black, suggesting an aerated heap – the new compost is nearest to the camera

ceased since then. 'All our fields and indicators show that our nitrogen levels are OK or not enough', Kaiser says (*Craftsmanship Quarterly* online magazine, Summer 2017 issue).

This quote is from the book *No Till Intensive Farming*, written by Bryan O'Hara, a grower of 35 years in Connecticut:

> 'We have seen the phosphorus levels on the Mehlich-3 soil test drop, even though we apply 30+ tons of compost per acre per year.' (p.188)

MYTH 15 – WATERING IN SUNLIGHT

Where does the oft-heard saying come from, that we should not water plants in bright sunlight? If it were true, all plants would suffer when the sun comes out, following rain storms in summer.

I have never observed any leaf damage from sunshine on water droplets, and, when one is not restricted by such a belief, it makes the day more flexible when there is much to do. I do hear comments from people in Texas and North Australia – that they would not water in bright sunlight – and am intrigued to know more, because tropical storms are often followed by strong sun.

MYTH 16 – DELEAFING CELERIAC

'You must remove the lower leaves of celeriac.' I have a feeling that this recommendation comes from a duke or duchess, wanting their crops to look tidy and smart (though celeriac does look lovely from about August, after old leaves have twisted away from the base of swelling bulbs).

However on two occasions, when I deleafed a few plants of celeriac while leaving others untouched, the latter grew larger. The leaves worth removing are only those nearest to ground level, the yellow and rotten ones.

Left, from top
I often water in sunlight, and this causes no problems whatsoever

When compost is thoroughly watered it holds a lot of moisture – these haven't been watered for three days, even in sunny March weather

Right, from top
Doing a trial on deleafing celeriac – after deleafing they ended up being smaller than their full-leaved neighbours

November 2018 – all I did here was remove some rotting leaves (but not before October)

Further reading
More information can be found in my book – *Gardening Myths and Misconceptions*, which can be purchased via my website: charlesdowding.co.uk

Quiz Lesson 6

	Question	Multiple choice
1	Rotation theory was created for gardeners in the 1700s, to increase yields and avoid disease, when growing vegetables on a small scale.	True or false?
2	When can you step on no dig beds? Choose two answers.	A Never, to avoid damaging the soil. B Occasional stepping on the bed is fine, to walk over or reach the middle. C Any time you need to, but don't dance on them after heavy rain!
3	How big should the planting hole be, for a tree on an M26 rootstock?	A Large enough to accommodate the roots or rootball. B One spade-width extra, to the size of the roots or rootball. C Twice the size of the roots or rootball.
4	Which type of commercial compost would you use to sow seeds? Choose the answer which covers most possibilities.	A Seed compost. B Potting compost. C Multi-purpose compost. D Any of these, as long as it is free draining.
5	What is the most important quality of a compost for sowing seeds?	A Nutrient level. B Good drainage and air. C An even texture, without too many lumps.
6	What is the principal benefit of adding cardboard sides to an open-sided compost heap?	A It stops weed seeds blowing in. B It adds carbon to the heap. C It retains warmth and moisture. D It stops rats getting in.
7	Sowings from the greenhouse must be hardened off outside, before being planted out.	True or false?
8	Choose the simplest, yet most effective way to store root vegetables for more than two weeks.	A In the fridge, in the chiller drawer. B In paper sacks, crates or boxes, washed. C In paper sacks, crates or boxes, unwashed. D Loose in a kitchen cupboard.
9	When your soil is healthy, fertile and mulched with compost, how often must you feed tomatoes growing in it?	A As often as the feed manufacturer recommends. B Every week. C Every two weeks. D You don't need to feed them.
10	Is it safe to water plant leaves in bright sunlight?	A No. B Wait for clouds to pass over. C Yes, it is.

Module 3
Plot layout, beds and paths

Lesson 7

Bed width and orientation, sides or not

This lesson is mainly for those who are starting out, because, once you have beds and paths in place, it's a lot of work to change their layout. I explain how best to align and create beds, using different areas of Homeacres as examples.

STARTING OUT AND CLEARING

In November 2012, when I moved into Homeacres, the 3,000 m² / 0.75 acre area of land was mostly grass, weeds and a few woody plants. Many of the weeds were perennial, such as creeping buttercup (*Ranunculus repens*), dandelion (*Taraxacum officinale*) and couch grass (*Elymus repens*) (*see Lesson 9 for descriptions of these*). I call this combination of plants 'pasture', meaning grass and weeds.

Homeacres' pasture had not been much grazed or mown, and I subsequently discovered how vigorous its roots were. It is an important distinction to be clear on because, for example, the roots and vigour of grass and weeds in a frequently mown lawn will be far less, making them quicker to die under a mulch.

- Use thicker cardboard and 15 cm / 6 in of compost when weeds are vigorous (*see Lesson 17 for an example of this*). Or, if not in a hurry to plant, spread compost on the ground then polythene on top.

- On a mown lawn, thinner cardboard and 5–7 cm / 2–3 in of compost can be enough to kill weeds, and also to sow / plant into immediately.

Start by looking at what is there, and imagining how you would like it to be, before you begin. Play with those ideas, and dare to imagine a few results and harvests.

STAGES OF MAKING THE SMALL GARDEN

1. When I started to create the Small Garden, my first job was to remove the concrete posts and wire fence. This entailed removal of the roots of stinging nettles (*Urtica dioica*) which were entangled in the wire. Normally I mulch over nettles, after cutting them very short to ground level.

2. I used a sharp spade to remove the top 10–15 cm / 4–6 in of the few docks I saw (*Rumex obtusifolius*). There were no other perennial weeds, perhaps because chickens had been running here for a year or two. Prior to that, in the 1960s–70s, this area was covered by a shed with boilers for the nursery, and the soil has slabs and pieces of concrete below the surface. This matters less in no dig, it is just annoying when pushing in posts and canes to support vegetables!

3 I cut back all growth from the neighbour's shrubs, as close to the fence as possible. I also pulled out many fat white roots of hedge bindweed (*Calystegia sepium*). It is common in his garden and continually spreads into the Small Garden (as does Euphorbia), but both are manageable.

4 I looked at the plot and decided that three beds of 1.4 m / 4.6 ft would make best use of the space, with one side 70 cm / 2.3 ft from the tin shed, and the other side 40 cm / 16 in from the brick lean-to on Homeacres' east wall. The two paths between the beds are 30 cm / 1 ft wide. If I had chosen to have four beds, each would have been 1 m / 3 ft wide, and that would have meant an extra path, resulting in a small loss of growing space and more maintenance per area. For anyone liking narrow beds this would be possible here; my preference is for wider beds. You can be creative in making such choices – it's about what you like to do, not what is right or wrong.

5 I kept a path at either end: it's easier to maintain a path near to a neighbour's garden than a bed, because the invading weeds make less progress into a path than into a bed – the path is like a quarantine zone.

From top The Small Garden in November 2012, when I had just arrived at Homeacres

Three days later – the Small Garden is underway; weeds are dying but I have not moved any soil

July, six months later – already growing a lot of food, despite stones and concrete in the soil

The Small Garden gave harvests of 93.7 kg / 207 lb of vegetables in 2018, with a steady 2–4 kg / 4.4–9 lb every week from mid-May, less before that. No dig makes it easy to keep resowing and planting throughout the season.

The photos right show how beautiful a vegetable garden can be. This is an important aspect, and helps you to stay involved. I strongly advise that you garden a small area to its full potential, for high productivity and full enjoyment, compared to a less intensive and larger area.

(*See Lesson 18 for a detailed plan of 2018's plantings in the Small Garden, and the results.*)

SHED AREA AND CONCRETE

The other side of the tin shed was a different challenge, because I mainly wanted it clean, clear and looking nice. In 2012 I was seeing Homeacres as a teaching and trials garden, more than one for producing and selling vegetables.

Originally, I also thought to have my new polytunnel closer to the shed, until I discovered the concrete under 10 cm / 4 in of soil and weeds. The whole area had been a shed or hard standing 40–50 years ago. I then started to worry about what else I might find under Homeacres' soil!

Every cloud has a silver lining, and I scraped off the soil (which had formed on the concrete) to fill a bed, which was then used in a soil / compost trial (*see Lesson 15*). Before filling the bed, I removed the roots of perennial weeds from the soil (such as nettles, buttercup and bindweed), and they went on the compost heap.

The concrete surface has proved ideal for stacking crates and washing salad leaves. The concrete is not thick, about 7 cm / 3 in, and could have been cleared if I had wanted the area for growing.

I could probably have made beds on it, because it is broken enough to allow water to drain through (although removal would be worthwhile before growing).

Drainage is best where materials are of the same or similar densities. For example, the various stages of compost decomposition are similar enough in nature for water to flow freely. Likewise in undisturbed soil, where changes in texture are gradual and do not impede drainage.

However, if you laid gravel on concrete as a 'drainage layer', water would resist flowing from the compost and into the gravel, because it makes a capillary layer across materials of different densities. This is why gravel or shards of clay are not a good idea for the base of pots before they are filled with compost. I fill pots and containers with compost only, for good drainage and more food plus moisture than if you had put gravel at the bottom.

If you should inherit a greenhouse with a concrete base, and you want to grow vegetables, it's probably worth hacking out the concrete to expose the soil. (*See the pictures overleaf for what the Catlows did, after attending a day course here. They are in Lancashire in the north west of England.*)

From top February 2018 – some overwintered vegetables, and beds ready for plantings

Mid-May – there is already a lot of growth, and some harvests

September – second crops and a few tall vegetables, as pretty as an ornamental garden!

From top December 2012 – the shed area, overgrown and with rubbish

Two days later – we had cleared the rubbish, and I had scraped soil and weeds off the concrete

This area is suitable for my salad washing – hard standing, and with some free water

NEARBY TREES AND TALL HEDGES

I was advising a gardener, who lamented how her squashes had wilted every afternoon of a hot summer despite her regular watering. Was that part of the garden just too hot for them? I was immediately suspicious of tree roots, which travel further than one might imagine. I asked her, and yes, they have tall acacia trees in the pavement just near their front garden. She had even seen suckers growing up – new little acacia trees from these roots – a long way from the trees.

Her squash plants wilted every afternoon because the trees could suck the moisture faster than vegetables; squash need to grow fast, from good access to moisture.

Many of us have borders and edges with our own or neighbours' trees nearby. Unless you can pollard the tree, or cut a hedge very short, there is not much that can be done. Cutting surface roots with a sharp spade is possible, but many roots run deeper than a spade can reach, and that rarely answers the problem.

Don't consider a membrane to 'keep roots down there'. They will eventually find a way through, and you will have poisoned your soil with a layer of plastic, restricting movement of soil life and of vegetable roots growing downwards.

From top Neil Catlow, removing the concrete in his greenhouse

The Catlows' greenhouse after removal of the concrete in November

The same greenhouse in the following July

From top
This bed is just 1 m / 3.3 ft wide

These new beds, for a trial, are 1.1 m square inside the larger frame (*see Lesson 15*)

1.2 m / 3.9 ft wide beds

December – beds and paths with no sides, and after a salad pick on the left weighing 1.07 kg / 2.36 lb

Near to deciduous trees, an option would be to have vegetables that grow in winter and spring, such as garlic, spinach, autumn-planted salads and spring cabbage. Even broad beans sown in November. They do much of their growing when tree leaves are not present and roots are therefore dormant – it's more about roots than shade.

BED WIDTH

Much of the conventional reasoning given for deciding how wide to make beds is based on a false assumption: that you cannot or should not walk on them. I have already explained how this is untrue, so deciding bed width is your call, according to what you are comfortable with and what will fit into your space.

Beds of 1 m / 3 ft width are my minimum, and are ideal for rows of tall peas, or one row of courgettes / zucchini; plus they are easier to pick leaves from. Bed widths of 1.2 m / 4 ft use space more efficiently, from a higher proportion of bed to path area, and up to 2 m / 7 ft is possible. At this width you can be creative with spacings of vegetables such as climbing beans, by making wide teepees for example.

Another consideration is square foot gardening, a method for growing a lot of variety in a small area. Your square feet can be other sizes, square 40 cm / 16 in for example, and on beds of varied width. Have fun trying out a few things.

I caution, however, that the common bed ingredients advised for square foot gardening are one third compost, one third peat and one third vermiculite. This combination is weak in nutrients; I had a mail from a gardener who had grown for ten years using this recipe and who had suffered declining harvests. He copied my advice to simply fill beds with compost of any kind, including old animal manure, and said that for the first time ever he now had more parsnips than they could eat.

From top
This bed is 1.6 m / 5.3 ft wide – we walked on its middle to pick the peas

You can walk on no dig beds, so bed width is flexible – this one is 2 m / 6 ft wide

December 2018 – the bed with rocket is 1.2 m / 3.9 ft wide; the two to the right of it are both 1.5 m / 3.3 ft wide

From top
22 May 2013 – shaping new beds in the Three-strip trial; they are each 1.2 m / 4 ft wide, with 30 cm / 12 in paths

The same day, and the new beds are ready to plant (*see Lesson 5*)

Just 39 days later, and there's strong growth from the new plantings; leeks have followed broad beans

BED LAYOUT AND ORIENTATION

How long to make beds? They are easier to manage when small, depending on how much you grow. Small Garden beds, 4.5 m / 15 ft long, grow four crops in each bed at any one time. My dig / no dig trial beds are slightly longer (*see Lesson 4*), and grow up to ten kinds of vegetable at any one time.

From top
The beds on Homeacres' west side have different orientations, and all work fine

A winter view, showing how bed orientation varies on the west side

You can see the same variation on this drone photo, with the west side on the left

Homeacres has bed lengths ranging from 2 m / 6.6 ft to 12 m / 39 ft, and I like them all. The garden is prettier when not totally geometric, and many of the longer beds have mixed crops at any time of year. Not being slave to a four-year rotation helps to achieve this exciting patchwork effect.

Orientation

The oft-advised north–south orientation, suggested to minimise shading effects, applies only if most plants are tall ones. On east–west beds these will shade plants on the north side at midday.

This happens in my polytunnel during summer, which I aligned almost east–west to be parallel with the neighbour's hedge, and to reduce wasted space. In summer I grow tomatoes and cucumbers in the middle beds, so the vegetables on their north side are somewhat shaded, but still good!

More inconvenient is hot afternoon sun stressing cucumbers in the southernmost row, because it dries the soil exposed to sun at their roots, more than elsewhere in the tunnel. However, this happens for only four months of the year; mostly the east–west orientation is fine, such as for salad plants and garlic in winter.

- The majority of vegetables are low growing, making a north–south factor redundant. Plus it is outweighed by important considerations of access and convenience – the entrance to a path needs to be where you enter the plot. Bear all this in mind when making your first bed, because the layout of all the others will usually follow these lines.

Slope

A final consideration is slope. Conventional advice recommends running beds across a slope, rather than up and down. This follows its own assumption that soil has been loosened by tools, which makes it less stable.

This does not apply to no dig, where erosion is minimised. In my garden at Lower Farm there were slopes of around 10°, and I found it worked better to run beds up and down, rather than across the slope.

From top
Water drains downhill on paths; with no dig you can align beds up and down a slope

An August view, showing how few vegetables grow tall enough to shade neighbouring beds

Even cucumbers can grow along the ground; this is a ridge cucumber – Tanya variety

From top
Dan's market garden in Devon, which is on a steep slope

Dan hired a digger to create terraces

For one thing, when beds are oriented across the slope, newly applied compost then runs down the bed (if going anywhere!), rather than into a path below. Similarly for water. Plus my access point was at the bottom, so it made sense for me to run paths straight up the hill.

Only in extreme rain did I find some of the paths' surface material run down, and, in just two years out of 13, I needed to load compost and soil at the bottom, and redistribute it at the top. It came to two wheelbarrows full for the 1440 m² / 0.35 acres.

If your slope is more than, say 12–15°, it's a different matter:

- Either run beds across the slope, and use wooden sides on their bottom edge only, to hold a reasonably level surface for each bed.

- Or, for larger areas, you could hire a digger to create terraces, as you see in the photos, left. This means you have steep slopes between each terrace, which will grow weeds unless you have a growing idea for them.

NEW BEDS

Creating new beds is simple, once you are clear about the layout you want and which width will work for you. You need mulching materials, and at least some must be organic matter.

- Organic mulches keep light off existing weeds *and* feed soil life, creating fertile soil even when it wasn't fertile before.

- Polythene / plastic mulches are quick to lay, but do not feed soil. I suggest not to use polythene mulches unless:
  – the weed problem is severe
  – time is limited
  – you don't need to crop for a while.

For most beds at Homeacres, I have laid temporary wooden sides to contain the compost. I made an exception for the two dig / no dig trial beds, whose oak sides are permanent.

From top
December, and the hardest decision was where to put these first beds!

By January I had made more beds, following the same orientation; plus there was mud

September open day – the garden is in good shape, with the greenhouse full

From top November 2017 – ready to make new beds; they will line up with existing ones

One hour later and the new beds are underway; I laid cardboard first as there was couch grass

Three months' growth in a new bed of winter salads, which have adapted to cool conditions

The wooden sides are temporary, and keep a clean line between the bed and the path in the first few months

In the area of the garden shown in the photos, left, the beds could have run either way, but generally it makes sense to follow existing path lines, which we did. This gives clear access from one end of the garden to the other.

As it happens, we often carry watering cans across the line between the old and new beds, from the water butt by the greenhouse to the polytunnel. Before the new beds were in place, this had been grass. Since it's fine to walk across the mulched surface of no dig beds, this is what we do, without there being a proper path. Which leads on to the next lesson about paths.

Quiz Lesson 7

	Question	Multiple choice
1	What sort of cardboard is good to use as a base layer, to clear perennial weeds?	A Some that is as thick as possible – brown not shiny, no tape or staples. B Any cardboard will work, including shiny card. C Amazon boxes laid side by side. D Food boxes with polythene between the cardboard.
2	What width should new vegetable beds be?	A The width that works best for you and your space. B 1 m / 3 ft wide. C 1.2 m / 4 ft wide. D 2 m / 7 ft wide.
3	It doesn't matter how long beds are.	True or false?
4	Why is it often said, in an all-embracing dictum, that 'you must never walk on beds'? Choose two answers.	A Because your footprints make a sunken mess of compacted soil. B Because you're likely to damage roots near the surface. C Because it's assumed that soil is loose after digging and tilling, and therefore will be squashed down again. D Because it's commonly thought that roots need mechanically-loosened soil to grow in.
5	Choose the best option for creating beds over concrete.	A A slight slope, or holes made in the concrete to ensure drainage, and 20 cm / 8 in of compost. B 10 cm / 4 in of compost. C A layer of gravel, then 15 cm / 6 in compost.
6	You always need to orientate beds north to south.	True or false?
7	What are two considerations for orientating beds?	A Access points for paths. B Your soil type. C The rotation of your plants. D Any general slope of the land.
8	Why is it better to run beds up and down, instead of across, slopes of less than about 10 degrees?	A No dig soil is firm and stable, so there is little erosion in heavy rain. B It looks more professional. C Plants prefer it.
9	Which factor is most relevant when deciding when to remove temporary wooden sides to new beds?	A When the compost has settled and won't roll into the path. B When the wood disintegrates. C When they stop looking nice.

Lesson 8

Paths – how they feed your plants and how to look after them

From top Paths are wet with rain water

The same area – the paths have now been mulched

A wider view of this area in October – small beds and narrow paths; a wider bed is in the foreground

WHY BOTHER WITH PATHS AND BEDS?

Forty years ago, most gardeners grew on level ground, with plants in rows and walking space between. Then, gradually, raised beds made appearances in a few gardens. Nowadays beds are almost the default method, as their benefits are acknowledged.

Yet there has been less attention paid to the spaces between and around beds. I see time and money being spent on paths, and bed sides too, but without always the necessary understandings on how to maintain paths, and how the soil in paths can work for us. This lesson considers many of the issues.

Path characteristics:

* They are permanent, in the same place every year.

* Mulched soil in paths maintains structure, fertility and moisture – available to plant roots from the bed edges.

* They are not just 'ground to walk on', but part of your growing space.

HOW PATHS RELATE TO BEDS

It is often assumed that beds are raised beds with sides, usually made of wood. If all of your beds are like this, and you wish to continue with sided beds, then you have different options for paths. This is because, for example, grass struggles to grow through a wooden plank! However, couch grass can sneak underneath, as we shall see.

Any grass path needs maintenance (mowing / cutting), and the roots will be feeding into soil at the bed edges, if not growing up into the beds. In preference to this, my advice is to achieve lower levels of maintenance. Most of this lesson is about beds with only a slight raise and no sides, which I find the cheapest and quickest way to establish and maintain a growing area.

Much of the reason for having paths is the definition of space, and to make planning and access easier, and spacing of plants more intensive.

Close planting on beds, to concentrate cropping, makes it possible to protect blocks of plants from pests, using just one cover. Plus it's a more economical use of water and compost, with many plants benefiting, rather than just a few.

WEED-FREE PATHS

The skill of maintaining weed-free paths is worth acquiring. This means that all goodness and moisture in the path soil is available for plants, once they are large enough for their roots to travel that far.

From top Gravel paths are an option, but need membranes underneath

Marestail grows up through a stone and cement path: it needs total light exclusion

Having paths clean of weeds is helped by feeding path soil with surface mulches of organic material, to feed soil life and maintain structure. This can be compost or woody materials, preferably in small pieces, and partly decomposed at the time of application. No weeds in paths means no weed roots spreading into beds, and no seeds arriving from path weeds that have gone to seed.

There are other options for paths, which I mention but do not recommend, because of cost, maintenance difficulties, and the soil not being fed:

- Gravel – this needs a membrane underneath, unless you fancy a lot of difficult weeding.

- Stone and cement – the marestail shows how perennial weeds can, and will, grow through surfaces that look impenetrable to us.

- Polypropylene membrane – this looks like an easy and time-saving option; however, it harbours slugs, is expensive, does not feed soil, and risks disappearing into the soil if enough mulch lands on top, and weeds then grow in that.

From top September – these beds are newly sown and I am firming the drills; you can walk on no dig beds

These beds are raised only slightly, and the paths just have light mulches – mostly of compost

December, with newly applied wood shavings; paths divide space and make planning easier

HOW NOT TO HAVE PATHS

To understand better what paths can offer when well maintained, it helps to look at the difficulties resulting from poor choices of path layout and surface. Nature never exists in a vacuum and, if you are not organised about your paths, she will take over.

From top A path edge, with couch grass and a thistle growing in the bed

A poor use of space, with grassy paths and narrow beds

All the grass needs cutting, and there is too much of it near the vegetables

Often the next stage: the grass is taking over

The photos, left, come from a nearby allotment site, and what they show is not uncommon – especially where there isn't an active committee to keep the site mown, and perhaps also to give advice.

The second photo shows a plot layout which must have been devised by gardeners of little experience, who have gone to some trouble over their beds. They are losing most of the moisture and goodness along the edges, and the ground is more path than bed. There will need to be frequent mowing and edging – wide and weedy paths create a lot of work, in proportion to the area cropped.

- I advise against paths of grass, except when you have only one or two beds surrounded by lawn.

- It's feasible to have wider beds and narrower paths – *see my examples in the next section.*

- Keep green edges to a minimum because they mean extra work. A square growing area is way more efficient than a long thin one, which has a high proportion of edge to middle.

- For Homeacres' main bed area, we spend as much time keeping the grass edges trimmed as in doing all necessary weeding.

PATH WIDTH

Paths at Homeacres are as narrow as feasible, to minimise waste of space and to reduce maintenance overall. The polytunnel and greenhouse are an extreme example of this – especially for winter leaf crops – because I want to maximise plantings in the precious covered area.

In the polytunnel I have three paths and slightly wider beds, rather than four paths and narrower beds. When picking salad from the 1.3 m / 51 in central beds, we place a foot on the bed to reach plants in the middle of each one.

Even if your wheelbarrow is wide, it can run along a narrow path when there are no wooden sides. And it's fine to rest the wheelbarrow legs on the beds either side, since their structure is firm.

From top Narrow paths of 40 cm / 16 in between narrow beds work fine

In the polytunnel, paths between salads are 30 cm / 12 in, just wide enough for access to harvest leaves

At Homeacres a few of my paths are wider, to allow easier access on open days, and for groups when I am teaching. Apart from that consideration, my preferred path width is 35 cm / 14 in.

How do you measure path width?

With non-sided beds it's harder to see a boundary between path and bed, and in any case it's a diffuse edge at best. The definition between bed and path is not a rigid one, because of how paths are part of the growing space.

Therefore the path widths I give are distances between approximate bed edges. Path widths are not the distance between the outermost rows of plants along each bed, because they run just inside the invisible bed edge.

For example, and in terms of running lengthwise along a bed:

- With salads, I plant the outside row 7 cm / 3 in inside each bed, with plants spaced at 22 cm / 9 in.

- For multi-sown beetroots, the outside row of plants is 10 cm / 4 in from the notional edge, with plants spaced at 30–35 cm / 12–14 in.

From top When beds are full of vegetables, pathways almost disappear and are full of roots

There is a path here!

A wider path of 50 cm / 20 in, along a 1.5 m / 5 ft bed; although the path could be narrower

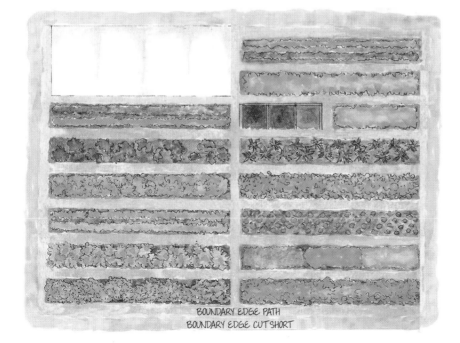

BOUNDARY EDGE PATH
BOUNDARY EDGE CUT SHORT

From top Laying cardboard on weeds, many of them perennials

Spreading wood shavings on new cardboard – the weeds underneath did grow through

Spreading wood shavings on old cardboard

So the distance between the path edge and first row of plants is around a third of the distance between each plant in the beds. A little more or less is fine.

Don't worry if your edges move a little, I find the main thing is to keep them straight – I do it by eye, or you could use a string.

PATH MULCHES

Think of mulches as feed for the soil, as well as being there to suppress weed growth. When soil is undisturbed and its inhabitants are well fed, fewer weeds grow, so the two go together.

This is one reason I do not recommend path mulches of membrane or polythene, which add nothing to soil fertility unless you lift them annually to spread an organic mulch underneath. The other reason is soil pollution.

There is a tendency for mulches of any kind of plastic to disappear below surface level. It seems impossible at first sight for this to happen, but I frequently hear stories of people taking on new allotments in the UK and then discovering synthetic carpet, plastic and membranes buried up to 15 cm / 6 in deep, and totally out of sight.

Once soil – or compost and weeds – lands on these plastic mulches, nature quickly colonises the surface. Once underground they become a layer that is impermeable, both to the roots of our plants and to larger organisms in the soil. A general hindrance to growth, which costs you time and money.

Cardboard is not pollutant-free, but I have not observed problems for worms or plants from using it just occasionally. In the case of path mulches, one to three layers of cardboard serve to kill most weeds, but this is necessary *only in year one* and, even then, only if there are many weeds to mulch.

Once weeds are gone, say at the end of year one, I usually spread a thin mulch of woody or half-decomposed compost as soil food, and to make weeding easier. It might seem like a waste to spread compost on paths, but it's worth it.

I like to use woody mulches on paths, where practical. However when beds have no sides, don't overdo the depth of woody mulch – this will prevent a lot of it from ending up on your beds.

Woody materials do not rob soil of nitrogen when on the surface; in fact they can then absorb nitrogen from the air, through azotobacter bacteria. A greater problem is that, on beds, they get in the way of seeding, or popping in small transplants. Plus they can harbour enough woodlice (pillbugs) that some plant stems and leaf edges get eaten, as well as the old wood.

The shavings in the photo, centre right, are from a heap of horse manure, in which they were the bedding. There is some horse poo in there, which helps the shavings to decompose. However, I would call that a mulch of shavings rather than manure, because the horses had been bedded with a large amount of wood.

The shavings in the photo, bottom right p.97, are also from kiln-dried wood, which takes longer to decompose than fresh wood chip. Plus they are oak, fresh from a joinery, and decomposition on paths is slow, taking up to two years.

The wood chip mulches in the photos, upper left p.100, are from a six-month-old heap, where they had started to decompose in April, with the mulching done in November. I would prefer it if they were older and more decomposed, but was happy enough with what you see there.

Generally I find that wood decomposes surprisingly fast when on the surface, partly because it is dampened frequently in our UK climate. The pieces of wood from the chips that you see here / there are not, in my experience, large enough to offer hiding places for slugs.

Pasture five months earlier, then mulched with wool carpet; I spread a little manure on the path, then new weeds started growing!

In November I laid cardboard on the weeds

In spring I spread wood shavings on the paths, on top of the decayed cardboard

This is after I had laid cardboard along the grassy edge; the crops are garlic and onions

Pasture was mulched a year earlier with polythene – some old grass is still visible on the path in the middle, which had not been mulched; the other paths just had some soil skimmed off, which was then put onto the beds

From top Mulched and narrow paths; there are no sides to the beds

Cloche hoops over spring onions, and a path mulch of wood shavings

After cutting, the old stems of asparagus have been used as a path mulch between two rows

Wherever there are bits of wood on the surface, we see white mycelial threads, and sometimes mushrooms or toadstools. A significant benefit of woody mulches is the fungi, which colonise their breakdown process.

In a similar vein, with asparagus you can use the old stems as a path mulch. We scythe them off every autumn and lay the 2 m / 7 ft stems lengthways along the path between two rows, then walk on it several times. At first it's a bulky mulch, but soon breaks up into pieces like straw and is then taken into the soil over 12–24 months.

A SEQUENCE, FROM WEEDS TO CLEAN PATHS

The photos below show the creation of a bed I made in my first Homeacres spring, on pasture which included a fair amount of couch grass (*Elymus repens*).

Instead of cardboard, I laid biodegradable polythene on one half of the bed area, to see if it made a difference. It turned out that this polythene is too soft for such a task, and the couch roots just speared through it. I advise you to save the expense of buying such a product, plus the 'biodegrade' time is more than a year, from what I saw.

In the end I kept pulling any new blades of couch grass, and it was all gone by early autumn. On the path nearest to what became a grass edge, there was couch grass spreading in, by rooting just under the path mulch. To save time pulling it, I laid new cardboard every three months or so, until midsummer of year two. Since then, we pull it when seen.

On one edge I experimented with a double layer of landscape fabric, on top of cardboard. This worked well and lasted longer than cardboard alone, but the fabric is a polythene product and I would not buy it again. Cardboard works.

You can really see the difference between the two photos, top left p.102. The photo from May 2015 is my objective every time: sloping sides and weed-free paths. In this case, I used 3 cm / 1 in of green waste compost as path mulch.

SUMMARISING PATHS

- Have paths as narrow as you are comfortable with, and keep them weed-free – easy when you have been thorough with mulching in year one.

- Look on your paths as living soil, not soil that is compact and dead. Walking on them does not damage structure when the surface is alive with food for organisms, which keep soil open as they move around and breed.

- Well maintained paths hold food and moisture for plants, whose roots into the paths benefit the structure, as well as increasing overall growth. This is a big reason for not having sides to beds, and for keeping paths clean and fed.

- Be friends with a local tree surgeon / arborist or garden contractor: they often have woody wastes they need to be rid of. Sometimes they would even have to pay for 'landfill', and will love you for accepting their 'waste' shreddings.

Edges to a whole plot

While we're talking about paths, it makes sense to consider the boundaries. Always keep an eye on these, because this is where weeds invade from. The easiest maintenance is with weed-free paths, to provide a clear boundary zone to the wildness beyond your growing space. The edge to the wilder boundary needs to be kept short and tidy, because otherwise grass and weeds encroach into beds.

March 2013 – a new path alongside an existing bed, which has a wooden side

Pasture weeds, covered with thick cardboard

A new bed, made with 15 cm / 6 in of compost – the surrounding paths have been carded

9 May – spinach and calabrese are now growing, and the cardboard is decaying (there is also a double layer of landscape fabric at the near end)

13 June – new cardboard has been laid on top of the old

September – lettuce and chicory in the bed, and a third layer of cardboard because some couch grass persisted

Near left, from top
Autumn brassicas are overgrowing the paths, and their roots are in the path soil

The beetroot next to the path have grown larger than those in the middle, thanks to accessing path moisture in dry conditions

No weeds and close planting – paths give an area to walk between

Above, from top
June 2014 – peas, cabbage, beetroot, and a last application of cardboard (still against couch grass which is now much weaker as it comes in from the edge)

May 2015 – finally, no more wooden sides and no more cardboard

Left A weed-free garden in November – the edges are mown and cut every three to eight weeks, depending on the weather; nettles and tormentil are on the boundary, between the membrane and a heap of compost

Left, from top
Leaves of couch grass are pushing sideways, to the edge of a cardboard overlap

This gives an idea of couch roots' movement, more lateral than downwards

A flower bed with no edge needs time spent on it; the tree bed behind has fabric right up to its edge

Right, from top
The new beds in the foreground still have cardboard and wooden sides

After large weeds had been cut down – the cardboard for paths will result in a clean edge

Edges again – this is creeping tormentil at an allotment

Lay cardboard along boundary edges if weeds are vigorously spreading into the outer path. Some cutting with long-handled shears is also necessary, because grass and weeds are always spreading horizontally, as well as growing upwards. This weakens their root systems, making them:

- Less able to spread in.
- Less likely to be giving shelter to pests.
- Less able to draw moisture and nutrients from the growing area.

Creeping tormentil, photo lower right, is a troublesome weed if you have it: always invading. The Latin name is *Potentilla*; other colloquial names of related plants are cinquefoil and silverweed.

Left, from top
Cutting the grass and weeds of a boundary edge, with long-handled shears at an angle

The cut is slightly into the soil and leaves a clean line; it may include some roots as well as leaves

Unless the weather is staying dry, it's best to collect the cut pieces for composting; this also allows you to check for any new, small weeds, and for any grass that may have rooted underneath

Right, from top
May – these beds are three to six months old, at a stage when the sides can be removed

After lifting the wooden side, we laid new cardboard and compost along the edges

11 days since the first photo, beds now open-sided

I maintain cardboard along edges for at least six months of year one. Thereafter I cut the edge line of grass and weeds with long-handled shears.

We always mow grass and weeds around the edge of growing areas. The mown strip in larger gardens may be 2–3 m / up to 10 ft wide, depending on how much space is available. Beyond it is wildness, where you want it: away from beds and paths.

Further reading & viewing
Fungi in the soil – Elaine Ingham and her Soil Food website: soilfoodweb.com

Quiz Lesson 8

	Question	Multiple choice
1	Paths have value, apart from being a means of access.	True or false?
2	What is the benefit of maintaining path soil at a good level of structure and fertility? Choose the answer with the most information.	A Plant roots in beds have access to extra moisture. B Plant roots in beds have access to extra nutrients. C Drainage is better in heavy rain. D All of these. E You can access your beds and plants in all weathers.
3	Which of these statements is true?	A Gravel paths never grow weeds. B Gravel paths ensure good drainage. C Gravel paths are always clean to walk on. D Gravel adds nothing for soil life, structure or drainage.
4	Which width do I suggest for your paths (not mine!)?	A 30 cm / 12 in. B 35 cm / 14 in. C 40 cm / 16 in. D Any width. E 60 cm / 24 in.
5	Paths need to be in a different place every year.	True or false?
6	Why is it good to regularly mow or cut grass and weeds that immediately surround your beds? Choose the answer which gives most information.	A To reduce entry of weed roots and seeds. B To fill your compost heap . C All of these. D To afford less habitat for slugs and other pests close to your growing area.
7	If you make paths too narrow, wheelbarrow legs will cause damage to the beds when put down.	True or false?
8	Growth will be good if plants are set literally at the edge of a bed with sloping sides, which merge into the path.	True or false?
9	Roughly how long might it take for thick cardboard used as surface mulch, say on paths, to have decomposed enough that surviving weeds start growing through any holes?	A 11–13 days, depending on the thickness of the cardboard. B 6–10 weeks, depending on the thickness of the cardboard. C Not until the cardboard has completely decomposed.
10	What impact do woody mulches have on nitrogen levels in the soil below?	A They remove nitrogen from the soil at all levels. B They make no difference at any stage of decomposition. C When on the surface, they do not deprive plants of nitrogen but even add some, once decomposed.

Module 4
Weeds –
understand
and clear with
no dig

Lesson 9

Know your weeds – the two types

I define weeds as plants you don't want growing where they have appeared. It's a personal call and does not mean they are evil plants, rather that they are strong growers and good at reproduction. Weed plants can spread over whole areas quite rapidly, either from seed or from roots.

This module is about having a clear strategy for clearing and staying clear of weeds. Neither underestimate weeds, nor fear them. Understand how they grow, so that you are well prepared for weeds that appear, and can stay ahead of their attempts to fill your growing space.

In the 1980s I visited the fields of other organic growers, and saw the work needed to prevent crops from being smothered by weeds. In 1987 I lost half an acre / 2,000 m² of carrots to chickweed, after having prepared the soil with a rotavator.

These experiences helped me to understand how fine the line is between having a few weeds and having too many. I recommend you ignore those who advocate tolerance of weeds, because that approach can so easily lead to a big drop in harvests and, more importantly, to a lot of time wasted.

Some advocate 'weeds as ground cover', but when your vegetables and flowers grow strongly, they cover the ground. The soil is also covered by mulches of organic matter, such as compost, so with no dig I feel that 'ground cover' is not an issue. One way or another it's always covered, but not with weeds.

From left Vegetables as weeds – squash seeds, 'weeds are plants in the wrong place'; these seeds had survived my composting process, as there was not quite enough heat

Having only a few weeds germinating makes interplanting these seedlings really easy – they are coriander, parsley and dill, between broccoli

After rotavating / tilling, annual weeds are a green manure but make new seeds; this is on a neighbour's farm – mostly chickweed, and after he had rotavated four months earlier

Here are the underlying themes of Module Four:

- Be thorough with mulching in year one, especially on perennial weeds.

- Having zero or almost no weeds is an achievable state, and saves much time.

- Develop the habit of little and often weeding – much easier than being occasionally overwhelmed.

- Tolerate weeds in wild areas – many have flowers that attract insects – but keep a tidy strip around your growing area.

HOW NO DIG REDUCES THE WEED BURDEN

In the 1980s, visitors were amazed when seeing my weed-free market garden. I thought the lack of weeds was due to my mulching, and diligence. I was conscientious and hard-working, with a keen desire for clean soil. That came partly from a fear of being overwhelmed by weeds and losing crops, which I had seen happen too often.

However the same weed-free effect has happened in all of my no dig gardens. I have come to understand how soil is actually calmer (for want of a better word) after being left undisturbed. It is calm rather than upset or disturbed, and therefore has no need to recover, or re-cover with weeds. Just like us: when disturbed, we need to recover.

- Soils which have been forked and pulverised, stirred, turned and lifted, are in a state of shock. They need to calm down and to recover – weeds are part of the healing process.

- Weed plants do a great job of growing fast, covering soil, and filling it with their healing roots when soil needs this help.

There are different weeds for different tasks, such as fast-growing, pioneer weeds for rapid colonisation of cultivated ground. Deep-rooting weeds, such as docks, are found on trampled and heavy soils.

Depending on the compost used, there may be a flush of weed seedlings on no dig beds in early spring, from seeds in the compost. Then, after you pull or hoe these, there is little growth of new weeds for the rest of the year.

By comparison, I notice that on the dig bed of my trial weeds keep germinating all year long. This is the more 'usual' situation faced by gardeners who dig and till. Plus the soil is sticky when wet, or hard when dry, and weeding is more difficult.

There are other considerations which I address in this module, such as weed seeds blowing in and weed roots zooming in from edges. The key approach is that, whatever their origin, you mulch weeds to clear them, with minimal disturbance. Your soil will love you for it!

Andy H by email, 20 October 2018:
I was close to giving up my allotment, partly due to the weeds!!! Your methods have given me the impetus I needed and I'm now working on the allotment!
No dig gardeners love having so few weeds, and this is one of the many such comments I receive.

From top 31 March – all weeds have been removed from the trial bed (dig on the left and no dig on the right)

August – Steph with the results of weeding the dig and no dig beds

A closer view of the weed seedlings – mostly buttercup, grass and nettles

The following one came from 'Offwego', when I had a website forum, 19 May 2018:

Shock horror, I actually found three weed seedings in my no dig onion bed today – the first of the year. Wind-blown from the adjoining overgrown plot.

Plot neighbours are asking if I am coming down very early in the morning as this year they never see me weeding; truth is I haven't had any.

This system is far easier to maintain, and I find water retention is far better as well. With my old soil, as soon as I watered it disappeared; now the water is held in the compost.'

PERENNIAL WEEDS

The most useful categorisation for understanding weeds is between perennial and annual types.

Perennial weed characteristics centre on the their persistence and durability:

- Roots survive removal of stems and leaves.
- Roots survive winter, often dormant with no leaves visible.
- Roots spread into new soil out of sight.

If left to grow, perennial weeds will also drop seeds when at a mature stage of growth. This means they have two ways to take over in a convincing fashion!

Woody perennial weeds

What I call a 'woody weed' has either stems of wood (brambles, any shrubs and young trees), or a fat and woody taproot (chiefly large docks). These are best dug out with a sharp spade, because otherwise their vigorous shoots grow through mulches.

You don't need to remove all the roots, only the central clump of stems in the case of brambles, or the top 10–12 cm / 4–5 in of dock root. Once the digging out is finished, use your foot or the spade to firm soil down again.

Tree seedlings

Below is an elder tree (*Sambucus nigra*), starting life as a little seedling. If left for half a year, it would develop a woody tap root and already be difficult to pull. At Homeacres we also pull many hawthorn seedlings in spring (*Crataegus monogyna*); like the elder, their seeds arrive in the droppings of birds, who have eaten their berries.

We also pull seedlings of sycamore (*Acer pseudoplatanus*) and ash trees (*Fraxinus excelsior*). These are blown in by the wind – have a look around to see where you may be gaining weed seeds, be vigilant for them, and keep nearby edges as tidy as possible.

No dig success with mulching perennial weeds

It fascinates me how successful one can be at eliminating 100% of perennial weeds, simply by mulching the surface.

From top The result of neglect and digging – hedge bindweed in full growth

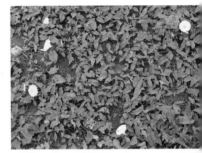

Hedge bindweed flowering, and climbing willowherb

Elder seedlings, usually from bird droppings after the birds have eaten the fruit

When I say this on courses at Homeacres, there are sometimes diggers present who look surprised, even disbelieving, after their years of attempting to remove every last root of whatever perennial weed it was.

If soil is continually sifted in that search for every root, the disturbance is cumulative and massive. Therefore every tiny bit of broken root will make a huge effort to recover itself and the soil.

With mulching it's the opposite, as roots gradually wither in situ from lack of food, due to no photosynthesis happening. Then suddenly they are completely gone, a happy moment for gardeners and a huge timesaver for years to come.

This was Evan on my forum, February 2018:
After 1.5 years not digging (mulching), what was once grass, oxalis, dead nettle, wild onion and the dreaded couch grass is now mostly weed-free! I remove occasional weeds from compost or ones that blow in, but the recurring culprits have died!

As well as the success we enjoy with mulching weeds, there is a feeling of the job being less intimidating and more achievable, fun even. This is Laura Evans after a day course at Homeacres, February 2020:
I spent several enjoyable hours renovating a neglected bed of raspberries using compost and polythene, a job so daunting I had put it off for months. Am feeling very empowered.

Some perennial weeds, and how long they take to die under mulches:

BINDWEED
There are two types of bindweed, and they both take more than a year to eradicate, often two years:

- Hedge bindweed or bellbind (*Calystegia sepium*) is a vigorous climber with white, trumpet-like flowers and thick, fleshy roots, many of which lie close to the surface.

- Field (or lesser) bindweed (*Convolvulus arvensis*) has smaller leaves, thinner roots going deep, and mostly pink flowers that are small and discreet.

Girly HR Gardener on my YouTube Bindweed video, August 2018:
I had bindweed in my original allotment plot and by following no dig I have got rid of it, so now in my 3rd year there is no bindweed at all.

BRAMBLE (*RUBUS FRUTICOSUS*)
To find the roots, cut and clear the thorny and trailing stems first. Brambles look more difficult to deal with than they actually are, because careful digging out of their relatively few root stems is enough to prevent regrowth, while the myriad small roots can stay in the soil to decompose.

Use a sharp spade to cut around each cluster of stems, making a circle of cut soil, perhaps the size of a football. Then, with the spade end at 15 cm / 6 in depth, cut diagonally through the main roots, and lever out the whole surface bundle.

- Mulching without doing this is not effective, because the strong stems will push up and through.

From top Field bindweed pushing up through a path mulch

After using a trowel to lever out some root, we see the older (parent) and newer roots

Clearing bramble (*Rubus fruticosus*)

Buttercup, creeping (*Ranunculus repens*), from existing roots – this is April, after mulching with compost in February; I levered out new growth with a trowel

Below, from top
Creeping thistle (*Cirsium arvense*)

Dandelion (*Taraxacum officinale*) has been mulched with old hay overwinter – it is still very much alive but I laid seed potatoes to grow, then put compost on top

BUTTERCUP, CREEPING (*RANUNCULUS REPENS*)

Roots are wiry and tenacious, although quite shallow. Mulching sees them gone within 4–6 months of the growing season. They often grow from seed, and can be hoed when small.

Also in this family is celandine (*Ranunculus ficaria*), whose tuberous roots are tricky to extricate, but can be mulched from late autumn to early summer during their period of growth. They are spreading if left to grow, and have pretty yellow flowers in early spring.

COUCH GRASS (*ELYMUS REPENS*)

In temperate climates, many gardeners have problems with couch grass, also called quack grass, crab grass and twitch. Its leaves are dark green and wider than many other grasses, and also a little hairy, while the white and spear-like root stems travel horizontally, and at some speed! This is a difficult weed to deal with if you are a digger. It grows in cool conditions as low as 6°C / 43°F, survives freezing, and stays dormant in dry soil.

Mulching reveals its weak point: that most roots are near the surface and hold less store of food than other perennials, like bindweed. The whole root system often dies within a year, but you must be thorough. Always mulch a strip around the edge of your growing area, to prevent re-invasion.

CREEPING THISTLE (*CIRSIUM ARVENSE*)

It looks bad but is not difficult to eradicate. Wearing a glove, insert your fingers below the leaves and gently grasp the fleshy but firm stem. Then pull evenly and gently to remove 7–10 cm / 3–4 in of white stem, which grows up through mulches from deeper roots. Persistence pays, and this weed – although of daunting appearance – can be completely eradicated within a year, or even half a year, by mulching and then regular pulling.

DANDELION (*TARAXACUM OFFICINALE*)

Along with many common salads such as lettuce and endive, dandelion is a member of the Asteraceae family. Its generic name derives from 'taraxos' meaning disorder, and 'akos' meaning remedy. The leaves are diuretic: cleansing for the liver and rich in minerals, and can be eaten in salads, even blanched. Roots dug out in autumn can be dried, roasted quite hot, and then ground to make a dark, earthy drink that is wrongly called a coffee substitute – I call it an acquired taste.

From top Dug soil that I saw at an allotment, with buried couch grass growing up to the light

January 2013 – roots of couch grass in a turf from my greenhouse

Leaves of couch grass pushing through compost mulch – notice the seedlings of annual weeds too

I used a trowel to ease out long roots – all of this went on the compost heap

Dandelions colonise large areas by seed dispersal, from their 'clock' heads, mostly in late spring and early summer. They pull easily at the two or three leaf stage.

In the darkness *under a mulch*, large roots can survive for up to six months before expiring. They die more quickly in spring when growth is fastest, meaning root resources are used up more rapidly. In year one at Homeacres, just three months (from March to May) saw vigorous dandelions die under polythene.

DOCK – BROAD LEAVED (*RUMEX OBTUSIFOLIUS*) AND CURLED OR YELLOW (*RUMEX CRISPUS*)

Docks of both types have large leaves, with reddish stems from the broad leaves, and both are prolific seeders. Large docks are easier to clear than it may appear at first sight, using a sharp spade to slice through taproots, 15 cm / 6 in down. The remaining root will be weak and die under a mulch, as will small dock plants.

Other weeds of notable vigour from their taproots are Alexanders or horse parsley (*Smyrnium olusatrum*) and burdock (*Arctium lappa*). As with docks, use a sharp spade to remove the top part of taproots.

GROUND ELDER OR GOUTWEED (*AEGOPODIUM PODAGRARIA*)

A member of the carrot or umbellifer family, famously introduced by the Romans for its edible leaves – tasty as a filling in omelettes, raw or steamed. They are greens for the hungry gap, when other vegetables are scarce.

Eradicable in one year of mulching, some weak regrowth may need pulling in year two until it expires completely. The roots are tough, white, and of medium thickness, and tend to snap as they are being pulled. They travel horizontally more than vertically, and entwine around roots of other plants, making mulching around existing plants difficult. Cut thick cardboard to shape so that it butts up to the stems of plants, then keep pulling any new weed shoots near the stems for a year or more.

HORSETAIL, MARESTAIL OR PADDYS PIPE (*EQUISETUM HYMALE*)

An extremely vigorous weed, whose spiky stems and leaves appear as remnants of a prehistoric time. Horsetail prefers soil that is continually damp, and takes six years or more to die when all methods are used: mulching as well as pulling, and even hoeing. However its vigour diminishes over the years, and it is not invincible. I need to do a composting trial on roots of horsetail to check their survival rate. Until that happens, I suggest not adding the roots to your compost heap.

STINGING NETTLE (*URTICA DIOICA*)

These are a sign of rich soil, and are not difficult to remove because their roots are shallow and spreading – just wear gloves when handling large plants. Harvest the tips in spring for excellent soups and even eat as salad, chopped very fine to dissipate the sting.

From top Dock, broad leaved (*Rumex obtusifolius*) and curled (*Rumex crispus*)

Ground elder or goutweed (*Aegopodium podagraria*)

Horsetail, marestail or paddys pipe (*Equisetum hymale*)

Stinging nettle (*Urtica dioica*), which we scythe three times yearly for the compost heap

Mulching works to kill nettles but may need a year. You can also slide a fork near the main roots, downwards at 30°, to lever out the main clump of pale yellow roots. Smaller roots do not regrow. Seeding is prolific, and seedlings can be hoed.

WILLOWHERB (*CHAMERION ANGUSTIFOLUM*)

An invasive weed, from seeds and roots. Seedling rosettes of shiny and dark green leaves can be mistaken for lamb's lettuce and then, if left to grow, develop tenacious roots and also white, fleshy stems below soil level – these endure for many years, but can be pulled out.

Pretty pink flowers on a long stem in late summer turn to hundreds or thousands of feathery seeds. Germination occurs whenever soil is moist enough, including in mild winters.

John McConville, comment on YouTube Spring video, May 2019:
I have a field which has always been a weed and stone infested problem. With no dig and composting it's turned into a small vegetable garden which is fantastic.

ANNUAL WEEDS

Annuals are easier to deal with – or are they? Their root systems are certainly less powerful than perennial weeds; however annual weeds can overwhelm from prolific seeding.

Two important qualities to be aware of are:

- Seed dispersal is their method of reproduction.
- They can flower and make viable seeds in a short time period.

Annual weeds do not regrow after being pulled, providing they are removed with some roots on the stem. All their fine roots can stay in the ground and do not regrow.

Alternatively, hoe them when so small as to be barely visible: you will be killing more weeds than you suspect, almost invisible ones with more root than leaf. After hoeing they can be left to dry and die in the disturbed mulch.

Annual weeds are in the group of pioneer plants, nature's tool for creating life out of apparently not much. On bare rocks, lichens and moss, they are the first colonisers. On damaged soils, pioneer weeds grow exceptionally fast, faster than most cultivated plants. This explains the saying 'chickweed follows the rototiller'. As do masses of perennial weeds, after the soil and their roots have been chopped up.

Pioneer weeds from seed, in temperate areas, include grasses, bittercress, groundsel, goosegrass, chickweed and charlock. Different climates and soils will see other weeds performing this valuable healing job.

With no dig there are many less pioneer weeds. At Homeacres we see them most often after compost containing weed seeds has been spread as a mulch. The main approach is to hoe, rake, scatter or pull seedlings of annual weeds, when they are barely visible. Mulches make this far easier (*which I explain further in Lesson 12*).

From top Willowherb (*Chamerion angustifolum*), at about a month old

Weeds germinating in the less-mulched path, beside a clean bed

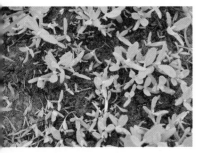

From top
Bittercress
(*Cardamine hirsuta*),
already flowering and
seeding – this could be
covered with cardboard
then compost, then it
would not regrow

Charlock
(*Brassica arvensis*), just
before it shot upwards

Chickweed
(*Stellaria media*), best
removed before it
reaches this size

Fat hen
(*Chenopodium album*),
where a seeding head
had fallen

Annual Meadow Grass
(*Poa annua*), and a
bonus groundsel!

Examples of annual weeds – their size, and how to react when seen

The measurements refer to a mature plant's height.

BITTERCRESS (*CARDAMINE HIRSUTA*)

3–5 cm / 1–2 in, with tiny white flowers that drop seeds just 4–6 weeks after appearing. Mostly a winter weed of cool and moist soil, with small leaves that are edible and tasty. Plants are small enough to go unnoticed, until they scatter hundreds of long-lived seeds at a young age. Remove when tiny and they pull out easily.

CHARLOCK (*BRASSICA ARVENSIS*)

6 cm / 2 in, with pale yellow flowers which seed in 8–10 weeks. It germinates in all seasons, though mostly in spring, and can overwinter as a seedling. Often full of flea beetle holes but still able to set hundreds of seeds. Easy to hoe when small, and easy to pull when larger; don't underestimate its ability to gain ground through speed and numerical advantage.

CHICKWEED (*STELLARIA MEDIA*)

5–7 cm / 2–3 in, a spreading habit with small white flowers within a month. It germinates in damp soil, often in early spring or autumn, and in mild winters too. The odd plant here and there is easy to remove, but its ability to set seed quickly can lead to a thick cover when it is often too damp for hoeing. Watch for it, and hoe seedlings or pull any small plants you see, with a firm tug of the almost wiry but shallow roots.

FAT HEN (*CHENOPODIUM ALBUM*)

75 cm / 30 in, with nondescript flowers turning to clusters of pale green seeds within six weeks, mostly in summer. A weed of rich soil, related to spinach and with edible leaves. Seedlings often appear in great number, and are tiny at first but subsequently grow large. Hoe tiny seedlings to avoid the pain of hand weeding high numbers of large fat hen.

ANNUAL MEADOW GRASS (*POA ANNUA*)

3–5 cm / 1–2 in, with feathery seedheads just 6–8 weeks after germination. A small, tough and common plant, growing whenever soil is mild and moist for a couple of weeks, and with mostly superficial roots, which dislike drought at least. Common in mild winters and in any other damp season, difficult to hoe and best pulled when small. Older clumps have tough roots which hang onto a lot of soil when pulled.

GROUNDSEL (SENECIO VULGARIS)

5–22 cm / 2–9 in, sets seeds 4–8 weeks after germination. Easy to hoe or pull but beware, because even one plant setting hundreds of seeds can lead to much extra weeding in subsequent years. It germinates and grows fast at all times except midwinter, mostly in fertile soil; if soil is dry or poor, plants seed when very small.

GOOSEGRASS (GALIUM APARINE)

1.5 m / 60 in if supported, and with sticky leaves and stem. The seeds are also sticky, called cleavers, and they follow small white flowers. Common in the cool and damp of late winter, spring and autumn; fast-growing, and the stem tips are fantastic for our lymph systems. A big seeder if you allow it, and perhaps the stickiest weed of all.

SHEPHERD'S PURSE (CAPSELLA BURSA-PASTORIS)

5–10 cm / 2–4 in, with a cluster of pointed leaves and then a spiky flowering stem, seeds in 4–6 weeks. It is most easily recognised by its stem of seed pods or purses. The plants have a vigorous taproot which may be hard to pull, and they can be killed by cutting this main root with a hoe or trowel, preferably when still small.

SOW THISTLE, PRICKLY (SONCHUS ASPER)

90 cm / 35 in, but often smaller, pale yellow flowers, which set seed in as little as 4–5 weeks if soil is dry. It germinates in a wide variety of conditions and can overwinter, but is most common in late summer and autumn. Its leaves are less prickly than creeping thistle, and it's related to perennial sow thistle (Sonchus arvensis), whose fleshy roots are quick to colonise new ground. All sow thistles need hoeing or pulling as small seedlings, to prevent them from invading.

SPEEDWELL (VERONICA PERSICA)

Mostly under 5 cm / 2 in, with slender stems and pale blue flowers, seeds in 4–6 weeks. Of the many kinds of speedwell, including the perennial ones, this is the most common. It grows mostly in winter and spring, has shallow roots, and is easy to pull when small. Be vigilant, as it seeds by the thousand, then being hard to control.

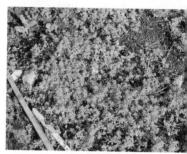

From top
Groundsel (*Senecio vulgaris*) close to seeding – it needs pulling straight away

Goosegrass (*Galium aparine*) many seedlings here; pull asap or cover

Shepherd's purse (*Capsella bursa-pastoris*) close to seeding

Sow Thistle, prickly (*Sonchus asper*) flowers 2–4 weeks after this stage

Speedwell (*Veronica persica*) in March, close to seeding

Quiz Lesson 9

	Question	Multiple choice
1	What is it about digging that encourages weeds to grow and regenerate?	A The soil is left in a state of shock, and weeds help recovery. B Breaking up the soil gives weeds the fresh air they need to grow. C Tools hitting the weed seeds awaken them from dormancy.
2	You need to dig out all perennial weeds from your plot or garden, before starting no dig.	True or false?
3	Why is bramble (*Rubus fruticosus*) one of the few perennial plants that is best removed before mulching?	A It makes strong, woody growth, which can push through the mulch. B The roots are too deep. C The mulch acts an an accelerant to growth.
4	Dandelion (*Taraxacum officinale*) must be removed by hand, as the roots can survive under mulch for many years.	True or false?
5	Which perennial weed has such a long and strong tap root that it's worth removing before mulching?	A Dock (*Rumex*, of either type). B Ground elder (*Aegopodium podagraria*). C Bindweed (*Calystegia* or *Convolvulus*). D Stinging nettle (*Urtica dioica*).
6	Which statement is false?	A Annual weeds need a year of light exclusion to die. B Couch grass can be cleared in year one. C You can grow plants in compost mulches, while perennial weeds are dying underneath. D Bindweed can be cleared within three years.
7	How do annual weeds reproduce?	A Through seed dispersal. B Through the roots spreading to make new plants. C Through stolons / runners.
8	Once the initial no dig mulching of weeds has happened, where do annual weeds come from? Choose the two correct answers.	A From seeds in new mulches. B From roots left in the soil. C From seeds blowing in. D From roots coming under the neighbour's fence.
9	Groundsel (*Senecio vulgaris*) has roots that can be left in the ground, if the main stem is twisted out and fully detached from the root system.	True or false?
10	What's the most time-saving way to stay clear of weeds?	A Weed little and often. B Allow weeds to provide ground cover. C Take on the weeds once every six weeks. D Learn to tolerate weeds.

Bob Paton CBE – Market Gardener at Hexhamshire Organics, October 2019:
Moving to no dig is the best thing we have ever done. Weeds such as chickweed which were such a problem to us last year are no longer an issue.

Organic mulches

Over the next two lessons we will explore mulching (covering) to smother existing weeds, so they die in darkness. In this lesson we focus on mulches of organic matter, and in Lesson 11 we look at non-organic mulches, such as plastic fabric and woven covers.

To consolidate what I have already shown and explained in earlier lessons, we'll concentrate on three aspects:

- What makes an organic mulch successful in killing weeds: the principles and requirements.
- Time sequences of mulching while also cropping: how the two can happen simultaneously.
- Potential problems with edges, and the need and methods for keeping them clean and in the same place.

Anna Mcleish on Facebook, September 2018:
Thanks to no dig I am – for the first time since starting an allotment five years ago – spending this time of year making the allotment nice and tidy, pruning trees, seeing to compost and planning next year. Normally I'm hacking down six foot plants and weeds and ranting that I'm giving it up. It is so much easier it's unreal.

ORGANIC MULCHES, YEAR ONE

Be thorough
It's essential to be methodical. Any 'weak point' in your mulches will be found by weed leaves searching for light, and some of them can move a long way, horizontally and under a mulch. Hence the importance of overlapping any cardboard sheets by 15 cm / 6 in, plus, if there are adjacent weedy areas, of maintaining a light-excluding mulch along its edge.

> **Membranes and carpet in the soil**
> *You may be unlucky enough to discover these under surface level: a mulch that someone laid as little as five years ago. As organic matter lands on the surface, they sink out of sight. Sadly it's a digging job to remove whatever you find. It cannot be left there or it makes an impenetrable layer for worms moving up and roots growing down.*

Level the surface
It's easiest to make beds and mulch paths on a level surface. If it's uneven, use a spade to move soil from the humps into the hollows. Remove any rocks and wood, including sides of old beds, old carpet, and any waste materials that you see. You can then apply mulches evenly and consistently, and in subsequent years you won't turn an ankle when gardening!

Decide mulch thickness

How much mulch you need depends on the amount of weeds present, and how many of them are perennials. Below are guidelines in relation to this starting point (*also bear in mind the descriptions of beds and paths in Lessons 7 and 8*).

FIVE STARTING POINTS IN TERMS OF WEEDS

Tamsin on forum topic: 'Parsnips for the first time', 14 October 2018:
After 15 years of struggling with weeds and digging on our allotment we gave it up in despair. Luckily I discovered your methods and now have a no dig veg plot in the back garden. It has been remarkable in its first year and so easy to maintain while juggling lots of small children. And for the first time ever, we have harvested parsnips! A tiny patch produced a huge amount. This is on undug pasture, with six inches of compost on top, first year. I am so surprised, I can grow parsnips! The children and I all say a big thank you.

These five categories of weed numbers and types are to help you decide your process of mulching in year one. Have a good look before starting; some areas of a new plot may need different mulches.

1 Few weeds and mostly soil visible
The easiest starting point. It might be ground which has been growing vegetables and flowers already, and was well looked after. Best to remove the few larger weeds, and then there are two possibilities:

— If the soil looks in good condition, cover the beds with 5–7 cm / 2–3 in of compost, enough to create a soft and fertile surface. That is all you need to do.

— If the soil looks stony and weed growth is not lush, apply a thicker layer of up to 15 cm / 6 in of organic matter and compost. This is my approximate upper limit for starting out, although I applied 20 cm / 8 in in the greenhouse, where cropping is more intense.

2 Many weeds, mostly annuals
Compared to the above, this simply needs a layer of cardboard to be laid before applying the compost. Cardboard slows weeds that are growing upwards as they strive to reach the light, and makes it unlikely that any annual weed leaves arrive at the surface before dying.

If weed growth is lush and tall I would cut them with a mower, strimmer or scythe, and then card over the cut leaves and stems. If you expect slug problems (in damp climates for example), you could remove the cut growth to your compost heap.

Watch for any regrowth, mostly of perennial weeds if there were some present, and pull any stems as soon as you see them.

A question on the forum from Zoe in Somerset:
If I am mulching onto neglected beds of seeded annual weeds, for instance a carpet of speedwell and chickweed, will a generous autumn mulch of rotted manure see it off by Spring?

The answer: Yes, for sure. These annuals are easy weeds to mulch because they have little energy in their root systems. Your mulch needs to be a level 5 cm / 2 in thick, or more if you have enough compost, with no weed leaves visible after spreading, so that no leaves can photosynthesise. Within a few weeks, and certainly by late winter, you will have clean soil underneath, with perhaps a few new weed seedlings to remove which will be growing in your manure or compost.

If she had been faced with more than a few perennial weeds I would have recommended thick cardboard first, before applying her manure on the cardboard, *see below*.

3 Many weeds and, say, a third or more perennials

This starting point needs more care, to be sure of not having perennial weeds coming back all the time. I suggest thick cardboard first, and 10–15 cm / 4–6 in of organic matter.

There will probably be some appearance of new leaves, straining for light and fuelled by energy stored in the weakening parent root. Don't panic! Just keep removing any new growth, by pulling or using a trowel to remove the new shoots. You can't lever out the parent root, but a time arrives when it just dies from having no more food.

How long this takes depends on the types of perennial weeds, and the vigour of their roots.

4 Woody growth and weeds underneath

Brambles are a common example (*see Lesson 9 for my advice on dealing with them*). For all plants with woody stems – including shrubs, honeysuckle, lavender and buddleia – you need a sharp spade. Perhaps even a pruning saw or axe, to cut or chop the thickest roots just below surface level.

The main non-woody weed that I find worthwhile to cut out with a spade is dock (*see Lesson 9*). Occasionally I take a spade or fork to the roots of stinging nettles, where they are overgrowing an edge for example. Otherwise I cut nettles to ground level, and mulch with thick cardboard.

Here are my tips on how to remove enough root of large woody plants:

First cut diagonally into the soil and through the main roots, in a circle around the main stem or clump of stems. The circle's diameter depends on the size of the plant, say from 15–45 cm / 6–18 in.

Left, from top
May – the membrane is rolled back, showing cow parsley and couch grass in a new bed made one month earlier, with no cardboard under 10 cm / 4 in compost

Using a trowel to lever out bindweed

The view from Zino's drone after Croatian TV filmed us creating a new bed on pasture, with cardboard under the compost

We planted salads and spinach into the new bed on 10 October – they all grew fine until flowering in the spring, with almost zero weed growth

Right, from top
Pulling out a wire fence with stinging nettles growing through the wire

Using a spade to loosen the nettle roots

From top A bed half cleared with tops cut – I then pulled ivy roots, and used a spade to remove roots of bramble

A bramble's new roots – the stems spread a long way and then root; best to pull them out at this stage

Once the lateral roots are severed, push firmly on the main stem one way then another, to loosen soil from deep roots underneath and to enable you to push the spade onto them to cut through. This part may be easier with two people.

When the plant is loose, lift it out and knock as much soil as you can off its roots. It's fine to leave many of the smaller roots where they were growing.

Use any nearby soil, or compost, to fill the hole and make it level. Then proceed as above, according to how many weeds there are.

5 Mostly perennial weeds of notable vigour

Using only organic mulches on these weeds can kill them, but not before you may have spent a lot of time removing the regrowth, while parent roots are gradually losing their reserves of food. In year one you may need to weed repeatedly, until you see no more regrowth.

In the next lesson I explain about using polythene / non-organic mulches, which is easier for thick growth of perennial weeds. The drawback is that it's less easy to grow vegetables in year one.

For those in the USA who suffer Bermuda grass (*Cyonodon dactylon*) I offer sympathy, because its root system is deeper and stronger than couch grass. However, I have heard from a few people on YouTube that mulching killed their Bermuda grass completely. Mulching, or total light exclusion needs to be:

- Probably for a minimum of one year, and preferably with plastic.
- 100% thorough, with nothing growing through holes in year one.
- Over a larger area than is planned for growing, to reduce subsequent invasion from edges.

To finish this section on a positive note, I saw this comment on Facebook, from Dawn Canham in London:
Bindweed has been completely manageable with cardboard and no dig – we just keep pulling up the shoots and it's giving up.

TYPES OF ORGANIC MULCHES

The table to the right summarises common mulches of organic matter. I have not mentioned them all in the text, because of the values of compost and cardboard as main mulches for clearing weeds and cropping straight away.

Mulches such as hay and straw are best for dry climates, where slugs will not be common. Like wood chips, they decompose in situ, and turn to compost at soil level in months or years. They have value for paths as well as beds.

- Preferably use organic hay and straw, to avoid the chemicals used by farmers to grow them.

- Hay usually has a lot of weed seeds, so what starts as a nice solution can create more work.

		MULCHES FOR KILLING WEEDS BY LIGHT EXCLUSION			
Mulch material	Thickness to clear weeds	Repeat application if needed	Suitability for paths	Advantages	Disadvantages
Compost of any kind, even partially decomposed	5–15 cm / 2–6 in, usually with cardboard	Annual 2–5 cm / 1–2 in for fertility	Only if there are no, or very few, weeds	Feeds soil, can grow vegetables while weeds are dying	Possibly expensive
Hay / grass, preferably organic	15 cm / 6 in when dense	If many weeds grow through	Perhaps, only where few slugs	Feeds soil, a use for spoiled hay	Cool in spring, weed seeds, slugs
Straw, preferably organic	20 cm / 8 in when dense	If many weeds grow through	Yes, preferably where few slugs	Often cheap, feeds soil	Cool in spring, weed seeds, slugs
Cardboard	Thick types or a double layer	Often after 8–10 weeks	Good, with shavings on top	A free resource	Need to remove any tape and staples, takes time to secure
Wood chips / shavings / sawdust	15–20 cm / 6–8 in	Perhaps, and especially for paths	Where few weeds – if weedy, lay card first	A free resource, easy to handle	Slow to decompose on beds, makes sowing difficult
Soil of the best quality possible	5–7 cm / 2–3 in with compost on top	n / a	You can scrape soil from path to bed	Uses up any unwanted topsoil	Weed seeds, stones, variable quality
Carpet, WOOL ONLY	One carpet	n / a	Yes	An effective weed suppressant	Slug build-up is possible
Newspaper	10–25 sheets	Perhaps after 8–10 weeks	Yes, but difficult to anchor in wind	A free resource	Cool in spring, slugs, securing edges and overlaps

For annual vegetables, some mulches make cropping difficult. You can't sow carrots in a mulch of wood chips for example. Hay mulches stick to lettuce leaves when you are picking them. Straw mulches are light in colour so reflect sunlight, which keeps soil cool through spring, just when you need it to warm up (especially in cooler climates). Which mulch or combination of mulches you use depends on:

1 Which are most available to you.

2 Your climate.

3 The weeds currently growing.

4 How soon you want to sow and / or transplant; the table above gives some pointers.

EXAMPLES

These sequences show how there is no fixed time between making a bed on top of weeds, and then sowing or planting. A big advantage of using compost mulches (rather than plastic) is the ease of sowing and planting straight away.

Because it's possible to make beds at any time of year, sometimes you will find yourself sowing and planting on the same day as you create them. If that is the case, be sure to tread the compost firm. We call it the no dig dance: you can't compact compost.

CREATING NEW BEDS TO DOUBLE CROP IN YEAR ONE

Winter is a great time to create beds, even when the ground is frozen (only not if snow is deep). Just look for any time in the quiet season when you can start. Then you will be ready to plant in spring, which, in my experience, always comes in a rush. So it pays to be ahead.

The 11 photos on this spread are of new beds that we laid out and filled in November, almost at the end of Homeacres' growing season. In one corner we popped in a few spare broad bean plants, and they gave harvests by late May. For the rest of this area I waited until March, the right season for the plantings I wanted to make.

The March plantings were helped to establish by having fleece over. It's a soggy area with squelching paths at this time of year, so the raised beds were helping plant roots stay aerated.

- In subsequent years the drainage has been noticeably better and, when the soil is saturated, these paths no longer squelch.

By May the coriander and dill were showing signs of flowering, and in early June we interplanted module-raised plants of beetroot between them.

Left, from top Measuring the new bed to 1.2 m / 48 in between the insides of the sides

Tipping compost which is old and lumpy cow manure, and best as a bottom layer

Using a rake to level the first batch of lumpy manure, before spreading finer compost

Homemade compost made up most of the surface

Right, from top New plantings on 27 March – coriander and dill; beyond are overwintered salads under fleece

Fleece over the new plants as soon as they were in the ground

So much changes in spring, and this is the wider area on 27 May – the herbs are still growing on the right

By that time the cabbages were making hearts, and we popped in French bean plants as soon as they had finished, after twisting out the cabbage stumps. The beds stayed full in summer and autumn, and sometimes even into winter. For example, after the French beans finished in October, we planted chervil and spring onions.

The beetroot harvest was in December. One beetroot weighed 1.9 kg / 4.2 lb; large roots grown like this are perfectly tender and juicy. They are also good to store over winter – we ate the last ones in late April.

Whenever cropping finishes for the year, we spread compost to protect and feed the soil throughout the coming year. In the case of the middle bed this was in October, after we had cut the French bean plants on their stems. Most roots remained in the soil, and we spread 3 cm / 1 in of old, fine compost, before the new plantings of chervil and spring onions. They were cropping until the following May, so it made sense to spread the compost mulch in September.

There is a myth that legume vegetables leave a lot of nitrogen in the soil, for the benefit of subsequent plantings. As with so many statements, this needs qualifying:

- Legume vegetables which have finished cropping do not add much nitrogen to the soil, because most of it (up to 97%) has been used by them to grow. They are not natural philanthropists.

- For soil to have a nitrogen boost from legumes' pink nodules, you need to cut off the plants before cropping, when in full flower.

- Nonetheless there is valuable organic matter, and other nutrients, in the roots of legumes and all vegetables. Old roots are food for microbes, and indirectly feed new plants.

After the beetroot harvest in December, we spread 5 cm / 2 in of slightly lumpy homemade compost, which was eight months old. In volume terms, it's probably an equivalent depth to 3 cm / 1 in of finer compost. The lumps shatter in frost, and after a light rake in early spring the bed is ready to start again. Preparation is so quick with no dig.

From top 15 July – a dry summer, and the new beetroot on the right have had very little water

7 October – we had recently planted chervil plus spring onions, and harvested beetroot

Two weeks later in the early morning – fennel leaves are top left

In a mild December – there are still many vegetables to harvest; the bed on the right has been mulched with 5 cm / 2 in of compost

MULCHING AND PLANTING UNDER COVER

Year one, greenhouse – mulching cleared 100% of the couch grass

Before the greenhouse was built, its whole area was full of couch roots.

123

In February, the first thing we did was lay some cardboard, when the wall was in place and before the greenhouse builders arrived. After that, my final compost spreading happened in March.

- Only a few blades of grass made it to the light and, by August, there were no more spears of new grass. Thick cardboard and 20 cm / 8 in of compost were more successful than I had dared to hope, after the amount of rhizomes I had seen when the builder took out soil to build the walls.

Year one, polytunnel – erection, mulching, cropping

We put up the polytunnel before doing any mulching, on pasture with weeds. It was an old tunnel and I dug a trench to lay the polythene in. In these eight photos you can see the mulching and planting in year one.

In January 2013, as soon as the initial mulch of cardboard and 10 cm / 4 in of old cow manure had been spread, I planted some of Steph's spare pea and broad bean plants into the mulch, during weather of frost and some snow. They provided welcome food by late May. By that time their roots were into the soil, below the compost and decaying cardboard.

In mid-April I planted multi-sown Boltardy beetroot, which had also cropped by the end of May, to everyone's amazement after a cold spring. Polytunnels are wonderful things, and great value per area covered.

Left, from top After banging in the 'foundation tubes', it then needed just two hours to erect the 11-year-old frame, taken from my previous garden

In January (once the polythene was secure) we began mulching the many perennial weeds, without using any polythene mulches

How it looked in February – with carrots sown bottom right; there was some soil under the composts

In early spring, some bindweed pushing through the first mulch – this was the first time I knew it was there as it is dormant through winter

Right, from top All finished by mid-April, and still some night frosts – now waiting for warmer weather before planting frost-tender plants

May 24 – a harvest of carrots, sown in January on a new bed of manure and some soil

30 May in the polytunnel – all tomatoes have been planted and legumes are cropping; beetroot are on the right

By mid-July vegetables are well grown – I had done hardly any weeding all year, and it was mostly bindweed

Quiz Lesson 10

	Question	Multiple choice
1	In year one, which is one of the key requirements of the mulch?	A It excludes light. B It stops moisture getting to the soil. C It is heavy enough to squash and kill weeds.
2	If starting no dig on soil with few weeds and mostly annuals, is it important to lay cardboard before spreading compost?	A Yes. B Only if the weather is warm. C No, although it's always an option.
3	How does cardboard on soil help as part of your initial mulch, in many but not all situations?	A Cardboard keeps the compost in place. B The decomposing cardboard speeds up weed decomposition. C Cardboard prevents weeds from growing upwards in search of light, for about six to ten weeks, until it decomposes.
4	What are some benefits of using cardboard, compared to other types of mulch? Choose two answers.	A It degrades. B The staples and tape help hold it together. C It's free. D It's high in nutrients.
5	It's fine to lay thick cardboard on moist soil, then 10–15 cm / 4–6 in of compost on top, and then to plant in the same day (if it's the right season for those plants).	True or false?
6	Before using an old carpet as mulch, why is it important to know the type of material it's made of?	A To establish how effective the carpet will be at killing weeds. B Because slugs prefer carpets made with wool. C Because it has to be all wool, yet most (but not all) carpets contain plastic threads and synthetic chemicals.
7	How would you deal with woody growth, such as brambles and buddleia, before mulching?	A Prune back to the base. B Dig out the main stems, and just a few of the larger roots attached to them. C Spray with a root killer.
8	It is necessary to start planting in a new no dig bed straight away.	True or false?
9	What time of year is best for creating new no dig beds? Choose the answer with the most information.	A Any time. D Winter. B Spring. E Autumn. C Summer.
10	Do you need to add mulch between any first and second crops?	A Yes – the extra nutrients are needed early on. B No – unless the soil life has eaten all the mulch, which is unlikely if you applied 5cm / 2in before the season began.
11	When do you need to apply the first mulch to beds in a newly erected greenhouse or polytunnel?	A Before erecting the greenhouse / polytunnel. B After erecting the greenhouse / polytunnel. C Either before or after – whichever is easier. D Six months before erecting the structure.

Lesson 11
Non-organic mulches

In this lesson we look at non-organic mulches, which are mostly plastic sheeting. We consider when they can be useful, and when they are best avoided.

CLEARING DIFFICULT WEEDS OR MULCHING QUICKLY

Large covers which exclude light are a delightfully easy way to clear weeds, for little time and effort. Sometimes you can grow vegetables at the same time, and I illustrate this here with potatoes and squash.

Other vegetables that you can grow through holes in the plastic are any of those that need a lot of space per plant. This results in fewer holes, cut into whatever material you are using. Suitable vegetables include broccoli, cauliflower, kale and Brussels sprouts.

However there are downsides:

- Vegetables grown through covers suffer an increased risk of slug damage, caused by moisture retention under the material.

- If using the non-woven polypropylene (landscape) fabric, you will need to lay cardboard first to achieve 100% light exclusion.

OR MULCH WITH NO CROPPING

Sometimes it may be simpler just to cover an area of problem weeds and grow nothing. This ensures total light exclusion, and is appropriate where you have other space ready to grow plants, or are simply happy to wait a year.

Thinking ahead and mulching like this can save so much time and effort in the following year.

May – we planted squash in holes cut in the polythene, which had been covering couch grass

May – potatoes emerging during a cold spring; they were planted through holes in the polythene (*see how this worked in 'Potatoes' section below*)

ATTRIBUTES OF NON-ORGANIC MULCHES					
Plastic covers to clear weeds	Cost	Life	% of light excluded	Advantages	Disadvantages
Black polythene	Low	3–15 years	100% if thick – hold up to light to check	Total darkness, cheap	Allows little rain to pass
Woven polypropylene	High	10–15 years	1% of light passes through	Rain passes through, durable	Cost, slugs, shreds when cut
Non-woven polypropylene fabric	Low	1–2 years	20–30% of light passes through	Cheap, looks ok, good on card	Not dark or strong, short life
Biodegradable black polythene	Medium	6–8 months	30% of light passes through	Biodegradable (in decades)	Admits light, does not compost

The prerequisite, especially if using polythene, is that the ground is moist before laying it. This keeps soil organisms happy, and means they build soil fertility when eating and secreting any organic matter that you have applied before covering with plastic.

MULCHING PERENNIAL WEEDS

However you go about it, be thorough and conscientious. Neither underestimate these weeds, nor be overawed by them. Don't try to dig any roots out before covering, except for woody plants.

Here are two cases showing the attention to detail you need in order to clean soil of perennial weeds. They quickly regrow towards any chinks of light.

Example 1
At an allotment that I visited, I saw a plot that had synthetic carpet laid over couch grass and buttercups, but with gaps between the carpet edges. Weed leaves easily find these gaps and start to grow again.

There were also gaps between carpet and plant – wide ones. Any mulch to kill weeds should butt up to the stems of existing plants.

To be clear, and despite what you may read, it's fine to sit mulches right against plant stems or tree trunks. I have never suffered or observed problems from doing this with cardboard, compost or polythene.

The photo, overleaf top, also shows another problem with synthetic mulches: some pieces of carpet have moved or been moved, and are starting to fragment and disappear into the ground. This sinking into the soil is a result of earthworms casting upwards, and debris landing on top.

The result is plastic debris buried in soil. A buried, invisible and possibly toxic barrier to both plant roots and soil organisms.

A globe artichoke, where the mulching has been half-hearted and not thorough enough

If this carpet were made of wool there would be no problem, because it would all be digested in the end and become food in the soil. Any synthetic carpet with nylon fibres will not degrade. Such carpets may also contain chemicals such as fire retardants.

Example 2

The six photos below are from Homeacres in 2018. It's an area with vigorous perennial plants, including brambles, cow parsley, thistles of different types, stinging nettles, couch grass and bindweed. I used a sharp spade to remove the main stems of brambles, then cut grass and weeds short, in order to facilitate laying the mulches.

Top row from left The far corner at Homeacres in June 2017 – showing weed growth in an area where we planted a hedge. Mulching weeds after planting the hedge – laying cardboard. Pulling a new tree through a hole in landscape fabric.

Bottom row from left 20 March – hedge trees have been planted, and the mulch has been pushed in with a blunt spade. 10 September – the edges had occasional mowing; a mulch covers Sea Buckthorn at the end. Six months of cardboard and thin landscape fabric did an amazing job for these trees

Before mulching we planted the small trees of Amelanchier and Sea Buckthorn into small holes, and without any loosening of other soil. Then we spread 3 cm / 1 in of compost.

The next steps were to:

- Butt thick cardboard up to the tree stems.

- Spread any organic amendments – here it was a little more compost and mostly wood shavings on top.

- Lay fabric over the top, and for each tree we cut a small cross-slit.

- Push fabric edges into the soil using a blunt spade, both to hold it down and to make it easier to mow weeds right up to the fabric edge.

I used some old and slightly torn fabric, and here it was helpful to hold the pieces of cardboard in place. In addition it slowed entry into the strip of the adjacent perennial weeds.

Another option, other than using fabric, would be to weigh down the card with say 10 cm / 4 in of wood chip. However this would allow more invasion of weeds from the sides.

During the summer we needed to pull significant amounts of bindweed off the tree stems, where it had found light through the planting holes. Plus the edges needed mowing every two to three weeks. Otherwise the tall weeds would have been able to grab a lot of moisture from soil in the strip, before the slower-growing tree roots could have found it. 2018 was a dry summer, and we did not water the trees.

I pulled the fabric off in September, and the only surviving weed was bindweed, in a much weakened state. Even after decades of mulching powerful weeds, this method still amazes me. The hedge was established, and we could now grow without mulching.

CLEAR DIFFICULT WEEDS AND CROP AT THE SAME TIME

This is a lovely combination: three worthwhile things are happening simultaneously, and in a short period of time too.

1 100% of weeds are killed, except the most persistent ones, in this case bindweed.

2 Soil organisms are fed, leaving soil more fertile than when we started, and ready to grow more great vegetables.

3 A harvest is taken.

Overleaf are a couple of examples of clearing and cropping: potato and cucurbit. Which of these you choose to grow depends on climate, timings, and what you wish to grow as a succeeding vegetable.

For example, you can plant potatoes earlier than squashes, and their harvest is often in summer rather than autumn. This allows time for replanting a wide range of vegetables. Squash, on the other hand, usually finish towards the end of a growing season, though not always.

Polythene and moisture

Gardeners sometimes worry about how polythene, as opposed to woven fabric, does not let any rain pass into the soil. In practice this rarely, if ever, matters:

- The aim is to lay polythene on moist soil, which then holds that humidity.

- Moisture under the polythene is replenished when it rains, because much of the water runs into planting holes.

- Often, and as in my examples, you are re-using old polythene which has a few slits. They are not large enough to allow weeds' upward growth, but rain can pass through them into the soil.

Potatoes

This area had a small bonfire in my first spring, after I had cut down a wild cherry close to where the polytunnel was going to be. The bonfire's heat killed many pasture plants, except for couch grass and bindweed. The compost I used, on an area about twice the size of the bonfire, was two-year-old cow manure. It had some straw bedding still visible, but was mostly well decomposed – dark and soft.

We planted the potatoes shallow because it was firm soil, and difficult to make any more than a small hole. As a result many tubers developed near the surface, and the polythene was not thick enough to keep all light off them. Therefore I laid cardboard on top of the polythene, between each potato plant, to prevent the potatoes from going green.

Lifting potatoes is easiest after you have cut all surface growth of the stems. I removed them to the compost heap, and then pulled back the polythene. This revealed many potatoes lying near the surface, easy to gather.

- Even if there is some damage to potato stems and tubers caused by late blight (*Phytopthora infestans*), it's fine to put everything on a compost heap. Blight spores can't survive in soil and compost.

If, when removing polythene, you see only a few weeds still growing, there is no need to put it back. When soil is already almost clear of weeds,

From top A month after the bonfire – spreading some old cow manure compost on the surface

1 April – Steph plants potatoes, after covering the compost with polythene

30 June – strong potato growth with little weed growth, and the potatoes are flowering

From top Mid-July – I removed the polythene and pulled the potatoes; this is one plant of Estima, a second early, waxy potato

Two hours later, and the soil is mostly clean of weeds – plus we had pulled all those potatoes

On the same day as the potato harvest I planted brassicas into the compost, with a net to stop pigeons

you can carry on without extra mulching. In this case I transplanted new vegetables into the now uncovered ground.

My polythene mulch had certainly given home to many slugs. They were already there in the old pasture, and you can see the result of a high slug population in the photos left. The plants had been fortunate to have had a dry summer for establishing, but once the rain returned in autumn, so did the molluscs!

Things improved the following year, when the mulch was only compost. With the grassy edge mown regularly, slugs found less habitat and their numbers decreased to manageable levels.

This area of the garden has now been absorbed into new beds.

Cucurbits
Many cucurbit plants ramble to cover a large area, with extensive root systems from trailing stems. Only a few plants are needed to pull value from a large area. Yields are even higher if polythene is not used, because roots from the trailing stems can then feed into the soil. However polythene is effective against perennial weeds, and cucurbits grow well through holes in the cover.

I am often asked by worried gardeners if there is a remedy for their white and mildewed squash and courgette leaves in late summer. The answer is not to worry, it is natural dieback as summer cedes to autumn.

From top 24 September – we now had a beetroot harvest, and broccoli has been damaged by slugs

A wet autumn in 2013 – the newly mulched ground resulted in many slugs

October 2014 – the crops are clean!

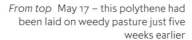

From top May 17 – this polythene had been laid on weedy pasture just five weeks earlier

We found slugs, leatherjackets and weeds – still alive, but weakening

The near end had the most couch grass, and we laid some cardboard as extra mulch

We spread a 7 cm / 3 in mulch of compost, then laid the polythene over once again

25 May – we made holes, and planted five Crown Prince squash for autumn harvests

Growth by July, with squashes on the right

Powdery mildew (of which there are various types) can be found on old leaves, and helps plant energy go into ripening the fruits. There are still new leaves and a high level of photosynthesis, until early or mid-autumn.

In the polytunnel, we cut mildewed leaves off cucumber plants. This makes it easier to see and harvest the fruits, and to prune the side shoots. Outside we leave courgette and squash plants unpruned, because the mildewed leaves are not in the way and do not harm new growth.

After harvest, we rolled up the polythene to use again, and used a trowel to lever out some roots of surviving perennial weeds (here it was bindweed). Then I spread another 7 cm / 3 in of compost on what became a wide bed of 2.1 m / 7 ft.

COMBINATION OF POLYTHENE AND ORGANIC MATTER TO KILL WEEDS, 2016

In another area of the garden there was a lot of couch grass and bindweed. I used polythene initially, then compost, cardboard and fabric.

I used several mulches, partly to check their relative merits, but also to be sure of killing all the couch grass, and to reduce the growth of bindweed. The strong growth of courgettes / zucchini also helped to suppress weed growth.

In early September, we pulled out half of the courgette plants and planted endives. There was still some bindweed, but all the couch roots had decomposed and subsequent plantings needed little weeding.

The following summer we found it easy to keep removing occasional bindweed, as it continued to weaken. By summer 2018 there was none at all in that area, just some in the adjoining old pasture (which we keep removing when seen as it spreads back in). You can reduce this reinvasion by keeping the edge cut short, to reduce vigour in roots.

From top
Growth by August, and the first natural dieback of squash leaves

Mid-October – we can now see the fruits, with just a few bindweed leaves

Over 50 kg / 110 lb of squash was taken for winter; the polythene wasn't needed any more, and there was weak growth of bindweed

The same bed after adding compost and sowing broad beans

From top
7 April – polythene laid on the pasture in February, after 5 cm / 2 in of compost

Under the polythene – light-deprived roots of couch grass, while bindweed is yet to appear

15 cm / 6 in of compost (mostly old manure with homemade compost on top) after we had covered the whole area with cardboard

Further viewing
My video on YouTube – *No dig, two ways to clear weeds*

Quiz Lesson 11

	Question	Multiple choice
1	When using plastic mulches, what is an important thing to know about the material you are using?	A How much light it excludes. B How much heat it generates. C What colour it is.
2	Before laying a large sheet of polythene (not woven polypropylene), what is the main requirement of soil condition?	A That it's moist. B That it's clear of weeds. C That it has a fine tilth.
3	Earthworms don't like the moist darkness under plastic mulches.	True or false?
4	Which of these weed categories, plus amounts, most justify the use of a plastic mulch?	A Many perennials. B A few annuals. C Many annuals. D A few perennials.
5	Which of these should you never do?	A Lay a plastic mulch with compost on top. B Walk over an area covered in plastic. C Lay plastic on top of compost, which is on top of weeds.
6	You need to use plastic mulches regularly, after clearing difficult weeds in year one.	True or false?
7	It's fine to butt any mulches up against stems of plants already growing.	True or false?
8	Which of these statements is false? Choose two answers.	A Mulches of organic matter feed soil life, unlike polythene mulches. B You can sow into mulches of compost, unlike polythene. C Polythene mulches, used for a few months to kill weeds, are bad for soil organisms. D It's quicker to mulch large areas with cardboard compared to polythene.

Left, from top

Three days later the beds are finished – they are ready to plant, but we are waiting for warmth

20 May – as weed roots were still growing, I put black polythene over and planted a few courgettes; we could have managed without the polythene, but it was a timesaver

Three weeks later and growth is strong – little chance for the couch grass there

Mid-September – one bed of courgettes has gone, and endives are now growing (on the right hand edge)

How this area looked by December, a view from the other end – normal beds and no more polythene, cardboard or wooden sides

Lesson 12
Staying weed-free – 'little and often'

Gardening is so much more fun when you are in control of the weed situation, rather than the other way around. No dig helps enormously, but even so you need to be in the habit of dealing with new weed growth. This is whenever it's mild and moist enough for seeds to germinate, or for perennial weed roots to grow.

There is a nice phrase used for dealing with the first flush of new weed germination in early spring – a weed strike. It's about catching them very young, and using minimum time for maximum effect.

The ideal period for weed strikes is before you sow and transplant, usually in late winter to early spring. Normally you use a hoe or rake, passing it lightly through the surface. Hand weeding is possible for smaller areas.

HAND WEEDING IS FUN WHEN THERE ARE FEW

Weeding by hand can be fun, as long as there are few enough for it not to be an overwhelming job. It's always such an opportunity to see what else is going on. At such close quarters you notice other things too: if there is any pest damage to vegetables, if there are any pods to harvest, or perhaps there is a need to water or give support; plus it's a chance to remove diseased leaves.

Hand weeding goes more quickly when weeds are small, really small. The habit you need is a willingness to be proactive, to pull those weed seedlings when it's *optional, rather than vital*. Stay alert and always be looking over your garden, searching for where you can make a worthwhile difference.

If you leave weeding until the last possible moment, just before they drop hundreds of seeds, the results are:

- More time and effort needed.
- A messy look to your garden.
- The likelihood of slugs hiding under the leaves.
- Reduced time to do other jobs of the season.
- A loss of enthusiasm for gardening!

From top 31 May, and new plantings in the polytunnel – if it weren't for no dig there would be many weeds at this stage; we have hardly weeded at all

September – close plantings result in less chance for weeds to grow

October – hunting for weeds; I did not find many, but it was still worth looking

WEED KNOWLEDGE – FEATURING OXALIS

Weeding is more interesting when you learn to recognise the different weeds. Then you can often work out how they came to be there, and better know the methods of control and level of attention needed. *Oxalis corniculata* and *Oxalis debilis*, both commonly called oxalis, are suitable for illustrating this point.

With its dark-coloured leaves, innocuous appearance and pretty pale flowers, oxalis can build a population fast and, unless you are familiar with the dark colour, *invisibly*. Your new plantings will then eventually suffer from its competition, as it drops seeds so readily.

It – or its seeds – often arrive in potted plants, because it's endemic in some nurseries. An added complication is that plants of *Oxalis debilis* grow bulbils in large areas of soil and become perennial weeds.

At a National Trust garden where I was advising the head gardener about weed control, the previous gardener had double dug every November for 26 years, to control perennial oxalis. After they switched strategies, and mulched with cardboard and then compost, the oxalis was immediately reduced and easily kept to a minimum with occasional hoeing.

The gardeners were happier for having an easier job, plus they enjoyed conversing with passing visitors, who were interested to see a new method.

From left Pulling a small sow thistle
A sow thistle in dug soil – the last chance to pull it before it flowers
Oxalis corniculata – always a candidate for hand weeding

HOEING WORKS FOR TINY WEEDS AND SAVES TIME IF THERE ARE MANY

In small gardens you may never need to hoe, because hand weeding is feasible. A hoe is handy for larger areas, and when there are hundreds or thousands of weeds at seedling stage.

The secret to success is 'hoe before you see the weeds', not literally but almost! The best time to hoe is when the weed seeds in new surface compost are starting to show life, that first hint of green as their small cotyledon (seedling) leaves unfurl.

Already at that stage of growth, seedlings have more root than you might imagine. Sometimes it's called the 'white thread stage', and you need to dislodge those threadlike roots before they make any kind of root network. When disturbed at this stage they die in place, without you needing to remove them.

Practice helps to train your muscles into working effectively:

- Learn to run the hoe blade through compost on the surface, as shallow as possible.

- Learn to rake sideways and shallowly through the surface compost, not moving it around too much.

- Hoeing becomes almost a pleasure: smooth, easy and rapid.

Develop the habit of hoeing the paths too, if needed; otherwise pull those few path weed seedlings. It's not hard work because mulches keep path surfaces soft.

Find a hoe you like, because there are so many designs and you need to be comfortable using it. Some have wires to run through the surface, rather than blades, and thin blades work most easily. Hand hoes are practical for close plantings.

In all of this, a top facet of no dig is that most of the time you will have few weeds, and occasional hand weeding will be sufficient.

RAKING CAN BE A WEEDING OPTION

Some people never get on with hoeing; if you are one of them, try raking. It's possible to use a rake for the weed strike before planting, and between widely planted vegetables. First, wait for conditions dry enough that the surface looks a little dry, and when there is either wind or sunshine, or best of all both.

It's important to run the rake horizontally, not downwards, so that it skims through the surface compost, just 3 cm / 1 in deep. I use it in a slightly circular motion, with the side edge of the rake's head being the first point of contact. Rotate to the left and then back to the right.

A light raking of the surface in early spring has three great results:

1 Weed seedlings are dislodged when many of them may have only white roots, which then die as they dry out. If there are many weed seeds in your compost, you will be saving a significant weeding job that would otherwise have to be done later on.

2 Lumps of compost break into smaller pieces as the rake hits them, creating a soft and friable surface for sowing and transplanting.

3 You leave the bed surface more level and even, which is then easier for sowing and planting into at a consistent depth.

STAGES OF GROWTH FOR WEEDING

The photos, far right, are to clarify some differences between stages of weed growth. The fat hen seedlings are already about to go beyond the 'small weeds' stage, when they are suitable for hoeing.

Chickweed roots are numerous and strong, despite being fine; they form a mat of root-filled soil, under and close to the leaves.

From top Hoeing lightly when weeds are very small and tender – using a swivel or oscillating hoe with a super thin blade

Running a hoe through soil of the dig bed, which grows many weeds!

Compare the weeds with those in the bottom photo, taken on the same day in early April – this is the dig bed

Weeds in the no dig bed – the spinach was planted in March, the parsnips were also sown in March

From top Running my rake through surface lumps in late winter

March – raking to break lumps, and to disturb germinating weeds and seedlings

The example you can see in the photo would be a candidate for hand weeding, unless the weather was hot and dry. Only in such weather do the roots die after being hoed, and only as long as no rain falls before the roots have shrivelled.

• The *grass weeds* are an example of weeds from a new spread of compost. I made the heap in my first winter at Homeacres, and the heap was never hot enough to kill the weed seeds.

Throughout those cold months of my first winter here, I had been clearing weeds which had soil on their roots from areas of old concrete. Also I had been levering out the roots of woody weeds, again with soil on. They all went into the compost heap and a year later, after spreading this compost, I could see how this soil contained thousands of weed seeds, including meadow grass.

The grass seedlings were emerging between mustards for salad, at a damp time of year when it's not feasible to hoe. Plus even if I had been able to hoe I wouldn't have, because grasses need hand weeding. Those tiny leaves are already attached to a root network which usually survives after hoeing, especially in October. I pulled them one by one; it did not take too long.

From top The last chance to hoe these fat hen seedlings, before their roots become too strong

Chickweed seedlings, now almost beyond the stage of hoeing – better hand weeded unless the weather stays dry

October 2013 – grasses from my first batch of Homeacres compost; I pulled them all

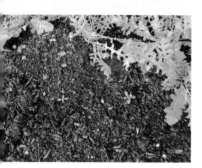

From top December – weeds between spring cabbage; I hand weeded these

Again this is December, so it's hand weeding; plus the spring onions are closely planted

Also December – here one could run a hoe through this open space, with the seedlings still very small

WHEN TO HAND WEED

These are three situations which dictate hand weeding as the best method:

1 When there is continual dampness – pull weed seedlings at any time of year when the weather is mild and moist. Hoeing and raking result in weeds making new roots, wherever you move them to.

2 When vegetables and flowers are planted close – there is no room to run a hoe between them, except perhaps for a hand hoe.

3 When new growth is from roots of perennial weeds – if you hoe or cut their roots, not only will they regrow from roots left at deeper level, but the cut root will regrow.

This third situation is the only time I use a trowel for weeding, to lever out some extra weed root and to weaken the parent roots. Trowels and hand forks should rarely be needed for weeding, because small weeds are so easy to pull out from a surface mulched with compost.

WEEDING MOTIVATION

In the summer months I hope you will be looking at beds full of vegetables and flowers, with clean paths and almost no weeds visible. Nonetheless, it's still time to stay vigilant for weeds. Go and hunt them, yet with a light heart!

Look under spreading leaves of carrots, beetroot, brassicas and asparagus. Some weeds go unnoticed and grow large quickly – it is then vital to remove them before they drop high numbers of seeds.

The important reason for this has nothing to do with weeds affecting and spoiling growth of the plants you are weeding amongst. It's about weeds multiplying, and then choking the *subsequent* plantings and the ones after that too.

- Give yourself more chance to establish new plantings successfully, with so much less time needed to weed.

If you are a beginner, you may need to experience what it's like when weeds take over a bed or a larger area, so you know that feeling of frustration and loss. It happened to me a few times in the 1980s, experiences from which I learned the importance of respecting weeds, and how to better manage them.

From top Bittercress in March – needs either laborious hand weeding or mulching as soon as possible, before the seedpods have time to fire their contents all around

Annual meadow grass close to shedding hundreds of seeds – another candidate for cardboard on top then compost on the card; if you tried to remove all of these weeds, you would waste time and be taking away a lot of soil on their roots, so better leave it all there!

In contrast, this (or when it is smaller) is the stage for pulling meadow grass

Quiz Lesson 12

	Question		Multiple choice
1	How often is it good to hand weed beds?	A	Whenever you see weed seedlings.
		B	Once a month.
		C	When you feel like it.
2	What is the key thing you are looking to achieve when hoeing a bed?	A	To aerate the surface.
		B	To cut stems and / or dislodge weed roots, so they die in situ.
		C	To create a finer tilth than previously.
3	For tackling tiny weed seedlings, how would you use a rake instead of a hoe?	A	Skim the surface shallowly, and in a circular motion – this also breaks up surface lumps.
		B	Pull the rake through the compost at a deep level.
		C	Turn it upside down, and scrape the top layer of compost.
4	After year one, why should you rarely need to use a trowel for weeding? Choose two answers.	A	Because you are mostly removing small weeds, which pull easily without a tool.
		B	Because the weeds need a spade to dig them out.
		C	Because there won't be many weeds.
5	With no dig, why is weeding enjoyable? Choose the false statement.	A	Because with no dig there are so few, from year two onwards.
		B	It's a chance to look closely at how the vegetables and flowers are growing.
		C	It's a relief to see the vegetables again, after having been covered by weeds.
6	Do you need to remove weeds after hoeing? Choose the two correct statements.	A	If they are grasses, and the weather is damp.
		B	Always, every tiny seedling.
		C	If the weeds have more than one true leaf, so are bigger than seedlings, and the weather is damp.
7	When would you not use a hoe for weeding? Choose the answer which covers the most possibilities.	A	All of these.
		B	When soil and weather are damp.
		C	When flowers and vegetables are closely planted, and touching leaves.
		D	When many of the weeds are perennials, and regrowing from roots in the soil.
8	Why is it important to remove weeds before they set seed?	A	To stop them competing with current plantings.
		B	To stop them blocking the light from neighbouring flowers and vegetables.
		C	To make success more likely with subsequent plantings, and to save time yourself.

Module 5
Soil, compost, fertility

Make your own compost

Fraser Sherrard by email, 2 July 2018:
At 67 years old I tried the no dig approach, spreading my own compost made last summer. Using row cover (fleece) here in Zone 5b, New Brunswick in Canada, we were eating salad in mid to late May, well before our normal planting time. The sheer abundance of produce, reduction in pests, and health of the plants is amazing; I am working less and enjoying more, thank you.

Making compost is a fascinating hobby, and if you have never tried it do have a go. You will convert wastes into value, perhaps enjoying the process as much as the result.

Compost varies enormously, and homemade compost is the most variable and interesting. Every batch is different, thanks to seasonally-changing ingredients and conditions. An added bonus is the range of local microbes in homemade compost, fantastic for human as well as garden health.

WHY MAKE COMPOST?

Wouldn't it be easier simply to lay undecomposed matter on the surface? This is called chop and drop, and in dry climates it may be the best course to take.

However, in damp climates undecomposed waste on the surface results in slugs. And decomposition is quicker in heaps, which are more than just 'decaying material'. Well made heaps convert waste matter quickly and tidily into stable organic matter, or humus.

From top Adding material to the compost heap, after trimming vegetables

The profile of a compost heap, where the bottom layer is 22 days old

A barrow-load of ripe compost, forked not sieved, and 8–12 months old

This is the Wikipedia definition of humus:
Fully humified humus has a uniformly dark, spongy, and jelly-like appearance. It has no determinate shape, structure, or quality. However, when examined under a microscope, humus may reveal tiny plant, animal, or microbial remains that have been mechanically, but not chemically, degraded. This suggests an ambiguous boundary between humus and soil organic matter. While distinct, humus is an integral part of soil organic matter.'

Albert Howard, who pioneered new ways of compost making in 1920s India, found that compost heaps could contain more nutrients than were in the materials added.[1]

DEFINING COMPOST

Compost is organic matter that has decomposed, including leaves, manure, weeds, kitchen scraps, ash, wood and paper. Compost provides food for soil organisms in a slow and steady manner. Their excretions feed plants, and their activity helps to aerate soil and create structure, such as aggregates of crumbs.

Compost holds nutrients in a stable, soil-enhancing form. Using it as mulch results in healthier plant growth plus better soil quality. A compost heap speeds up nature's process of decomposition, and allows us to add other wastes to our own.

From top Lifting the side of a compost heap

It has been three months since the first additions were made to this heap, and two months since the last

SO WHAT IS COMPOST TEA?

This term is used to describe two completely different liquids: *aerated* and *anaerobic* tea. In gardens you don't need to use either, though you may choose to. Aerated tea makes sense on farms where there isn't enough compost for mulching, and also on golf courses, because you can't lay compost on the greens.

Aerated compost tea is made with small amounts of the highest quality compost, aerated for at least 24 hours by an aquarium air pump. Add sugar such as molasses, to feed and help multiply the bacteria and fungi. This tea is all about stimulating soil microbiology; it is not a nutrient feed, but it helps nutrients to become available.

Aerated compost tea gives great results for such a small input of material. You need the kit and time to set it up and run it, then to apply it. However, in a garden with mulches of composted and decomposing materials, I see little benefit from using it, in proportion to the time needed.

Anaerobic compost tea is smelly, made by soaking compost in water, and is a weak feed of nutrients. I have used this a few times over the years and have been unimpressed by the difference it has made, in proportion to the time needed and the unpleasant odours. It's simpler to mulch with compost, or comfrey leaves for that matter, and let nature do the work.

ORGANIC MATTER

Organic matter is food for soil's billions of mostly unseen inhabitants. They aggregate soil into crumbs, resulting in structure, drainage and aeration.

From top Using a manure fork to turn the two- to three-month-old compost

How it looked after being turned and aerated, with the lumps being mixed while turning

How compost can develop – this is four months after a heap was turned; it has had black polythene on top to keep it moist

- Organic matter is carbon based – more in the soil means less in the atmosphere.

Fresh manure is also organic matter. However, compared to compost, it contains fewer living organisms and its nutrients are more water-soluble. Hence the worries over nitrate leaching from slurry, worries which confusingly and wrongly have become associated with compost.

The nutrients in compost are generally insoluble in water, and do not leach into rainfall. At the same time, compost is about way more than fertiliser and feeding plants. Its biology is more important than its chemistry. Don't worry about compost's 'low' NPK figures, compared to when you may have used synthetic fertilisers. Compost and no dig serve to unlock food in soil which was previously unavailable.

COMPOST PROCESS

Decomposition happens within a spectrum of possible ways. Garden heaps have a mixture of processes enabling decomposition:

- Bacteria are at one end of the spectrum – heat builds from their proliferation, and the rapid decomposition of organic matter which they bring about.
- Fungi are at the other end – breakdown happens at lower temperatures and more slowly (through mycelial activity), in piles of leaves and woody materials for example.

One stage of maturity is when a heap's warmth has mostly gone, because the bacterial processing is finished. Then fungi multiply, especially in heaps with woody materials.

Often brandling or tiger worms arrive when heat reduces, and heaps effectively become wormeries for a while. They reduce in quantity and increase in quality. At Homeacres it takes three to six months before worms appear in my heaps. Before that it is too warm for them, except in winter months.

Contrast this with green waste or municipal compost, which looks fine and 'finished' after just a few weeks, from being shredded and then turned regularly. However its blackness is from carbonisation caused by high temperatures, up to 80°C / 176°F. This is a result of thermophilic bacteria being encouraged by the regular turning and introduction of air.

I take deliveries of such compost in this so-called 'ready-to-use' state, and measure temperatures of 60°C / 140°F at the time of delivery, even though the appearance is black and crumbly. I have tried spreading this compost and then planting through it. The resulting growth was poor, compared to when I spread it after four to six months of extra fermentation. Lesson 16 compares and explains the qualities of several different composts.

MOISTURE LEVELS

In climates where the air itself is often damp, as are the materials that you are adding to a heap, watering is rarely necessary. As damp materials decompose, their moisture is free to seep into the heap.

Check your compost's moisture by squeezing a handful to see how much comes out. A rule of thumb is that more than two droplets of water suggest soggy compost, which therefore needs more air.

If there is enough brown matter in a heap, excess moisture can either drain out or be absorbed by drier materials. Too little brown results in compost becoming soggy and airless, called anaerobic. This slows or halts the process of breakdown. A remedy would be to turn the heap and add paper, soil and other brown ingredients.

Maintaining correct moisture

Moisture levels are hard to assess when adding materials, but during dry summers you probably need to water. For example 2018 was unusually dry here, and when turning heaps made in the summer we found many dry pockets.

This afforded a chance to water with as fine a rose as possible, otherwise water droplets would have run through and away. Plus, in dry conditions, it's worth firming materials or even walking on the heap. This reduces air pockets, holds moisture and builds warmth.

From top Shredding stems of broccoli, which are half green and half brown

This is how the stems look after shredding

COMPOST INGREDIENTS – GREEN AND BROWN

GREEN compost ingredients are soft, leafy, high in nitrogen, usually moist and low in fibre.

- Kitchen peelings, grass, weeds and food wastes are mostly green. Some green ingredients, such as coffee grounds and horse poo (both 3% nitrogen), look brown.

- Brown ingredients are fibrous, drier, and more woody than leafy.

- Some materials are both green and brown, see the broccoli stems in the photos above.

Why differentiate? When you achieve the desired balance of about 50:50, this contributes to having the correct level of moisture, warmth and structure for air. The result is decent aeration and sweet compost.

An excess of green results in high heat, bacterial dominance and a lack of air – making the compost sour and anaerobic, often dark black. A dominance of brown material results in moderate warmth, more fungi and a slower process.

Fresh manure from any animals, especially chickens, is green and so is urine. Both are excellent for speeding decomposition. Should you have large animals, such as a cow or a horse, their manure and bedding would 'take over' the compost heap volume-wise, meaning your compost heap would become more of a manure heap.

From top Trying a different method of assembling a heap in one day – this compost is 12 days old, and has already been turned three times

The same heap, now 24 days old – there is no more heat as it was a little too moist

Beware of adding too much wood-flake bedding, because it's kiln dried and very slow to decompose. Old manure with a fair balance of poo and bedding becomes great compost, just with different qualities to garden wastes.

BROWN compost includes chipped and shredded materials, which are woody. Their speed of composting depends on size, the type of tree wood, and whether they have been crushed or simply cut – crushed results in more surface area and faster decomposition.

Coniferous wood is better kept for mulching rather than composting because it rots so slowly, thanks to oils in the wood. However, if you are given a pile of chips and it contains, say, a third or less conifer, then that can work for adding to a compost heap when half decomposed and in small pieces. Other brown materials are:

- Shredded and crumpled paper.

- Cardboard in medium pieces, say 20 cm / 8 in diameter, and not shiny cardboard or food packaging with hidden polythene.

- Soil and yard sweepings (only they often contain many weed seeds).

- Tree leaves.

- Wood ash up to, say, 5%.

- Straw, which gives good structure and aeration, and works best when already wet and half rotten.

Summer sees a surplus of green, so I keep a pile of decomposing wood chips near to the compost bays. We add them to any large additions of grass mowings and fresh leaves. They can be anything from six to eighteen months old – I find the older the better. To speed up decomposition, we run a lawnmower over them before adding to heaps.

GOOD TO COMPOST

Weeds (green) often include soil (brown) on their roots, which means you can make fine compost from them alone. Shake off as much soil as possible, to create a chance for heat to be created from a sufficient amount of green.

You can compost perennial weeds too. I add roots and leaves of bindweed, docks, nettles, buttercups, dandelions and couch grass. They break down even in winter's cooler heaps, and regrow only if left exposed to light. Save time by not separating out perennial weeds and allow them to add value to your compost.

With no dig you apply compost on the surface. This gives the chance to see and remove anything you don't want in the finished compost, such as an odd root of bindweed.

This comment is from Stringfellow, in a forum topic about horsetail, June 2018:

I had a lawn of horsetail covering my plot. Being a total beginner back then, and paranoid about horsetail growing through concrete bunkers etc. we mowed the top growth and skipped the lot. Now wish I'd composted it all. Just keep an eye on the heap, you'll get little if any regrowth – I've found they quickly wither and die. It all ends up back on your plot to help grow vegetables.

Tree leaves start green and older leaves become more brown, so autumn's tree leaves are mostly 'brown' in compost terms. They compost better if chopped by a rotary lawnmower. Large amounts may be better left to decompose slowly into valuable leaf mould – in their own heap, through fungi.

Rhubarb leaves and citrus peel are green, and good to compost.

Eggshells are brown and bring structure to a heap but decompose slowly. After spreading the compost they may sit as a mulch on top, which is fine.

Above, from top
Pasture weeds after four months under a woollen carpet – only bindweed has survived

Diseased materials are fine to add

Diseased leaves are good to compost, such as mildewed courgette and lettuce, blighted potato and tomato. Also tubers, and fruits with late blight. Blight, and other fungal spores which cause disease on leaves and stems, need living plant tissue *in which to survive*, hence they die in a compost heap, and likewise in soil.

Below, from top
Starting a heap – on soil is fine, and better than concrete, for example

We used trowels to lever out some of the roots, and all this went on the compost heap

Layers of brown and green compost in a new heap

- On two occasions I have spread compost made with blighted leaves around tomatoes in the polytunnel, with no ensuing problems.

- Because blight spores do not survive in soil, there is no need to empty greenhouses of their soil after blight occurs.

SIZE / LENGTH OF MATERIALS

It is worthwhile to cut and split longer lengths of stems and wood into pieces of 10 cm / 4 in or less. Otherwise they don't pack down, and only very slowly convert to compost. As much as a heap needs air, it also needs an even density, and this keeps moisture consistent too.

We use a rotary lawnmower to chop stems of broad bean and pea, and a shredder for woody stems including hedge prunings. Softer wastes which are long and thin can be cut with secateurs or a knife.

Left, from top
Even in December you can have heat, if there are enough green materials to add

This heap was finished two months earlier, but still has some warmth!

Coffee grounds and cardboard are creating warmth, even in cool weather

Right, from top
The plastic compost bin has been lifted off, after four weeks of adding materials in May

A heap made from pallets, with wooden posts at the corners

Using planks of wood at the front, slotted into the frame at each end; new planks are added as the heap rises

Open compost bays at Sissinghurst Market Garden in Kent

TEMPERATURE –
DOES A HEAP NEED TO BE HOT?

In a word, no. Heat is not vital, but it speeds up the process and kills weed seeds. You can also make excellent compost at temperatures of 30–50°C / 86–122°F. To know the temperature, buy a 'compost thermometer' like the one in my photos. It has a probe of 30 cm / 12 in.

These are some of the differences between compost from cooler and hotter heaps:

- Temperatures below 55°C / 131°F do not kill weed seeds.
- Hotter heaps decay more bacterially, especially when temperatures are over about 50°C / 122°F.
- Cooler heaps below about 50°C / 122°F decay in a more fungal manner.
- Cooler heaps result in browner compost, compared to the black colour of hot heaps.
- Cooler heaps take longer to decompose.
- There is a greater range of microbes in cooler heaps.

CHOICE OF BIN – SOLID OR OPEN?

A bin with plastic or wooden sides keeps materials together, increases warmth and moisture, and allows you to keep rain out if there is a lid or cover. It's said that wooden bins need slatted sides to allow entry of air, but this can result in dry edges.

Homeacres' heaps with solid wooden sides make great compost, the wood conserving both heat and moisture. I screw them onto the shed posts, then it's simple to unscrew them when turning and emptying heaps.

Or, if you have heaps made from pallets, line the sides with thick cardboard.

Plastic bins are usually smaller, and this restricts the heat they can maintain. My trial with a Rotol 'dalek' bin saw temperatures rarely exceed 45°C / 113°F, and weed seeds survived the process. Nonetheless it was good compost, and the bin is easy to lift off when you want to use it.

In 2016 I designed my seven bay system at Homeacres, including a roof to keep rain off the heaps. I had wanted a roof for years, because too much rain entering heaps can change aerobic composting to anaerobic, by excluding air.

BUILDING A HEAP

Add your garden waste as it is produced, in level layers rather than as a mound in the middle, in order to have uniform spreads of different materials. Sometimes you need 'balancing materials', in terms of green and brown:

- In the growing season keep a reserve of brown: paper, small wood of any kind, autumn leaves, cardboard, soil and twiggy materials.

- In winter you need extra green, such as fresh manure, coffee grounds and spent hops.

Richard Loader on Facebook – UK Here We Grow, 13 August 2018:
Since visiting Charles Dowding's garden and seeing his composting system we have started to see our compost heaps very differently. Previously weeding, trimming, mowing seemed like chores but these activities have transformed into harvests of food for what we now call 'the beast'. We gather the 'browns and greens' and blend them so as to satisfy the appetite of the beast and enjoy monitoring the process of decay and heating with a long probe thermometer. It's like having a new pet to care for.

The photos, right, were all taken on the same day, after I had added several barrowfuls of material to finish a heap which was already four weeks old.

WHEN TO STOP ADDING MORE MATERIAL

Small gardens generate less material and may struggle to fill a bin, even over a whole year. Use the smallest bin you can because a small, full bin makes better compost than a larger, half-empty one.

After perhaps a year of filling, lift up the bin (it will be light!) and place it close to the now exposed heap. Then you can fork out the top, undecomposed part and put it at the bottom of the empty bin. Finally, help yourself to compost from the bottom part.

- In large gardens, pallet sized heaps may fill to a height of 1.5 m / 5 ft within perhaps a month.

- Continue filling for another 2–4 weeks, until the heap is hardly sinking any more.

- Unless you have a roof, cover with straw / carpet / cardboard / woodchip / polythene, while filling a new heap.

- Optional for a faster finish: turn the heap 1–2 months after the final additions.

Left, from top Compost making – a layer of six-month-old wood chips and coffee grounds, on a four-week-old heap

Next a layer of Homeacres soil that came from some building work

Old straw, and a little fresh horse poo from a neighbour's manure heap

Four loads of lawnmower cuttings and leaves from the garden's edge

Centre, from top A new board is screwed to the front – now at full height

My pile of six-month-old wood chips, and a homemade sieve

I added a layer of half soil, half wood chip on top of the grass

Already the new additions are warmed from below, and the 30 cm / 12 in probe reads 66°C / 131°F

Right, from top The final addition is a layer of more soil and old wood chip

And finally thick cardboard, to hold moisture and warmth

Eight weeks later – we are about to turn the heap

After the turn – everything you see was added 8–12 weeks ago

TURNING COMPOST – IS IT NECESSARY?

Turning is worthwhile for larger scale compost makers with several heaps, in order to mix and aerate, and to create a more even compost in a shorter time. For most of us, just one turn of a larger heap makes a worthwhile difference. Two hours of turning is sufficient for a Homeacres heap of about a tonne.

You need an empty space or bin next to the heap you are turning. Use a manure fork with long prongs – good for shaking out dense lumps to introduce air. Turning is about mixing, aerating and checking the quality. If you discover dry portions, add a little water; or conversely, add some dry paper if it's soggy.

For a small heap that perhaps barely fills during a whole year, turning is not worthwhile.

A simpler way to 'turn' is by occasionally using a proprietary compost aerator, to lift and mix the materials.

The law of diminishing returns applies to compost turning. Gains are marginal from a second turn.

From top A summer heap – this took six weeks, and the oldest addition is 11 weeks; it is still 55°C / 131°F in the middle

After turning we found several dry pockets, so added some water to correct the moisture level

From top Compost with worms like this is not 100% 'finished', but your soil organisms will love it

December – spreading eight-month-old compost, after a harvest of celeriac

FINISHED COMPOST

Within a year, or perhaps within months in the summer, your compost will have a crumbly texture of variable quality. A dark brown colour is better than black, which suggests a lack of air and too much moisture.

Any large lumps need breaking up with a fork while loading a wheelbarrow. Sieving compost before use *is not worth the effort and time needed*, unless you want it for propagation. If there are large pieces of undecomposed material, simply pull them out while loading a wheelbarrow, to add to your current heap.

You may find the odd root of perennial weeds, which are white and therefore noticeable. There is nothing to fear from such roots because, even if you miss them while spreading, you will have another chance to remove them later when you notice regrowth. This visibility, and the easy removal, are both advantages of no dig – compost being on the surface rather than incorporated.

VARIATIONS

I have described the principles of easily composting mixed wastes (the variety that many of us have) without too much effort.

You can also make compost more rapidly, in as little as 14 days. I have tried this a few times, but find it inefficient in terms of the time and energy needed, say three turns. Also I preferred the quality of my slower, once-turned heaps.

The Johnson-Su bioreactor contains only wood ingredients, in a fully aerated and moistened pile. The intention is for there to be fungal rather than bacterial decomposition, and without any turning. I made one of these in spring 2020. I like that it's low-tech, uncomplicated, and uses common wastes of chipped or shredded wood. It took six hours to make the frame and add a tonne of wood chip.

Microbial richness is a key asset of good compost, as much as are the nutrients. Lesson 14 now considers definitions of fertility, and the values of compost for soil and plants.

From top I cut holes in the pallet, for slotting in drain pipes to create ventilation holes

Adding sides and five pipes to the bio-reactor compost heap

Lifting recently cut wood chip into the bio-reactor

Removing pipes from the bio-reactor – on day four the wood chip is 30°C / 86°F

1   Sir Albert Howard, *Farming and Gardening for Health and Disease*, Soil Association Ltd, 2006 and *The Soil and Health*, Benediction Classics, 2011 (both books are based on tropical agriculture and gardening). Also see 'the-compost-gardener.com' for more information on Albert Howard's work.

Quiz Lesson 13

	Question	Multiple choice
1	In damp climates, why is it better not to lay undecomposed materials on the soil surface?	A They give shelter to slugs. B They don't decompose. C They smell unpleasant for a long time.
2	Which statement is true? Choose one answer only.	A Compost is organic matter, in a stable, soil-enhancing form. B Organic matter is compost, with extra nutrients from kitchen waste. C Compost is organic matter in its freshest form. D Organic matter is compost mixed with soil.
3	Compost is created by the breakdown of organic material, through which of the following? Choose the answer which covers the most possibilities.	A Bacteria. B Fungi. C Fungi and bacteria, then worms – all or any of these. D Brandling (red) worms.
4	During the compost-making process, when are worms likely to appear in a compost heap? Choose two correct answers.	A After bacterial decomposition has happened, and the temperature has fallen. B As soon as you begin the heap. C After about a month, and when the temperature is high. D When only small and occasional additions mean little heat, therefore the heap behaves more like a wormery.
5	Approximately which proportions of green and brown ingredients do you need in your compost heap, for steady decomposition without excessive heat?	A 50:50. B 25% green, 75% brown. C 75% green, 25% brown. D It doesn't really matter, as long as the moisture is right.
6	Which of these compost materials are mostly 'green'? Choose five answers.	A Kitchen scraps. B Cardboard. C Soil. D Weed leaves. E Grass cuttings. F Coffee grounds. G Horse poo.

Question	Multiple choice
7 Which of these materials are approximately half green, half brown? Choose the answer which covers the most possibilities.	A Brassica stalks (e.g. broccoli), recently pulled. B Weeds with soil on their roots. C Prunings of new wood in summer. D All of these.
8 Compost heaps, in the process of being assembled, may need to be watered at which of the following times?	A As soon as the air temperature is regularly over 10°C / 50°F. B During spells of hot summer weather, when you are adding few fresh, moist leaves. C When you add some paper or cardboard to a heap, and half of the other ingredients are fresh green leaves.
9 Can you compost all parts of perennial weeds, including their roots?	A Sometimes, but only if the weather is warm. B Yes. C No.
10 Heaps need to be hot (above 55°C / 131°F) for roots of perennial weeds to die.	True or false?
11 How would you deal with diseased leaves?	A Burn them. B Add them to the compost heap. C Create a separate heap to contain the disease.
12 Which are differences between hotter and cooler compost heaps? Choose the two correct statements.	A Temperatures above approx 55°C / 130°F kill most weed seeds. B The higher microbial count from cooler heaps (less than 50°C / 122°F), especially of fungi, is excellent for soil biology. C Hotter heaps create more fungi. D Cooler heaps never result in good compost.
13 How is it best to add materials to a larger compost heap?	A Piled in the centre of the heap, all mixed together. B In level layers. C It doesn't matter, just throw it on.
14 Over a period of say, three months, which of the following is it better to do?	A Half fill a large compost bin / bay / heap. B Completely fill a smaller compost bin / bay / heap.
15 For larger compost heaps, the most time-efficient way to improve quality (and save time later when spreading compost) is by doing which of the following?	A Leaving it alone. B Turning it twice. C Turning it once. D Doing extra watering.

Lesson 14

What compost offers, when to apply and amounts needed

My second most asked question[1] is:
Do you spread compost in summer before second plantings?

The answer is simple: there is no need. This lesson considers why decomposing organic matter on the surface works so well to feed plants, indirectly. Appreciating how this process works will give you a deeper understanding of how no dig works, and the value of organic matter as a mulch.

THREE USEFUL POINTS

1. Soil organisms are more active and numerous in undisturbed soil, therefore more able to help plant roots find food and moisture, as and when they need it. There is continual symbiosis, or 'mutual back scratching'. In return for helping plants to grow, soil organisms receive 'exudates' of food for their own survival and breeding.

2. Soil organisms eat and digest organic matter, with their excretions adding to soil fertility. Worm casts, for example, contain thousands of bacteria and enzymes, as well as nutrients. They are also colonised by fungal filaments, as discovered by J.N. Parle in 1962, at Rothamsted Research Station, UK.[2]

3. Compost holds nutrients in a stable, insoluble form, so they do not leach out and are available over a long period. One dressing of compost helps to unlock food when needed, for two or more plantings. It is indirect fertility, made available to plant roots through a biological process.

HOW TO DEFINE FERTILITY?

J. Arthur Bower is one of my heroes. He took on a holding at Wisbech, UK, in 1934, and became famous for selling organic flowers at a 40% price premium because they were of such high quality. J. Arthur Bower is still used as a brand name on sacks of potting compost in the UK.

From top Eight second crops in September, plus tomatoes, aubergines and peppers (first crops) – no compost or any other feeds for nine months

After spinach in the spring, this is November – 10.66 kg / 23.5 lb of carrots from 50 × 150 cm / 20 × 60 in, sown in June with no feeds or extra compost

154

He wrote this for the Soil Association's *Mother Earth* magazine in April 1957:

> 'Soil fertility is a fascinating subject to discuss, as I have found in the many talks I give. But it is a very difficult thing to define. Here is an outline:
>
> - Simple, standard, and constant despite weather vagaries.
>
> - Assuring permanent "field capacity" for water, which implies good drainage *plus* a high capacity to absorb.
>
> - Soil can supply growing crops with their needs for warmth and nutrients according to age and size.
>
> Let me enlarge upon the word – "simple".
>
> When I was a young man learning my profession, soil fertility was simple. The only tricks were products employed for giving a fillip to exhibition blooms, such as Epsom salts or nitrate of potash.
>
> But in the last 50 years, complications have come thick and fast. The plant breeder has to work hard to keep pace with ravages wrought by the interference of the chemist, who has never really had a true picture of fertility.
>
> The basic needs of plants are: (i) moisture, (ii) warmth, (iii) light. The question of nutrients is secondary to these; but it has been made the dominant one, and the most intricate of all. Why?'

Bower continues on this theme, explaining how chemistry and commerce have taken over farming, while soil structure and quality have become ignored. This was in the 1940s and 50s, and in his market garden he practised no dig. However this was rarely discussed, and his reputation was based more visibly on growing organically.

Bower recounted to a friend how a cement lorry had once driven into his no dig field by mistake, and then driven out, leaving deep wheel marks in the wet soil. However, by the end of that day, all the soil had rebounded upwards. He could hardly see where the lorry had passed, illustrating the health of his soil.

From top The first crop was of Charlotte potatoes, harvested by Finn in late July

Second plantings exactly four weeks after they went in the ground – pak choi, kale and kohlrabi

2 September 2017 – mostly second crops, and nine to ten months after adding any compost

AUTUMNAL ABUNDANCE, WITHOUT FEEDING IN SUMMER

All of my autumn photos show abundant growth from summer plantings, when nothing has been added to the soil since the previous year. We mostly spread the annual dressing of compost in late autumn to early winter.

Despite this, I often see it claimed that compost should be 'either covered through winter with polythene, or spread in the spring just before planting, to ensure no leaching of nutrients'.

In my experience, which is now 38 years of spreading compost before Christmas, this is not true. Growth has always been phenomenal, and consistently good throughout every year following, on different soils.

I read claims that sandy soils 'cannot hold the nutrients like heavier soils can'. Yet the Facebook photos from Karen Drexler in Lesson 4, whose beds are sand, suggest otherwise. She applies compost once a year, for two to three crops, and in a climate of heavy rainfall.

- Claims about scientific studies showing nutrients leaching out of soil are almost all based on cultivated soil. This factor is not stated. The biology and structure have been harmed by cultivation and problems ensue, such as nutrient leaching.

- The 'scientific' focus on movement of nutrients misses what would be a more complex and worthwhile study: the quality of soil.

More on nutrients

Another aspect of second plantings in summer is whether you can follow with a vegetable of the same family, or even the same vegetable. My plantings suggest you can, as with these two photos, right, of calabrese in 2016.

In terms of nutrients, calabrese is called a 'heavy feeder'. It grows fast and large. I did not give any more 'food', yet it found the necessaries thanks to biological activity in the soil.

For second plantings, this means you have options. My preference is to plant vegetables of a different family to the first, as we discussed in Lesson 6. Sometimes you may need to replant with a vegetable of the same family as the one that has just finished. This is possible!

2019 HARVESTS FROM ONE BED, 1.5 × 5 M / 5 × 16 FT

These harvest figures follow one application of compost in a year, from the no dig bed of my trial. In mid-March 2019, we filled the bed with new plantings (*see details in Lesson 4*).

Through May, June and July these gave 44.02 kg / 97 lb of edible roots, fruits and leaves. This figure is after trimming and grading – it's kitchen-ready produce.

From top 21 June – calabrese from a spring planting in April; after the harvest we cleared plants to the compost heap

27 September – we had planted calabrese in the same space in July, with no feeds or compost given for the second planting

Below, from left 23 March 2019 – mostly ten days after transplanting; the carrots have been sown

21 May – some harvests are already happening

28 August – the bed is full of new plantings made in summer; no compost has been added, and no feeds given

As soon as these harvests finish, we plant again in summer. Sometimes I overlap the first and second plantings. For example I sowed carrots between lettuce that were still cropping, celeriac between cabbage, and kale between carrots which we were still pulling.

The second plantings gave food from August to November, and there was even a third planting of Florence fennel after the second planting of cucumber, which had followed the first planting of beetroot.

The second and third wave of harvests totalled 51.71 kg / 114 lb, with no feeds or compost given in the second half of the year.

The year's total was 107 kg / 236 lb of vegetables from this one bed of 7.5 m^2 / 81 ft^2, after applying 4–5 cm / almost 2 in of compost in the previous December. This bed had started with 20 cm / 8 in compost in 2012, then had 8 cm / 3 in in both 2013 and 2014, and 5 cm / 2 in in every December since, and also one small bucket of rockdust in 2016.

The seven applications of compost total 54 cm / 21 in, yet the bed still contains the same 20 cm / 8 in depth of compost.

THREE-BED COMPARISON OF GROWTH FROM DIFFERENT COMPOSTS

In February 2013 we used three different mixes of compost (and some soil) to fill three beds, all adjacent in a line. We used the same wooden frame – measuring 1.2 x 2.4 m / 4 x 8 ft – as the template for each bed, filled to a depth of 15 cm / 6 in.

After filling and then firming the compost with your feet, a frame like this can be lifted off to put on new ground for refilling. We again used feet to push the bed sides into a 45° slope.

The contents of each bed were as follows:
- Bed 1 – old cow manure, two years old and dark.
- Bed 2 – a bottom layer of 5 cm / 2 in soil, and old cow manure on top.
- Bed 3 – recently delivered green waste compost (still warm) from the local facility, who sieve it to 15 mm / 0.6 in.

All three beds were planted with onion sets in early April.

Growth through the spring was similar between Beds 1 and 2, but noticeably different in Bed 3. Some onions in Bed 3 did not appear, a higher proportion went to seed,

From top The compost trial has been set up – Bed 1 is nearest, Bed 3 is furthest

The onion harvest in August gave 100% more on Beds 1 and 2, but some beetroot planted in the summer gave more on Bed 3

Two beds with different fillings, divided in the middle – the compost-filled bed is on the left, the soil-filled bed is on the right; both beds have been planted with oca, yacon and peas

and bulbs were smaller at harvest in August. Beds 1 and 2 gave strong growth and large bulbs, with hardly any going to flower. I saw little difference between those two beds.

In June I found space between the onions to interplant multi-sown beetroot. It grew well in all three beds, with noticeably *the largest beetroots in Bed 3*.

This all suggests that the green waste compost was too fresh when delivered to give good growth – until about June it was continuing to decompose. This made some of its nutrients unavailable, because they were being used for the decomposition of its woody fragments.

However, by summer (once the decomposition had mostly finished) growth was stronger in Bed 3, even more than in Beds 1 and 2.

This is why I now buy such compost in the summer, for use in the late autumn and winter. Plus you often get more for your money, because it's drier and weighs less in summer.

This nutrient grabbing – by immature compost and woody mulches – occurs much less when roots are growing in soil beneath any thin woody layer on top. The difference, in my 2013 example, was how a whole bed was filled with immature compost.

COMMERCIAL FERTILISERS VS. COMPOST

Early in 2013 I was given some 'Grochar' to trial. It was charcoal, with added mycorrhizal fungi, seaweed, worm casts and a nutrient blend. The label says it is 5-5-5 in terms of NPK, what a chemical gardener would call a balanced fertiliser, suitable for many types of plants.

Grochar is expensive to buy and advertised as an 'organic biochar fertiliser', with application rates much lower than one would use if it were compost, so we filled the sacks accordingly. The main fill of all three sacks was topsoil, from trenches made when building my greenhouse wall in January.

- Sack 1 had wood ash, dried seaweed, basalt rockdust and some dust of volcanic lava – about one third of a bucket mixed with the soil.
- Sack 2 had 10% Grochar mixed with the soil.
- Sack 3 had 30% homemade compost (8–10 months old) mixed with the soil.

Rockdust is ground rock, not literally dust, of basalt / volcanic origin. It supplies trace elements, and often improves growth on problem soils. Best to search for a local supplier. If I lived near the sea, I would spread seaweed instead, as soil and plant food.

I planted Sungold tomato plants (sown in March) on 23 May, and they cropped from early July. I did not weigh the harvests, but the pictures give an idea of how those in Sack 3 grew most strongly, and with the highest harvest from the earliest date.

In late May I also planted a Genovese basil and trailing lobelia in each sack, just to see! Sack 3's basil grew the largest.

This was not a 'scientific' trial, but a conclusion was not difficult to find: that it is simplest, cheapest and most reliable to use compost as your source of fertility. I felt that the Grochar was oversold in terms of its capabilities.

Compost is much better value to buy than any fertiliser. It is so much more than fertiliser, and gives the extras (beyond NPK) to grow large and healthy plants. Moisture, structure, microbes and trace elements are all found in good compost.

THREE-SACK POTATO TRIAL			
Sack	Stem width 5 September	Stem weight 5 September	Potato harvest 14 October
Sack 1 Minerals	1.5 cm	125 g	160 g
Sack 2 Charcoal	1.6 cm	155 g	250 g
Sack 3 Compost	2.2 cm	325 g	310 g

After a final pick from each sack in the trial on 5 September, I measured the width of the stems at three feet high, and weighed the bottom three feet of stem from each sack. Also shown in the table are harvests six weeks later from Charlotte potatoes, planted on 5 September.

Grochar had also sent me some of their potting compost. I used it when filling a propagation tray at one end, and I filled the other end with my standard potting compost, from West Riding Organics. The bean photo overleaf shows you what happened, with the Grochar nutrients running out quickly (or perhaps not readily available to the bean plants), while the seedling growth is variable – I am unsure why.

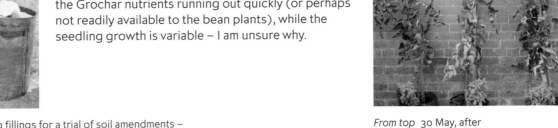

From top Preparing fillings for a trial of soil amendments – the mix for Sack 1 was wood ash, seaweed and rockdust

The mix for Sack 2 was soil and 10% of the expensive Grochar

The mix for Sack 3 was soil with 30% homemade compost (nine months old)

Sacks 1, 2 and 3 are ready for planting – one Sungold tomato plant in each

From top 30 May, after planting the tomatoes in mid-May – left to right are minerals, Grochar, compost

Growth on 15 June

17 July – the only ripe tomatoes are in Sack 3

Growth by 26 August

From top The same beans sown in two different composts – West Riding multi-purpose on the left, Grochar on the right

Lettuce germination was variable in this Grochar potting compost

ANOTHER LOOK AT FERTILITY – GLOMALIN

This substance was discovered as recently as 1996, by scientist Sara F. Wright, while she was working for the USA Agriculture Research Service. She discovered how to extract the sticky material glomalin, which binds soil particles into aggregates, giving structure and tilth. She believes glomalin could account for a quarter or more of soil carbon, and exists for decades in undisturbed soil.

Glomalin is probably produced by mycorrhizal fungi, as Sara describes:

> 'We've seen glomalin on the outside of the hyphae, and we believe this is how the hyphae seal themselves so they can carry water and nutrients. It may also be what gives them the rigidity they need to span the air spaces between soil particles.'[3]

During plant growth – as roots extend further into soil – fungi close to the original roots die off at the same time as new fungi colonise, and work with the developing root extensions. The decaying fungi shed their glomalin, and it remains in soil as a glue-like sheath around nearby particles.

This raises the intriguing point that all plant growth helps to build soil organic matter, as long as soil remains undisturbed.

> 'In a 4-year study at the Henry A. Wallace Beltsville Agricultural Research Center (Maryland), Wright found that glomalin levels rose each year after no-till was started, with no plowing. Soil was protected from erosion by keeping fields covered with crop residue . . . Glomalin went from 1.3 milligrams per gram of soil (mg / g) after the first year, to 1.7 mg / g after the third. A nearby field that was plowed and planted each year had only 0.7 mg / g. In comparison, the soil under a 15-year-old buffer strip of grass had 2.7 mg / g.'[3]

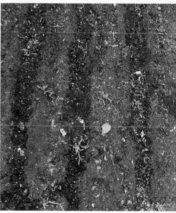

From top Soil fungi made visible, after a leek harvest in winter

Drills for sowing in June – watering the drills highlights the fungi

COMPOST AND FUNGI

New knowledge about glomalin ties in with older work by Albert Howard in the 1920s[4], on the value of compost. He developed methods to make high quality, aerobic compost at the Indore Research Station in India. Next he discovered how just a small application of such compost could transform the soil of tea plantations, enabling plants to rediscover lost vigour.

Howard trained as a chemist, and had initially thought of compost in terms of chemical constituents, or a content of nutrients. At that time he assumed the composting process was about recycling and efficient use of waste organic matter.

On that basis alone he saw the potential of composting for Indian small farmers, who already had the ingredients to hand. He subsequently discovered that the compost they made actually *increased* the amount of total nitrogen, compared to each heap's ingredients.

The results from using Indore compost, coupled with Howard's knowledge – that nutrient levels had barely increased because he was adding so few – helped him to see compost as a game changer in many ways. He championed the role of soil fungi, even though they were little understood at the time, and he clarified the ability of compost to help fungi multiply.

During this same time (in the 1930s), mycorrhizal fungi were first being noticed and appreciated by scientists such as Dr Rayner. She worked for the Forestry Commission, on Wareham Heath in Dorset. Her obituary in the *Empire Forestry Review*, June 1949[5], describes the huge impact of her research. This extract illustrates how scientific findings of great value get lost in a world of commercial applications:

> 'There can be few countries in Europe and few states in the USA and Canada from which foresters have not visited Wareham. The correspondence regarding mycorrhizal relationships has been world-wide, embracing tea, coffee, rubber, oil palm and so on, as well as timber trees and herbaceous crops.'

Since that was written, over 70 years ago, mycorrhizal fungi have been overlooked in mainstream farming until recently.

Which brings us back to the value of transforming manure and other wastes into compost. I notice at Homeacres how crops grow better where the compost applied is ripe – dark, crumbly and with a sweet smell; not the ammonia or sulphur smells of manure stacked in an airless state.

There is much to discover about the relative benefits of different age composts.

MORE ON SECOND CROPPING VEGETABLES, WITHOUT FEEDING –
WHICH VEGETABLES GROW BEST IN WHICH HALF OF THE YEAR

Here are more stories of first and second plantings, with no summer feeding of any kind. The photos overleaf also give an idea of which vegetables grow best in each half of the year, for example:

- Potatoes yield most highly from spring planting, and suffer less blight than in late summer and autumn.

- Brassicas grow most healthily in late summer and autumn, when there are fewer of their pests, and they are less inclined to flower.

From top Fruiting bodies of Homeacres' lovely soil fungi

A December harvest of oca reveals the soil fungi

In the Three-strip trial we harvest second early potatoes in midsummer, then plant leeks for autumn harvests (*see Lesson 5*). Yields in 2019, from an area of 1.2 × 7 m / 4 × 23 ft, were 48.2 kg / 106 lb of potatoes, and 25.41 kg / 56 lb of leeks, all from one application of 5 cm / 2 in compost, applied during the previous December.

Peas and broad beans, then chicories, then the annual mulch

Peas and broad beans grow most strongly in the spring, making leaf and stem before their flowering season of early summer. Therefore, to have a maximum of flowers and pods, it makes sense to sow them as early as possible (even in November for broad / fava beans), if winter temperatures stay above approximately –10°C / 14°F.

Chicory and endive flower in the early summer, so are best sown after mid-June, for cropping in autumn. We had a fantastic harvest of radicchio from these plantings of 26 July (sown on 7 July), when the module-raised plants were three weeks old.

The sequel to autumn harvests is clearing all debris, including (in this case) the plant stems, which otherwise grow again. Leave all the small roots in place, rake the beds level, then spread 3–5 cm / 1–2 in of compost, and you can relax while knowing that your soil organisms are fed and protected for the coming year.

On the paths we spread about 3 cm / 1 in of wood chip, from a pile which had been delivered in April. The wood was partly decomposed, with larger pieces still woody.

POLYTUNNEL PLANTINGS –
TWO CROPS FROM ONE APPLICATION OF COMPOST IN MAY

My timing of compost application is different undercover to outside, for practical reasons and not to do with plant growth. There are two times during the year when the space is clear: after summer crops finish in early October, and after winter vegetables finish in April / early May.

From top Mid-June – first plantings include tall peas on the left, and onions next to them; peas suffer less damage from mildew and pea moth in June, compared to in July and August

A close-up of the tall peas Alderman on 15 June – in 2018 they cropped for only two weeks because of heat; at least they had done most of their growing in the cooler spring

Chicory, following peas and onions – 91 days from sowing, and planted in dry heat on 26 July; we watered the plants every two days in their first week

From top Late November – chicory beds after we had harvested two thirds of the hearts, and pulled the six weeds

Raking the beds level after another harvest of all but two of the chicories; we twisted out the main stems

Finally we mulched the beds with ten-month-old homemade compost, and the paths with old wood chips

From top Recent plantings for summer harvests – ten days after the annual mulch of 6 cm / 2 in of compost

The same view on 24 July – no feeds were given to anything, only the compost we spread in May

The same view in late March – the salads were planted in October, with no compost or feeds for ten months

I like to spread compost before the summer plantings because:

- We have more time to spread compost in May than in October: in autumn the days are short and there is so much harvesting to do, as well as the new plantings of salads for winter.

- The beds' surface is a little lumpy for a while after spreading compost – an easier surface for planting and growing tall summer crops, compared to ground-hugging salad plants such as lettuce, endive, mustards and chervil.

SUMMARY OF MAINTAINING FERTILITY

Mulching once a year with high quality compost – and using the no dig method – makes it quick and straightforward to keep soil in top condition. All these benefits follow: great crops, healthy growth, steady drainage, good moisture retention and few weeds.

Timing is flexible, and occasionally you are spreading compost while plants are growing.

- You can spread the annual dose of compost in autumn, while vegetables and flowers are still growing, as long as there is space between. For example, spread compost in any rows which are wide enough, as with the leeks above right.

- You can spread the annual mulch of compost under tall brassicas in autumn. The aim is to feed soil organisms rather than plants, but the plants will also benefit (from improved soil structure and drainage for example).

1   The most asked question is: 'Do I need to dig before starting no dig?' The answer is similar: there is no need, but with an exception or two.
2   'A microbiological study of earthworm casts', microbiologyresearch.org, 1 April 1963
3   USDA *AgResearch Magazine*, September 2002
4   Albert Howard, by Keith Addison, *Journey to Forever*, journeytoforever.org
5   'The importance of the mycorrhizal habit: an appreciation of Dr Rayner's work', D.W. Young, *Empire Forestry Review*, Vol.28, No.2, June 1949, pp. 162–165

From top We mulched these leeks with compost of nine-month-old horse manure in December, while they were still growing

Something different – a mulch of spent hops, c.3% N when dry (I would not use this for new plantings)

Seven-month-old woodchip – suitable for paths, and small amounts can be added to compost

Quiz Lesson 14

	Question	Multiple choice
1	Which of these statements about soil fertility links to this lesson's quote, by J. Arthur Bower?	A Soil fertility is a complex matter of nutrient availability. B Soil structure and moisture retention / drainage of excess water are more important for growth than soil chemistry. C Understanding chemistry is the only way to understand soil fertility.
2	What does J. Arthur Bower define as being the basic needs of a plant? Choose the answer which covers the most factors.	A Moisture. C All of these. B Warmth. D Light.
3	If you had spread my recommended 5 cm / 2 in mulch in winter, would you then need to spread more compost in summer, before second plantings?	A Yes, always. B Yes, but only every other year. C No, not normally.
4	Which of the following statements is the most true?	A Compost must be covered over the winter, to stop nutrients from leaching. B Nutrients stay in compost when rain droplets run through. C Nutrient levels in compost drop after a ground frost .
5	Can you plant the same crops in the same place for second plantings?	A No, it's not a good idea. B Yes, if you need to, and the first planting grew healthily. C Yes, if the phosphate levels are correct.
6	Why is glomalin important to soil fertility?	A It's a vital micro-nutrient for all plants. B It regulates the temperature of the soil, to ensure it stays fertile. C It builds structure by helping to aggregate soil into crumbs, when soil is undisturbed. D It makes soil loose and fine grained.
7	Compost heaps, which have not been too hot, grow fungi, and this boosts soil fertility when the compost is spread.	True or false?
8	When do new brassica plants grow most healthily?	A From mid-spring, as the weather warms up. B In late summer and autumn, when there are fewer brassica pests. C In winter, when they are prolific in lower temperatures.
9	Peas grow most strongly in spring.	True or false?
10	In one year of growing, why do you need a second application of compost under cover?	A The additional heat tends to bake the soil, and reduce the nutrient levels. B The intense cropping means that nutrients are depleted more quickly. C You don't.
11	You can't spread compost on beds while plants are growing.	True or false?

Understanding soil, and comparing it with compost

How can I mulch on top of my raised bed without it overflowing?
This question, frequently asked by gardeners, suggests that
a lot of the bed's original content was soil.

- Compared to compost, soil reduces little in volume through
  time, and therefore the surface level of a soil-filled bed will
  barely reduce from one year to the next. This leaves no empty
  space on top to add compost and maintain fertility.

In contrast, compost does reduce in volume, so one can fill beds
with compost to a depth of say 15 cm / 6 in initially; then, within
a year, the surface level may be 5 cm / 2 in lower. Or lower than
that if, when first filling the bed, you did not firm the compost by
walking on it.

SOIL PROFILE AND QUALITY

A great aspect of no dig is being less involved with soil such as
sticky clay, which is difficult to work and to pull weeds from. You
rarely even see your soil, let alone need to work it.

When starting out I recommend digging a hole to see what is
there, for your information. I did this before making an offer to
buy Homeacres back in 2012. The selling agent found this very
funny – her first house-viewer to have brought a spade!

The most noticeable thing you see when digging a hole of
more than about 30 cm / 12 in deep, is the paler colour and

From top The different colour
and texture of soil compost, left,
and mushroom compost, right

No dig lettuce in a bed with
no compost mulch – the soil is
cracking open in the dry weather

No dig lettuce in a bed with
compost mulch – dry weather,
and 0.75 kg / 1.7 lb has just been
harvested

denser nature of soil at lower levels. This is called 'subsoil', to differentiate it from the darker 'topsoil'. Depth of the layers varies, and the main differences are:

- Topsoil has more organic matter (carbon) which gives the darker colour.
- Topsoil has more organisms living, moving, eating and excreting.
- Soil organisms maintain more structure, drainage and air in the topsoil.

The topsoil you can buy is probably low in microbes, and often contains some subsoil. If using it for vegetables you will probably be disappointed with their growth. I have seen samples of supposed topsoil which looked very pale and shiny rather than crumbly, and contained gravel, roots of perennial weeds, and thousands of annual weed seeds.

Stones are interesting, because sometimes they add fertility and hold some moisture, especially limestone. However, although on the whole they reduce the chances of roots finding food and water, I don't recommend sifting soil to remove them. Best to use a thicker compost mulch if your soil is very stony.

BIOLOGY MATTERS

A big reason to avoid buying topsoil is that it has usually been heaped in a stack. When this happens many of its organisms die, from lack of air and food.

This was unintentionally proved by the UK National Coal Board (NCB) in the 1940s–70s. Some of their mines had coal near the surface, and they would scrape off soil to remove the coal, called 'opencast mining'.

After removing the seams of coal, they put the soil back so that farmers could 'carry on farming as before'. Except they couldn't: growth was so poor, and nobody understood why.

The NCB sought advice and struggled to discover what the problem was. Finally it was the insights

From top Checking the soil before buying Homeacres – lovely topsoil, and subsoil in my hand

A soil profile from April 2017 – a mulch layer on a four-year-old bed

From top Soil from underneath a raised bed, and the top mulch of compost – the texture difference is clearly visible

Parsnip seedlings on the dig bed at Lower Farm – the clay soil had been dug, and here the surface is cracking in a dry spring

of a soil biologist in the 1970s, Professor Victor Stewart, that revealed why plants were struggling.

He discovered that the soils contained enough nutrients, but were slumping and 'dead' from being stacked too long in heaps. They needed bringing back to life with additions of organic matter. Stewart's work, on these farms and elsewhere, highlighted the importance of soil biology and structure to maintain a balance of air and moisture, with a free flow of both.

I was privileged to meet Victor and discuss this with him in the 1980s, and we agreed that his work was still ahead of its time. In other words, not many farmers or scientists were asking him for advice.

In the 1980s, and even for another 30 years or so, soil research majored on nutrient status and chemistry, rather than biology. Soil was seen as a 'bank balance' for an NPK chequebook, receiving nutrients in and sending/allowing nutrients out.

Chemists and farmers controlled growth through managing the input–output equation, for which you needed to know which plants are heavy feeders, which are light feeders, and when they all like to feed. As Bower commented, it was getting mighty complicated.

More confusions were happening on the cultivation front. Roots were seen as accessing their nutrient 'bank' by free movement in a loose soil. In this scenario (but not in reality), if soil was not mechanically loosened, growth would be compromised.

COMPACTED SOIL? NEEDS AERATION?

The word 'compact' is overused and causes confusion, linked to the false belief that soil must be opened up by tools for growth to happen. This misunderstanding results in the incorrect labelling of firm and healthy soil as 'compact'.

However, firm soil is not the same as true compaction, which happens rarely. A definition of compacted soil is that air and moisture cannot pass through any free channels. Soil then changes colour to orange, grey, or even pale blue. And it becomes smelly, like a mildly sulphurous swamp. Plant roots can't survive in compacted soil.

Nonetheless plant roots do like firm soil, into which they can anchor themselves and be stable. Ideally, there is an 'aggregation' of soil into lumps of different sizes. Roots and associated fungi travel within this matrix of soil aggregates, both between and into them, in search of moisture and food.

Aggregated soil particles are coated in organic matter, the glomalin that we looked at in Lesson 14.

There is a slow flow of air in and out of soil, enough for roots to breathe. Soil with air smells 'sweet'.

Aeration is helped by the good drainage of no dig soil, so that air is not displaced by water.

From top A profile of the soil in 2013, from under the new conservatory at Homeacres – you can see the compacted orange clay

A closer view of the trench – there is dark loam over clay, and we also see areas of true compaction

The orange clay in the photos, preceding page, was probably a result of earlier work by builders, because it is close to Homeacres' house wall. Some compaction at this depth is not good for growth, and there was a slight smell of putrefaction. However most of the soil at Homeacres is healthy so this was not a major problem, and aeration improves when soil organisms are active and can penetrate any compacted layers.

As ever there are exceptions, such as where excessive passage of heavy machines in wet weather has squashed soil into such density that almost nothing can pass. In this case using a broad fork once makes sense, but just once. Then mulch the surface, and allow soil life to work quietly.

WEEDS

You can avoid much of the difficult work of dealing with new weeds by filling beds with compost rather than soil, and always making compost the surface layer.

- All soil contains weed seeds, and sometimes roots of perennial weeds.
- After soil is moved, weed seeds germinate when exposed to light.
- Soil is sticky and heavy compared to compost, and weeds pull out less easily.

On the left are some photos of a trial I did, just to see which growing medium led to the most weeds growing: soil, homemade compost, fresh horse poo or old horse manure.

It was in winter and growth was slow, but there was still extra germination of weeds in the disturbed soil (*we'll look at this again in Lesson 16*).

Most soil you can buy is of a lower quality than any you may have on site, say from building work at your property. Only use soil from the top 30 cm /12 in or so of darker topsoil, depending on how deep a layer you see.

NUTRITION

Soil holds fewer nutrients than most composts, especially potting composts. Hence, for propagation, it's worth buying commercial products designed for that use. You can use multi-purpose compost, also called all-purpose, for every stage of propagation, including seed sowing.

From top A trial for weed growth at the end of October, clockwise from top left: soil, Homeacres compost, fresh horse poo, old horse manure

The same trays in January – they've been in the greenhouse for ten weeks, and the soil tray has the most weeds

April – a trial of a soil-filled tray, to see which weeds would grow (nothing had been sown); the soil was from an allotment

From top A trial on 4 July – the same amount of cow manure has been added to all the pots; soil is on the left, and compost is on the right, with added vermiculite on the top row

The same pots on 26 August – Cavolo Nero and oak leaf lettuce Navara; the soil plants have less food and the soil holds less moisture

The same pots on 2 October – soil on the left, compost on the right; the best growth is in the front pots, which had no vermiculite

From top January 2013 – soil from the trenches made for the greenhouse was dropped by a dumper truck

I raked it level and removed any couch grass I saw – most of the soil was from a level below the couch roots

April 2013 – the last of my greenhouse soil for new beds; cow manure was then spread on the soil

Incidentally, in the US I have noticed that potting compost is called potting soil. Until I realised this, I was often having confused conversations with American gardeners.

I did a trial on soil for potting, and you can see the results in the three photos, on the right, p.168. The soil pots had one third of cow manure mixed in, to see how viable that might be as a mix. It would have been interesting to grow some plants in soil only, without the nutrients of the old manure. Even so, my conclusion is to stick to compost for propagation, for the extra nutrients and better retention of moisture.

SOIL AS A BASE INGREDIENT IN NEW BEDS

However, if you are a garden landscaper making permanent features and new contours, it does make sense to use mostly soil. The shapes and undulations will endure!

In contrast, for vegetables you want mostly compost, but with two exceptions:

For making beds more than 25 cm / 10 in high, a bottom layer of up to 50% soil serves to maintain the volume needed to keep it full. For beds of 60 cm / 24 in and higher, use two thirds of soil at the bottom.

To 'lose' unwanted soil, it can be the base of any bed. This happened at Homeacres when the builder was digging trenches for my greenhouse. They dropped soil on the pasture where I was about to make new beds, as a 5 cm / 2 in base layer. It took a lot of effort to spread the sticky soil into a bed shape.

SOIL AND COMPOST TRIAL

To discover more about the differences between growing in soil and in compost, I filled two beds at Homeacres in November 2012 – one with compost and one with soil. The compost bed was actually my very first Homeacres bed, next to where I would soon establish the dig / no dig trial beds.

The beds both measured 1.2 × 2.4 m / 4 × 8 ft, and the sides were 2.5 cm / 1 in thick planks of softwood, of 15 cm / 6 in depth.

Each bed had 15 cm / 6 in of ingredients, with no cardboard on the weeds. There were enough dense ingredients that only a few small dandelions, buttercups and weak blades of couch grass made it to the surface. However, annual weeds were another matter.

- The soil was fertile and had been growing strong weeds. I pulled out any roots of dandelions and couch grass, but a lot of weed seeds remained.

From top December 2012 – old wooden frames laid on the pasture grass and weeds

Filling one of the frames with homemade compost from my previous garden

The compost bed is full – now filling the soil bed with recently lifted Homeacres soil

From top December 2012 – a wheelbarrow of soil from the shed area I was clearing

The soil bed is now full – it is all 'living soil', because it had not been stacked in a heap

- Because the soil was freshly moved, many of its organisms survived to carry on their work, although some would have perished in the move.

- It was true topsoil, from the surface 15 cm / 6 in.

My method was to grow and compare the same vegetables in each bed. However, I now realise that perennial kale was not a good choice for the middle section, where the beds were adjoining, and only separated by a plank of wood.

The kale plants grew to over 2 m / 7 ft, and their extensive root networks could access the adjoining bed, as well as the one they were in. I could not say that either pair of kale plants were growing exclusively in a soil-filled or a compost-filled bed.

COMPARING WEED GROWTH

The main, and almost immediate difference between the beds was a massive quantity of new weeds germinating on the soil bed, while there were only a few on the compost bed. The soil had a lot of weed seeds and they wanted to grow, a healing job I imagine.

The soil weeds were time-consuming because there were so many to pull, one by one – the only option in early 2013 when it was too damp to hoe. This mass of seedlings were even more difficult to remove as the soil was extra sticky from having recently been moved.

Twice, in early spring, Steph and I spent a whole hour on the soil bed. We pulled speedwell, grass, celandines, buttercups, nettles and bittercress. Although small seedlings, their roots hung onto the soil as though glued to it, and our fingers became less nimble, coated in sticky soil.

You rarely suffer this stickiness with compost mulches. In fact no weeds grew in the compost bed, thanks to two factors:

1   I had added few weed seeds when filling the compost heaps, thanks to my garden almost never having seeding weeds.

2   The compost heaps had mostly attained a high enough temperature to kill any weed seeds.

By late spring the surface of the soil bed was clean and drier, and I could hoe lightly. Superficial hoeing is quick, and from then onwards it was easy to keep the soil surface clean. By autumn there were almost no new weeds. At that point in a dig garden, the spade or fork would have returned things to square one: disturbed soil with many weed seeds germinating.

COMPARING PLANTINGS

The growth differences were smaller than I had expected, as the year one results show in the table overleaf. In 2013 some vegetables even grew larger in the soil bed, mostly first plantings such as early potatoes, garlic and shallots.

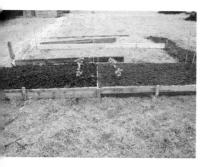

From top December 2012 – the first planting of perennial kale; compost on the left, soil on the right

By mid-spring the growth on both beds is quite similar, with the same plantings on each bed

Mid-July – we've already had harvests of broad beans, potatoes and garlic

Possibly this is because working and moving soil admits air, which stimulates bacterial activity, causing conversion of organic matter into nutrients. Hence, when diggers start with a reasonable level of organic matter in the soil, they can 'use' that for a while to have reasonable growth, while reducing soil organic matter.

Growth was good for all plantings on the compost bed. By autumn, most of its second plantings were more productive, and had glossier leaves than the same plantings on the soil bed.

I think that the high quality of the soil used here made a big difference. If I had bought soil, it would have been different in these two ways:

1 Older, and therefore less full of microbes and organisms, which diminish in heaps of soil.

2 Less aggregated/structured in lumps, from being less fresh, and having a higher proportion of subsoil compared to topsoil.

In subsequent years, because the soil was not diminishing in volume, it became difficult to add compost to feed the soil bed – the surface rose higher and above the boards. The compost bed gave stronger growth throughout 2014 and 2015, until I stopped doing comparative plantings in 2016. We removed the wooden sides, now eight years old, and discovered many slugs in rotten cavities inside each plank.

In 2013, the total yield of vegetables was 20 kg / 44 lb 1 oz from the compost bed, and 19.1 kg / 42 lb 1 oz from the soil bed.

See overleaf, table of 2013 yields from beds on undisturbed pasture.

From top 30 August – a beetroot harvest from a planting nine weeks earlier; from compost on the left, and soil on the right

December 2014 – a parsnip harvest, from compost on the left and soil on the right (the soil bed had a compost mulch)

August 2015 – the same beds (compost left and soil right) with oca, yacon and peas

Further reading
Professor Victor Stewart's work, *Principles of managing man-made soils*, first published in 1989: onlinelibrary.wiley.com

			2013 – BEDS ON UNDISTURBED PASTURE, FILLED WITH SOIL OR COMPOST	
Vegetable	**Planted**	**Harvested**	**Bed with higher yield**	**Comments**
Daubenton kale (perennial)	Dec	Apr–Dec	Compost	Prolific on both beds
Broad bean Aquadulce	Dec	Jul	Soil	Similar harvests
Garlic	Dec	Jul	Soil	Lovely bulbs, similar
Shallot Red Sun	Mar	Jun	Soil	Shallots on soil bed all bigger
Potato Swift	Mar	Jun	Soil	Stronger plants on soil bed
Onion sets Stuttgarter	Apr	Jul	Compost	Bulbs larger on compost bed (opposite of shallots)
Beetroot Boltardy	Jun	Aug–Dec	Compost	Large roots over a long period of harvest
Cabbage Christmas Drumhead	Jul	Oct–Dec	Soil	Firmer hearts on the soil bed, only two on each
Kale Redbor	Jul	Oct–Dec	Compost	One plant on each bed, both good
Endive Aery	Sep	Nov	Compost	Brighter green on compost bed

Quiz Lesson 15

	Question	Multiple choice
1	What is the most likely reason for there not being empty space at the top of a bed with sides, meaning you cannot add mulch without it overflowing?	A Because the bed was originally filled with soil, which, unlike compost, doesn't condense. B Because the bed was mulched with compost a year ago. C Because, in raised beds, the mulch should only be very thin. D Because compost in raised beds doesn't condense.
2	In terms of growing plants, what are the differences between topsoil and subsoil? Choose the answer which covers most aspects.	A Subsoil has nutrients, but they are less available to plant roots. B Topsoil has more biological activity. C Topsoil has more organic matter, hence is a darker colour. D All of these.
3	Which is the most reliable indication that soil is truly compacted?	A It will be firm to the touch. B You can walk on it without sinking much. C It has irregular air channels. D It has changed colour to orange, grey or pale blue, with a smell of putrefaction.
4	Should you use soil as a base layer in a new shallow bed, 15 cm / 6 in or less, for vegetables?	A Yes – because you can't sow and plant in 100% compost. B No – best results are from using only compost. C It's better to mix soil and compost when filling the bed.
5	Why is it worth adding soil as a base layer in deeper beds, say more than 30 cm / 12 in deep?	A In order to increase fertility. B Because it helps to retain the volume of the bed. C To hold more moisture.

In 2015, I dug a hole in a bed, for course students to see what Homeacres soil is like at a depth of 40 cm / 16 in – we found dense yet crumbly silt, as shown on my copper spade; it smelt earthy and not sour, suggesting good drainage

Homeacres topsoil, from where we built the cabin in 2018 – this is 20 months later, after having added some to compost heaps; we spread compost on top and transplanted the squash six weeks earlier – the soil is cracking from dryness

	Question	Multiple choice
6	For a bed with sides, why is it good that the contents shrink?	A Because you can fit taller crops in and still reach them. B Because it allows earthworms to reach the top more easily. C Because you then have space to add surface compost each year.
7	Why might it take longer to weed a bed of soil, compared to a same size bed of compost?	A The weeds have deeper roots in soil. B Hoeing is impossible in soil. C Wet soil sticks to the weed roots and fingers, while dry soil is often hard.
8	Bought topsoil is generally of less good quality than topsoil in your own garden.	True or false?
9	In the comparison beds, one of soil and one of compost, did you notice whether it was generally the first or second plantings which gave bigger harvests in the soil bed, compared to the compost bed?	A Second plantings (beetroot, cabbage, kale). B First plantings (potatoes, shallots, garlic).
10	What might be the reason for this?	A As the soil hadn't had a crop in it recently, it was full of the nutrients required. B The compost must have been badly made, and lacking in certain nutrients which these particular plants needed. C Moving / loosening / digging soil exposes some of it to air (oxygen), which stimulates bacteria, thus decomposing some nutrients and making them available to plants.

Lesson 16
Types of compost

This lesson is to clarify the qualities of compost. This will give you more confidence in choosing and using it, and also in discussing it with other gardeners, who often mistake compost for fertiliser and don't understand its biological qualities.

Compost is a little word of many meanings, and you see it used to describe materials of totally different quality. The basic description is decomposed organic matter, with a great variability in life content, colour, consistency, aroma and weed seeds.

MANURE

A commonly used compost is old manure, and manure is another confusing word. If you are discussing manure, and to avoid confusion, I suggest to precede the word manure with an adjective to describe its age and origin, such as old / fresh / horse / rabbit. Even describe whether you mean just poo (excretions / faeces), or poo and bedding, such as straw or wood shavings.

Most manure includes animal bedding such as straw, wood shavings and shredded paper. In farming, and most gardening language, the word manure assumes bedding as being part of it.

Dung and slurry are terms for pure cow manure, often fresh and with a strong odour. Avoid confusing these terms with the word compost, because they refer to something completely different in terms of texture, nutrients, leaching, smell, and value to soil and plants.

From top Homemade compost – seven months old and full of life; it has not been sieved, the lumps have just been knocked open with a fork

Mid-September – filling a bed on grass and weeds using only old cow manure, half a tonne so far

It has now been topped with 80 l / 2.8 ft³ of potting compost – this is an option if you want a smooth surface

Mid-October – exactly one month after planting the new bed with autumn salads and oriental vegetables

From the Three-strip trial, different composts to compare growth – the left-hand strip is green waste and mushroom compost, the right-hand strip is old cow manure

AGE OF COMPOST

Quality changes all the time as heaps age. Compost can reach ripeness or maturity in anything from 2 to 24 months, depending how quickly a heap was filled, the materials used, and the amount of turning. Differences you may observe include:

1 Fresh compost and manure is lighter in colour, fibrous and lumpy, and usually contains many weed seeds.

2 Half-mature composts are darker in colour, and still have a few recognisable ingredients. They probably have some odour and red worms, and half-ripe compost can be used for mulching around larger plants, but not where you want to sow seeds or plant closely.

3 Mature or ripe composts are sweet smelling and crumble into smaller pieces, dark brown or black in colour. Sometimes there are bright red brandling worms, but not always, and compost can be good without worms. There may or may not be weed seeds, depending on the temperatures during the composting.

4 A further stage is old compost, say two years or more: the volume has reduced, the texture is dryer and finer, and the colour almost black.

WEED SEEDS IN COMPOST

Homemade compost has a bad reputation for its quantity of weed seeds, as a result of heaps being insufficiently hot to kill the seeds. Mostly they are fast-flowering annual weeds, such as chickweed, groundsel and shepherd's purse, depending what is native to the soil and climate. Other 'weed seeds' may be flowers such as forget-me-nots and calendulas, depending on which flowers you grow, and whether you add them to the compost heap after clearing.

> I was advising a head gardener about conversion to no dig, and recommended spreading their homemade compost on top. She looked hesitant, and confided a fear of coping with the compost's chickweed seeds. However the garden had been dug every winter, and her worry was based on how chickweed proliferated in that disturbed soil, then becoming difficult to hoe or hand weed. She decided to spread the compost as mulch and the weed levels decreased.

From top Fresh horse manure, less than a day old and with a bedding of straw – suitable for a compost heap where it will heat up

Horse manure – a year old but it still has much undecomposed wood bedding; it could be a thin mulch, and would also be good for paths

Horse manure, composted for eight months – it was 60–70°C / 140–160°F, and is now garden-ready compost; notice straw visible at the bottom, where there was the least air for decomposition

I advise you never to let a fear of weeds stop you from using compost. Rather, adopt strategies for dealing with them. A combination of hoeing tiny weeds, pulling some larger ones, or mulching with cardboard when there is a mass of weeds, solves most of the problem. Then your garden has fewer weeds seeding, resulting in compost with fewer weed seeds the following year.

To check the content of weed seeds in various composts, I filled four trays with different samples – soil, homemade compost, old horse manure and fresh horse poo. It was late autumn and weed growth was slow, even in the greenhouse. Even so, the results bear out my mistrust of disturbed soil, in terms of new weeds. Plus I was surprised to see so few weeds in the fresh horse poo:

- There were only a few weeds in my homemade compost, mainly meadow grass.
- The largest amount of weeds, including plenty of buttercups, had grown in Homeacres soil.
- There were no weeds at all in the old horse manure, taken from my hotbed of the spring – the result of sufficient heat.
- Interestingly there were only a few weeds in the fresh horse poo – perhaps the horses had eaten more grass than hay.

COMPOST TYPES

Here we look at the different qualities of composts that you can buy and make. The descriptions are not 'absolute values', because of the extent to which compost can vary. However they are a starting point, to help you choose from what is available to buy in your area, and to give you an idea of how this compares with composts that you can make.

Green waste compost

The name is taken from its main ingredients – garden wastes – even though in composting terms a lot of these wastes are 'brown'. The compost is sold (and occasionally donated) by municipal or private garden processors. Usually it has been shredded, and you can see a lot of woody pieces.

Decomposing wood reduces the nutrient value of compost, especially when it's under about nine months old and much of the wood is still decomposing. The fungi and insects involved in wood decomposition need more nitrogen to survive and thrive than is contained in the wood itself. Once decomposition has mostly finished, nitrogen becomes more available – it's a temporary shortage.

Heaps in commercial facilities are turned frequently, and may reach 80°C / 176°F, which assures their guarantee of no weed seeds or pathogens. In the UK, all suppliers of compost adhere to a PAS 100 scheme, one part of which 'requires that the number of weed seeds and propagules does not exceed zero germinating weed seeds and propagules per litre of compost. Propagules are seeds and other parts plants necessary for their reproduction'.

The heat, however, also 'cooks' many organisms, resulting in a lack of aggregation in the compost. Such compost can go to sludge when wet, and to powder when dry.

From top After ten weeks with no seeds sown – from left to right, fresh horse poo, eight-month-old homemade compost, soil, eight-month-old horse manure

Seedlings of mayweed in March – these need hoeing or light raking as soon as possible; they came from soil which the compost heap was sitting on – I had scraped some of it up when filling the wheelbarrow

Weed seedlings from composted cow manure – many are fat hen, a weed which seeds on neglected manure heaps

I advise three approaches when buying and using it:

- Check that it has been sieved, to a size no wider than 15 mm / 0.6 in, in order to reduce the amount of large wood and plastics.

- Buy the compost, or have it delivered, at least two (though preferably four to six) months before you need to use it.

- Spread it thinly on a large area, rather than in depth on one or two beds, so that soil life can colonise it more quickly.

I did a growing test, to see how six-month-old green waste compost would compare with other composts, for seedlings of mustards and salad rocket. The photos say it all in terms of ready nutrients, but it's still a good compost for mulching. *(Also see the trial of different composts in Lesson 14.)* A more recent trial showed stronger growth in five-month-old PAS 100 compost.

Spent mushroom compost (SMC)

This is made from straw and some stable manure, with proprietary extras. Some peat is used in mushroom houses as a capping layer.

The composting process takes less than a month, and the mushroom-growing period is only 20–25 days. After that the mycelia find less food, mushroom growth decreases, and the compost is 'spent' for mushrooms, but highly suitable for garden use.

It's valuable for mulching, even though there are two myths that you may hear. Be informed, and ignore them.

- 'Mushroom compost has a high pH.' This was the case in times past, but current formulations in Europe are resulting in a pH of around 6.8. When at Lower Farm, I used the high pH mushroom compost on soils of high pH (7.8), with no problems ensuing over many years of use.

- 'The high nutrient/salt levels may burn roots.' This is nonsense, totally contradicted by the experiences of hundreds of thousands of gardeners. I am sure this myth originated from manufacturers of soluble fertilisers, who are afraid of losing sales. Ironically, theirs is the product whose soluble salts may burn roots.

You can use SMC when delivered straight from a mushroom farm, but only as a mulch, and not as the only compost for filling a bed. At this stage you will notice fibres of straw, lumps of peat, white threads of myceliae, and also that its colour is more brown than black.

After a few months it becomes finer and darker, with no weed seeds or other problems. The texture is soft and fibrous, while nutrient status varies. I find it more nutritious than green waste compost and less nutritious than composted manures, as the photos overleaf demonstrate.

From top Green waste compost – it has been sieved to 15 mm / 0.6 in before purchase

Seed sown at the same time – in multi-purpose compost on the left and green waste compost on the right

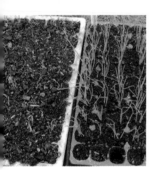

From top
Mushroom
compost, two
months after
delivery

February sowing
of lettuce into
six-month-old
mushroom
compost – variable
from seed
differences

Onions sown at
the same time – in
six-month-old
mushroom
compost, left, and
multi-purpose
compost, right

COMPOST TRIAL WITH MARAVILLA LETTUCE IN POTS IN THE GREENHOUSE

I sowed lettuce in July, then potted them as four-week-old seedlings into four different composts. Every ten days or so I harvested their outer leaves, giving the results below.

There was a lack of quality in the lettuce leaves from the green waste compost, with some holes and brown tips, while the leaves of lettuce in the other composts were 99% good. By December, and after its slow start, the green waste compost was releasing more nutrients – probably related to the wood content having decomposed, and therefore not taking nutrients ahead of the lettuce.

COMPOST TRIAL WITH MARAVILLA LETTUCE					
	Sept	Oct	Nov	Dec	Total
Type of compost			Harvests (g) Leaf numbers		
Own compost (8 months old)	136	106	47	19	**308 g**
	23	20	10	8	**61 leaves**
Cow manure (18 months old)	137	93	40	20	**290 g**
	24	18	9	10	**61 leaves**
West Riding multi-purpose potting compost	110	54	29	15	**208 g**
	22	16	8	7	**53 leaves**
Green waste compost 15 mm sieve (6 months old)	73	47	38	24	**182 g**
	19	14	10	10	**53 leaves**

The West Riding multi-purpose compost was disappointing, although I had expected it to run out of nutrients by November. Both the homemade and cow manure composts were somewhat lumpy, but dark and crumbly too, and growth was good throughout. Put another way, the lumpy composts grew better plants than the very fine ones, perhaps from more air around the roots.

WOOD AS MULCH

The best thing about mulches of wood is their fungal decomposition. Look under wood and you will often see many white mycelial threads near the surface. Plus there are organisms such as millipedes, who eat and breed, excreting food for plants and adding to soil structure.

From top Four composts with Maravilla lettuce, sown four weeks previously

My own compost bottom left, and cow manure bottom right – five weeks and one pick later

However there are confusions about wood as soil and plant food, partly from misconceptions about the excellent 'Back to Eden' gardens. I understand that Paul Gautschi ages his wood chips before spreading them, often in the hen run where chickens rummage and add their nitrogenous droppings. Plus he is spreading only thin mulches every year.

A thin layer of wood mulch on the surface breaks down reasonably fast, especially if the wood was shredded as well as chopped, into short lengths. Small pieces decompose more quickly than larger chips, thanks to the greater surface area.

Further differences are with green wood, sometimes called 'ramial', from branches grown since spring. When used as a mulch, this decomposes faster than brown wood (which takes a year). Another difference is that conifer wood takes longer to decompose than wood from broadleaf trees, because of the oils it contains.

Green wood is an effective mulch for beds, if you are lucky enough to have some. Sometimes it contains green leaves which bring further value, and speeds up decomposition when in a heap.

A summary of wood for garden use:

- Wood chips are usually short lengths of wood, in a range of diameters.

- Shredded wood means that a crushing process has opened a larger surface area, therefore decomposition is faster.

- Green wood describes branches that have grown within the past year – the wood is soft and decomposes more rapidly.

- Brown wood is a year or more old, making it harder and drier than green wood.

- Shavings and sawdust are by-products of working wood, and they decompose quickly thanks to a high surface area, depending on the type of wood.

- Do not use wood shavings or dust from workshops that cut timber with glues, such as chipboard.

From top Wood of various sizes/ages – six-month-old oak shavings on the left, new larch in the middle, and six-month-old tree prunings on the right

Woodchip at 15 months, with many worms – larger pieces of hardwood make this better for paths; small amounts could be used in a compost heap

A pile of woodchip at two and a half years old is now compost – it was turned once and now could be used as a bed mulch, or even for potting

Wood chip comes in so many shapes and sizes that it's difficult to offer a simple description of its uses in the garden. As a mulch, it's best to use wood chip for paths only, and preferably when a few months old, although it can be used when fresh. Add half-composted wood chip as a brown ingredient for compost heaps, to balance any excess of green (*see Lesson 13*). You can spread 18- to 24-month-old wood chips on beds, when they're looking more like compost.

If your only source of organic matter for beds is woody material, I would wait for it to break down over 18 to 24 months. The only issue with this would be how much space was available for a heap of wood chips. Another option would be to spread fresh wood chips around trees, shrubs, fruit bushes and perennial vegetables.

From top After mowing, Finn lays down a wooden edge to contain the shavings

December 2017 – after mulching paths with six-month-old oak wood shavings, which are yellow at first then turn a darker colour as in the paths beyond

March 2018 – the first steps in setting up a trial of four composts; there are old wood shavings on the soil

I suggest you avoid deep mulches of wood on beds, not because of how they would affect soil, but more because of the difficulty of sowing and planting. Seeds and plants need to be in contact with compost or soil, not pieces of wood, hence my advice to use woody mulches as a thin layer only, say 2–3 cm / 1 in. Even in this case, transplanting is more viable than sowing direct.

Don't ever fill a bed with wood that is not decomposed – see the photos, right!

WATCH OUT FOR WOODLICE!

Woodlice (also known as chuggypigs, pillbugs, slaters or grammasows) eat certain leaves, and their numbers grow when there is plenty of old wood for food. Plus the babies sometimes eat stems of green plants, when tired of chewing dry wood!

Above all be careful in your propagating area, to keep it clear of decaying wood. Woodlice like seedlings, and tender leaves that are close to the surface, including stems of cucumber and tomato.

A message from Holly Mock on Instagram (peacefulpandemonium), 26 September 2019:
I have been gardening in a no till way for five years, but struggled with using wood chip or hay as a mulch, since it causes all sorts of pest problems. So in 2017 I started using compost instead and I have not looked back.

A COMPOST TRIAL

I was given two proprietary composts to try – Dalefoot wool and Melcourt farmyard manure – and we filled new beds to compare their effects on plant growth. Two other beds were mulched with my own compost (seven months old and less mature than I would have liked) and green waste compost.

This was in a corner of the garden which a year earlier had been totally overgrown with brambles and weeds. In June 2017 we had mown the grass and weeds, (photo, top left) and then dropped a half-tonne of wood shavings,

From top Woodlice damage to spinach leaves and stems – small nibbles, and lots of them

Woodlice have been eating this aubergine leaf

Woody horse manure in the bed at rooting level means nitrogen starved the cabbages!

to decompose and reduce new weed growth. By December it had started to decompose, and we spread it as a mulch on paths (*see top two photos p.100*).

It would have been interesting to have had more volume of the proprietary composts, to fill the whole depth of each bed. Since I could not do that, each one had a base layer of old cow manure and green waste compost, added in March 2018.

COMPOST TRIAL RESULTS 2018
FIRST AND SECOND PLANTINGS
SMALL CHICORY HARVESTS ADDED TO CABBAGE

Type of compost	Harvests (kg)			
	Potatoes Colleen	Onion sets	Red cabbage	Total Jun-Sep
Dalefoot wool	2.2	1.63	1.53	**5.36**
Green waste 10 months old	1.7	1.02	0.41	**3.13**
Homeacres 7 months old	1.68	1.24	1.67	**4.59**
Melcourt stable manure	1.31	1.14	0.76	**3.21**

Trials like this are always fascinating: plants tell you things! A notable result here was growth in all four squares being less abundant than I had expected, probably because of the residue of wood shavings under the compost. It was not a thick layer, but enough to deprive plants of nitrogen as the shavings continued to decompose in the rooting zone.

Early potatoes are excellent as a first crop, because after their harvest there is time to grow more vegetables.

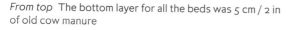

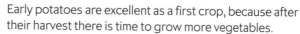

From top The bottom layer for all the beds was 5 cm / 2 in of old cow manure

Thin wooden strips serve to delineate the four squares

Next we spread a 5 cm / 2 in layer of nine-month-old green waste compost

The final layers – Dalefoot wool (green sack), Homeacres compost, Melcourt farmyard manure (yellow sack), and green waste

From top Walking on the beds to firm the compost – always worthwhile unless compost is wet

31 March – Steph is planting Colleen first early potatoes and onion sets

A mesh cover sits on the leaves, to protect plants from rabbits and cold winds

40 days after planting – I was surprised by the growth in the green waste compost!

In mid-June, and straight after the potato harvest, we planted Granat red cabbage as five-week-old plants. In July we harvested the onions, planted a Cabbice cabbage on each bed, and three Treviso chicories.

The trial had to finish early, as a new cabin was being built in this area. The cabbages and chicories did not have time to make firm hearts or heads.

Overall, there was more difference than I had expected:

- The Dalefoot compost did particularly well, all summer.

- The Melcourt compost had what looked like too high a proportion of bedding. It was pale in colour and had many undecomposed fibres – its plants were not impressive.

- The green waste compost showed its low nutrient status, while growing reasonable plants.

- My homemade compost disappointed me a little, though the results weren't bad. It would have grown bigger harvests if the compost had aged another two to three months. Younger compost is good for mulching, but use older compost for filling beds.

From top 16 days later on 25 May after three warm weeks, 18–21°C (high sixties °F)

13 June, just before the potato harvest – the total was 6.9 kg / 15.2 lb

Potato harvest – my own compost bottom left, and Dalefoot bottom right

A FINAL THOUGHT

Hay and horse manure, in particular, have a small risk of contamination by aminopyralid weedkiller, which is occasionally sprayed on grass intended for making hay. In my experience it's the only weedkiller which persists, and it is lethal to solanums and legumes, whose growing tips become curled and twisted.

Most horse owners have no idea how their hay was grown, unless it's from their land. Ask them for as much information as possible, because this poison persists in manure heaps for many years.

- You can check for its presence by growing susceptible plants in pots, such as pea, bean, potato and tomato. The manure can even be quite fresh for a test like this.

- A very few green waste composts contain clopyralid, from lawn weedkillers. It's an equally strong and persistent poison.

The photos, far right, are to help you identify the negative effects. If you experience any of these, complain to your supplier at least, and email the government and manufacturers – CRDEnforcement@hse.gov.uk and UKHotline@corteva.com, headed 'Aminopyralid contamination'.

The mulch would then need either to be scraped off – with the aim of removing the poison, but where to put it? – or left in place, where soil microbes will break it down. You could still grow brassicas, sweetcorn and umbellifers while this is happening (over the period of a year, or hopefully less), depending on the concentration of aminopyralid. Alternatively, you could sow green manures.

From top The wild area in the background is how the trial area looked a year earlier

By September the second plantings look fair – they were meshed against insects but only a little watered

10 September – Homeacres compost bottom left, Dalefoot bottom right, green waste top right, Melcourt top left

Right from top

Broad bean test for aminopyralid – they have been sown into old horse manure and the plants are fine

A broad bean test for aminopyralid – they have been sown into fresh horse poo and, although there are seasonal and nutrient issues, the growing tips are not curling

Aminopyralid in horse manure – the effect on broad beans

An aminopyralid test of my own compost, with affected horse manure nearest to the camera, and the same transplants in Morland Gold organic potting compost above – beans, chard, and lettuce

Tomatoes in Morland Gold organic potting compost on the left, and compost with affected horse manure on the right

Quiz Lesson 16

	Question	Multiple choice
1	Animal manure, say one year old or more, can be used as compost for mulching.	True or false?
2	Which of these describes mature compost which is suitable for mulching beds? Choose the answer which covers most aspects.	A The colour is more dark than light. B Texture is open and crumbly, rather than large, sticky lumps. C Most of the original ingredients are not recognisable. D The smell is neutral, even a little earthy and pleasant. E All of these.
3	Why should animal manure be mostly decomposed before being applied as a mulch?	A To increase the nutrients in the mulch. B It then holds most nutrients in a water-insoluble form, and is more crumbly – easier for sowing and planting. C To remove the smell.
4	It is not worthwhile to use compost which you know contains many weed seeds.	True or false?
5	When buying green waste compost (made from municipal garden waste), which is most worth checking?	A Which recycling centre it's from. B That it doesn't contain any wood. C That it contains Christmas trees collected by the local authority. D That it has been through a 15 mm / 0.6 in sieve, or finer.
6	What do you need to remember about the pH of spent mushroom compost (SMC)?	A That it's usually fairly acidic, and must be tested on a small area of garden first. B That's it's usually fairly alkaline, and needs to have sulphur added to it. C That it's usually neutral and fine for all uses (but check with your supplier).
7	Can you use wood chips as a mulch on beds and paths? Choose two answers.	A On paths yes, in a thin layer. B On beds only if decomposed – and mostly like compost – if sowing carrots, or planting salads and small seedlings. C No, never.
8	Which type of organism is mostly responsible for the decay of wood? Choose three answers.	A Earthworms. C Millipedes. B Fungi. D Woodlice.
9	How do you ensure woodlice don't cause damage in your propagating area?	A Keep sowings on the ground. B Remove decaying wood from the whole area. C Keep the lights on overnight. D Keep it dark at all times.
10	What is the simplest way to discover whether horse manure is contaminated with aminopyralid weedkiller?	A Smell the manure – it will have a strong chemical smell. B It will have a darker colour. C You will still be able to see bits of bedding in it. D Test it by sowing some peas, beans, potatoes or tomatoes. E Use a commercial testing kit, even though they are rare and expensive.

Module 6
A new bed
and the
Small Garden

A new bed – plantings and harvests over five years

This lesson is about one bed. We assembled, filled and planted it on 7 May 2015.

Below I describe the timeline of harvesting those May plantings, followed by a second and a few third plantings in that same year. We then look at subsequent years of growth in this bed. I used it to trial some exotic vegetables, in terms of the UK climate, and some rarely grown ones too.

BED CONSTRUCTION

The sides are treated softwood, measuring 15 × 5 cm / 6 × 2 in. The treatment, as much as I could discover, was with micronised copper applied under pressure. If softwood is not treated, it goes rotten within about five years. I prefer beds without sides, partly to avoid this issue of treated wood. On the other hand, single beds, in grassy/weedy areas like this, work better with permanent sides.

The end pieces measure 1.27 m / 50 in, and the sides 2.26 m / 89 in. The inside area is 3.66 m^2 / 39 ft^2.

The compost volume was half a cubic metre by measure, but three quarters in practice, because of how we firmed it down. In weight, this is at least half a tonne, depending on moisture content.

In our area you can buy this amount of compost for around £40 / ≈ $50, which is excellent value for the produce it grows over many years. Ask around for deals in your area, and buy in bulk if you can, to save money and packaging.

The compost was cow manure on the bottom layer, and green waste on the top layer. I had wanted to use homemade compost, but that May I had none spare because we had spread it all.

PLANT SPACINGS 2015

I've plotted out the spacings I used in the drawing, opposite. The drawing is to scale and the numbers on left are distances in cm between each row. The numbers in brackets are how many plants were in each row. Only carrots and radish were direct sown as seeds.

Correct spacing comes from understanding which vegetables can be closely planted, as opposed to those needing room to grow. Two extremes are radish and broccoli:

- A May sowing of radish is harvested and gone within six to eight weeks; here they were a 'catch crop' between the lettuce, using space that was free while the lettuce became established. The lettuce continued cropping after the last harvest of radish, whose speed of growth allows close spacing of 1 cm / 0.5 in between each radish in the row.

- At the other end I planted just three broccoli plants, because I know how large they grow, and how long they crop for. They look too spaced out when newly planted, but soon fill the space and use it for a long time.

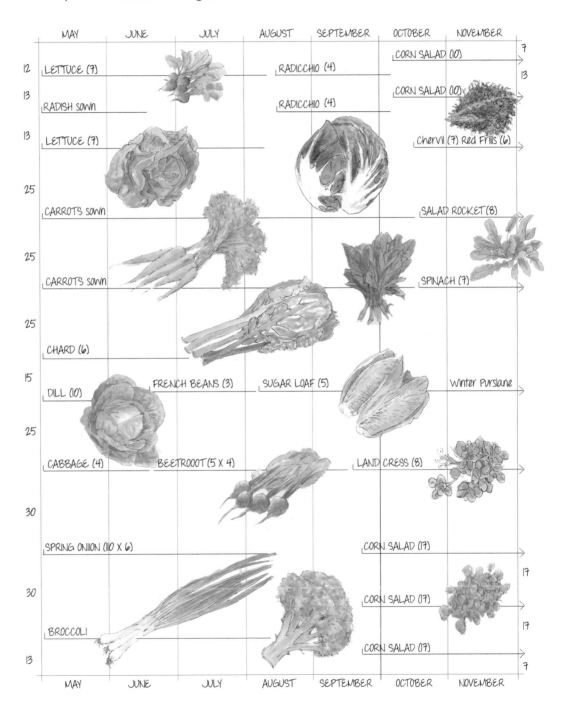

	MAY	JUNE	JULY	AUGUST	SEPTEMBER	OCTOBER	NOVEMBER	
						CORN SALAD (10)		7
12	LETTUCE (7)				RADICCHIO (4)			13
13	RADISH sown				RADICCHIO (4)	CORN SALAD (10)		
13	LETTUCE (7)					Chervil (7) Red Frills (6)		
25	CARROTS sown					SALAD ROCKET (8)		
25	CARROTS sown					SPINACH (7)		
25	CHARD (6)							
15	DILL (10)		FRENCH BEANS (3)	SUGAR LOAF (5)		Winter Purslane		
25	CABBAGE (4)		BEETROOOT (5 X 4)		LAND CRESS (8)			
30	SPRING ONIION (110 X 6)				CORN SALAD (17)			
30					CORN SALAD (17)			17
13	BROCCOLI				CORN SALAD (17)			17
	MAY	JUNE	JULY	AUGUST	SEPTEMBER	OCTOBER	NOVEMBER	7

187

PLANTINGS / SOWINGS AND HARVEST

May

Everything we planted could also have been planted in April, because these are frost tolerant vegetables. Fleece / row covers are advisable in April because of cold winds (more so than against frost), but are optional in May. The bird netting was more important, to protect seedlings from pigeons, sparrows and rabbits.

The frame which supports my netting here is a commercial product, rather more elaborate than needed. You can make your own hoops from 4 mm / 0.2 in high tensile wire, or use alkathene water pipe, with wood such as bamboo inserted in the ends, to push in the soil.

June

We enter summer and growth speeds to a maximum. You can see it has taken carrots four whole weeks to 'get going' and reach the small seedling stage, but now they are growing fast. It's similar for spring onions, flimsy for a long time then suddenly strong and tall.

On 10 June I transplanted three module-sown French bean plants, close to the dill which was soon to finish.

Harvests through June were all leaves: lettuce, 400–500 g / ≈ 1 lb weekly, radish and chard, and I cut all the cabbage hearts on 20 June, giving 0.8 kg / 1.8 lb. I twisted (not pulled) out the stalks, and then planted five clumps of multi-sown beetroot (three to four plants in each), in the row where the cabbage had been growing just an hour earlier.

Although there was no cardboard under the compost, you can see how few weeds managed to grow up to the surface. Only couch grass needed a few brief sessions with a trowel, where it was creeping in along the edge.

From top 7 May – edges are ready to screw together for the new bed

The bed is assembled, filled, and ready to sow or plant

Making holes for module-raised plants on the same day

From top Six days later – a slight frost, but no harm to these plants; we then fleeced over

24 May – Edward helped to roll up the fleece, and to place hoops for bird netting

4 June – it has now been four weeks since the bed was made

4 June – first harvests of lettuce, chard, and radish

Every seven to ten days, from March to November, we mow close to the edge to keep it tidy, reduce slug numbers and diminish the vigour of grass and weeds. Every month we pull the longer grasses and weeds next to the boards (you could also use shears to keep that edge tidy).

July

The chard had been sown in early April, and was flowering by early July when I twisted it out. We harvested spring onions every week in July, and lettuce leaves as needed. Towards the end of the month we picked 260 g / 0.6 lb of broccoli and 350 g / 0.8 lb of French beans.

August

August saw a few final spring onions and lettuce, 560 g / 1.2 lb of broccoli, the last beans, and 4.61 kg / 10.2 lb of carrots. I gently pulled the largest carrots, as they started to push upwards a little. The carrots were straight and lovely, even though it's commonly claimed that adding compost makes them fork.

On 10 August the lettuce finally rose to flower after nine weeks of harvests, and I planted six chicories of a hearting variety, which produce red radicchios in autumn.

September

This was a month of many plantings, like a second spring. Our oceanic climate, with mild winters (see Lesson 2), makes it feasible to grow winter salads outside. In colder climates, grow these in a cloche, a polytunnel or in boxes/containers – wherever you have weather protection and light.

The final carrot total from this small area was 6.9 kg / 15.2 lb. I was fortunate to suffer no damage from root fly maggots; if they are a problem in your area, use a mesh cover.

I propagate more plants than I think I need, and this helped in keeping the bed full.

From top 20 June – cabbage and more lettuce ready to pick

Couch grass roots, removed from the inside edge using a trowel

8 July – strong new growth, with spring onions ready and beans flowering

These lettuce have given five weeks of harvests from the outer leaves, and there is more to come

From top 2 August – the main harvests are beans (nearly finished), broccoli and first beetroot

20 August – a carrot harvest, 17 weeks since sowing seeds in compost and two-year-old manure

For example, every August I module-sow masses of coriander, chervil, spinach, salad rocket and mustards, for plantings after summer harvests, and to fill any gaps. Think of these vegetables as an alternative to green manure for ground cover; other possibilities are mizuna and radish, which both grow quickly.

The lamb's lettuce (corn salad) were sown two seeds per module on 5 September, and I transplanted some when still tiny, after clearing the broccoli on 26 September. The rest remained in modules in the greenhouse until mid-October, after I had harvested the last radicchios.

AUTUMN HARVESTS AND LAST PLANTINGS

Chicories deserve to be more widely grown – here are their advantages:

- They grow best in autumn, from summer sowing (here, early July works well).

- They have few insect pests – only seedlings are at risk of slug damage in wet weather.

- They give high yields and often with dense hearts, and their self-blanched leaves are half bitter, half sweet.

Every few days in November, I cut a sugarloaf chicory from the five on this bed, photos right, and the hearts/heads averaged 700 g / 1.5 lb each. They are tasty in salads, stir-fries and roasted too (*see Stephanie Hafferty's book,* The Creative Kitchen[1], *for more recipe ideas*).

From mid-October there were decent harvests of mustard, rocket and chervil, but less so of spinach, which I had sown a little too late. The best date here for sowing spinach is 10 August.

After the final harvest of sugarloaf chicory, and twisting out the stumps, came the year's final planting. It was winter purslane / Claytonia / miners' lettuce, module-sown in late September – it crops well outside in winter months.

From top 16 September – 4.6 kg / 10.1 lb carrots have already been taken from these two rows

16 September – the final harvest of carrots gave 2.3 kg / 5.1 lb

From top 16 September – new plantings of module-sown mustards, salad rocket, spinach and land cress

19 October – lamb's lettuce at both ends after broccoli and radicchio; the sugarloaf is hearting

From top 29 November – the bed has harvests of lamb's lettuce, mustards, rocket, spinach and land cress; purslane has just been planted

13 January – the unprotected salads are keeping healthy, growing slowly in the short days

11 April – after a winter of occasional harvests there are still leaves to eat, while salad rocket is now flowering

The winter was unusually mild, as the photos, left, show, with so much new growth. There were only 29 nights of frost altogether, against an average of 48, and no nights were colder than –4°C / 25°F. Daytime maxima averaged around 10°C / 50°F, above average by 1.5°C / 2.7°F. However, at the solstice there are only eight hours between sunrise and sunset, and the low amount of light restricts growth, sometimes more than low temperatures.

Most weeks during December to April saw small harvests, including lamb's lettuce, mustards, rocket, spinach, chervil, land cress, and Claytonia.

THE NEXT FOUR YEARS

2016

I added no more compost until after the harvests of August 2016. We reaped the benefit of having trodden the contents firm when making this bed in 2015: it sank very little during the first year. Then in 2016 I tried some different plants:

In mid-April I module-sowed green lentils from the kitchen jar, just to see how they might perform in the UK. Germination and growth were both excellent, but in August the harvest of dry lentils was only 230 g / 0.5 lb, from masses of small pods and with just two lentils in each – fiddly to pick and shell. After twisting out the plants, I popped in some spinach.

Yacon (*Smallanthus sonchifolius*) grows sweet and watery tubers, of low calorie content. I had kept root buds from the previous year's plants. In November, after a slight frost, I levered out the tubers, and the weight from six plants totalled 11.3 kg / 25 lb. They have a great flavour and are worth growing, if you have the space and can find plants.

The Carlin peas are an old British variety, grown for harvests of dry peas in late summer. In August we picked and podded 0.94 kg / 2.07 lb of dry peas, a labour of love but more worthwhile than the lentils! They cook up to a firm texture, and have a decent flavour. Spinach followed these peas as well.

2017

The compost level was still good, and, since there was little shrinkage, I spread just one 40 l / 1.4 ft³ sack of

From top Mid-June 2016 – spring plantings of lentils, yacon and Carlin peas

August 2016 – left to right, lentil, yacon, and dry pea pods on the Carlin plants

Above, from top August 2017 – Chinese artichoke (*Stachys*) on the left and French beans on the right, interplanted with leeks

December 2017 – the leeks grew well after the French beans had finished in September; *Stachys'* leaves die in winter

Left, from top 10 August – soybeans are ready to harvest for edamame; Green Shell are on the left and Siverka are on the right

16 October – the soybeans have been cleared, and 60 l /21.1 ft³ of Dalefoot wool compost has been spread as a 2 cm / 0.8 in mulch

multi-purpose compost in late winter. It would then be another 20 months before adding more compost, in October 2018.

Ten years earlier I had grown Chinese artichoke (*Stachys affinins*, related to mint), and had been disappointed with the small harvest. Meanwhile I kept hearing about their amazing flavour, so grew them again in half of the bed, planting the small, ribbed tubers in April after removing the spinach.

At the other end I let the Medania spinach crop until June, then twisted it out to plant French beans. In July I also popped in eight modules of multi-sown leeks (two or three leeks in each), in the small spaces between French bean plants, with the leeks barely visible at first.

The harvest of Chinese artichokes was again small, fiddly and disappointing. Unless you are a chef looking for something different, I advise you not to bother. They also regrow from any tiny tubers left in the ground, so you need to keep pulling those until June.

French beans cropped well through summer and into September, while the leeks struggled for light and moisture. However they had clearly made some strong roots because they grew superbly in autumn, after I had removed the bean plants. I did a similar interplant in 2018, again with good results.

2018

After clearing the artichokes and a final leek harvest in April, the bed was empty until mid-May, and I didn't add any compost at this stage.

SOYBEANS

I grew these for edamame, or green soybeans. I like their flavour and texture, and had been reading that they can be grown in our climate (Zone 8b). However it's a cool 8b, and summer afternoons average only 21–22°C (low seventies °F).

I was unsure what to expect, as soybeans prefer warmer weather. Plant breeders have responded by producing a variety called Siverka, adapted to cooler weather by fruiting more quickly, partly through growing fewer leaves.

Soy plants are killed by frost but need a long season of growth, so I sowed them in modules in the greenhouse. Also in the greenhouse, I dared to sow a different variety of Green Shell in mid-April (earlier than I ever sow French beans for outdoor growing), while I sowed the Siverka at a more 'correct' time, in early May.

It turns out that soy plants resist cold (not frost) better than French beans, and the April sown Green Shell grew fast in a warm May, after being planted on the 10th. The later planting of Siverka was more affected by a June drought, despite watering.

The compost of this bed now has some invading roots from the dwarf plum tree, which is next to the shed. In a wet summer this is not important, but, in 2018, the moisture taken by those tree roots caused smaller harvests. I gave water, but not enough for maximum growth.

Picking began in early August and continued for a month, until the beans became drier and harder. I did not weigh the fresh harvests, but they contributed to several tasty meals. Green Shell gave the most edamame, because they stayed green for longer than the Siverka.

For dry soybeans (shelled), the Siverka gave 790 g / 1.74 lb in early September, and the Green Shell gave 770 g / 1.69 lb in mid-September. I found soybeans worthwhile, but 2018 was unusually warm.

The bed was then empty for a month, until we planted winter salads in October. These would have been better planted in September – the late planting resulted from an unexpected trial of new varieties for a magazine photoshoot.

Before planting, I spread 60 l / 2.1 ft³ of Dalefoot wool compost, the one which performed so well in the trial from Lesson 16.

The fastest grower through winter was pak choi, despite most of its larger leaves suffering insect holes, probably from flea beetles – a result of warm weather. Normally flea beetles are less common in autumn. On the other hand, something always eats pak choi.

The best result was Valentin lamb's lettuce, so hardy and with few pests eating its leaves. I started cutting in January, while the nearby cos lettuce were looking woeful – not helped by fleece having blown off in December. It was mid-January before some cold weather established, then I relaid the fleece/row cover. It sat directly on the plants, just above ground level: less prone to being ripped by wind than if suspended on hoops.

From top 18 October – new plantings are Valentin lamb's lettuce, Winter Density lettuce, Samish spinach F1, and Yuushou pak choi, all sown 36 days earlier in modules in the greenhouse

December – we had laid fleece on hoops over the bed in October, but it kept blowing off; these plants have frozen a few times

From top 26 March 2019 – a frost of
−3°C / 37°F, and this is the morning
that I planted the bed

26 March – after transplanting
seedlings and sowing carrots, which
I then covered with fleece; I also
transplanted fennel between the
spinach – small module plants

9 May – clearing spinach by twisting,
to make room for the fennel to grow
and swell

30 May – just six weeks since planting
and sowing; the harvests are lettuce
and pea shoots

2019

Following the mulch in October 2018, a layer of just 3 cm /
1 in, we didn't spread any more compost or feeds in 2019.
During the summer there were many second plantings,
even third and fourth ones.

I had no precise plan but this is what happened. I mention
'no plan' because it shows how you can improvise when
you have some experience. Also, you need a 'backlist' of
plants and seeds ready at any time.

- For beginners, I recommend making a rough plan in
  winter, and to start raising plants by late February if
  you can.

*It's always good to have more plants than you need,
for popping in unexpected places where gaps
arise. Also for when you change your mind about
plantings, perhaps because of unforeseen weather,
or because pests eat some plantings and you need
replacements.*

Through winter 2018–19, lamb's lettuce, spinach and pak
choi were all growing. By March I had removed these
winter vegetables, except for the spinach.

The plantings on 26 March were all new. This was
prompted by the arrival of Huw Richards with his camera:
he wanted to film me planting *One Bed*, a video which is
still buried in his archives – he had a mighty busy year as
it turned out. His *One Bed* book became 2019's largest-
grossing garden book in the UK.

I carried on making the video, at four different dates
through the year; it shows the progression of growth and
new plantings, and you can see it on YouTube: *One bed,
results of succession plantings all year*.

Do follow these photos closely, to see the incredible
results of interplanting. I was thrilled to have three
plantings in the same year, in the same place and with no
feeding. Then I managed a fourth planting in the same
year, which is unusual in this climate.

On 29 July I sowed winter radish in modules: a green
mooli type, long and firm. We transplanted them three
weeks later, in the small amount of free space between the
French beans, which were still cropping. All four of the
2019 plantings in the bed's middle section grew without
any new additions of compost or other feeds.

Like all summer plantings of brassicas, insects ate the radish leaves at first, but through autumn this reduced, and the radish grew enough healthy leaf to end up weighing 220 g / 0.5 lb each. They are colourful, dense, and way more long-lasting than spring radish.

The next step was to spread 3 cm / 1 in of compost in December, and to make a rough plan by March. In early 2020 I needed space for trial plantings of different vegetables (for magazine photoshoots) and this bed has proven ideal, as illustrated in the two photos, right, from April 2020.

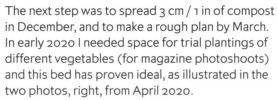

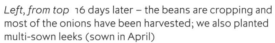

Left, from top 16 days later – the beans are cropping and most of the onions have been harvested; we also planted multi-sown leeks (sown in April)

After another eight days – you can see strong growth again, plus new plantings of chicory and leeks

By 31 August – radish are planted between the beans, and growth is strong after some thundery rain

By 18 September – harvests could now be made from chard, celery, radish, leeks or beetroot

23 October – a harvest of radicchio, radish, celery, leeks, chard and beetroot; the main job now is harvesting

Right, from top 20 April before picking leaves from plantings of 16th March, all fleeced throughout

Same day after picking 2.3 kg / 5.1 lb leaves of pak choi, rocket, spinach and lettuce

On 12 May we had a −2°C / 28°F frost, and all plants survivied including the fennel, and two lettuce for hearts

Further viewing

YouTube – *Space race: see how closer or wider spacings speed growth and harvests*. In this video I explain how closer or wider spacings speed growth and harvests

More tips on growing chicory in my YouTube video – *Grow chicory for beautiful hearts of radicchio, dense and bittersweet, or for chicons*

1   *The Creative Kitchen*, Stephanie Hafferty – available to buy from Stephanie's website: nodighome.com

Quiz Lesson 17

	Question	Multiple choice
1	How much time do you need to wait before planting a newly filled bed, which has weeds below the bed filling?	A You don't need to wait. B Wait until it has rained a couple of times. C One week. D Three to four weeks.
2	How much new compost did this bed need before spring plantings, in its second year (2016)?	A 5 cm / 2 in of multi-purpose compost. B A thin layer of homemade compost. C None.
3	Why did the bed need so little new compost in 2016?	A Because we walked on the compost to make it firm, before the first plantings in May 2015. B Because of the compost types we used. C Because the bed always had plants growing in it.
4	Can you plant vegetables in the same holes / exact place in which the previous planting grew?	A This works only with beetroot. B No. C Yes.
5	In early spring, why might you use a fleece / row cover / reemay to protect plants? Choose two answers.	A To shelter leaves and stems from cold winds. B To shield plants from hot sun. C To increase the temperature of the bed, before sowing and planting. D To protect plants from birds and rabbits.
6	Do root vegetables fork when they are sown in compost, spread as a mulch on a no dig soil surface?	A No, this is a myth. B Sometimes, if the soil had been particularly weedy. C Always, because the soil below is too firm.
7	In temperate climates (not polar or tropical), which is the best time to sow salad plants for winter picking?	A Late summer and early autumn (August and September at Homeacres). B Midsummer (July at Homeacres). C Mid to late autumn (October and November at Homeacres).
8	New plantings grow poorly after you clear soybeans.	True or false?

Growing abundance – two years of planting and cropping in the Small Garden

I crop the Small Garden here at Homeacres in a varied and productive way. There are three beds of 1.5 × 4.5 m / 5 ×14.7 ft, and I plant four blocks on each bed with different vegetables.

With 12 different vegetables growing at any one time, and throughout most of the growing season, my aim is to demonstrate and explain:

- No dig in a small area, and how to manage it for a high output.
- How to crop a diverse range of vegetables over a long period, say three fresh each day from May to November, and some in winter too.

This was how my son Edward and I envisaged it, when starting the *Small Garden Project* on YouTube in September 2017. Then he left for university, and we now film during his vacations; some filming is also done by David Adams, my local videographer.

HISTORY

In the 1960s to 1980s, this area was a shed with a hard floor and a coal fired boiler, which heated the nursery greenhouses. There are still slabs and gravel in the soil, making it difficult in places to push in a cane, or hammer in a stake. From the 1990s the nursery fell derelict; until later there were a few chickens plus many weeds.

In November 2012 I set to work, and it was my first clearing job for vegetables at Homeacres. First harvests were in April 2013, when there were also a lot of slugs. Now the ground is mostly slug free, from being tidy.

A GOOD SPACE, SMALL DRAWBACKS

Lack of sun is only a small negative because you can grow a lot with say a half, or even a quarter, of a day of direct sunlight. There is still daylight when the sun itself is not shining and plants still grow, as you can observe a little in winter's dull weather. This garden has sun for about two thirds of the time.

We keep the edges pruned and weeded, with extra time needed because of a wild border beyond the fence.

Above, clockwise from top left 25 November 2012 – creeping shrubs and weeds from the neighbouring garden, all to cut off. Clearing underway – shrubby stems will either be burnt, or chopped for the base of the middle bed. The next day – I have cut down the large weeds and left their roots in the soil; we are now mulching. 28 November – all done, and I have planted the nearest bed with salad from my old greenhouse

Below, from left A paving slab that I found in April 2013, when trying to plant perennial kale.
13 May shows the light contrasts – both the shed and the house create some shade.

- Bindweed, spurges and ivy appear regularly in summer, from Gert's garden on the other side.
- Ivy and honeysuckle need pulling off the wood, two or three times a year.
- Three times a year we cut the stinging nettles behind the shed, and pull some out if they spread in.
- The grass edge is mown and trimmed.

Edge maintenance takes longer than weeding the beds and paths, where very few weeds appear, and there are no perennial weeds.

We also apply 3 cm / 1 in of new compost once a year, between autumn and early spring. This happens either before planting vegetables to overwinter – such as spinach, spring onions and lamb's lettuce – or after a last harvest in autumn. One application of compost grows two crops, and I use no other amendments.

In November 2018 I started mulching paths with old wood chips. Prior to that, the paths had received 3 cm / 1 in of compost in 2013 and 2014, then nothing for four years. However there are always bits of wood and compost spreading out from the bed mulches.

A YEAR OF PLANTING – 2018

Overleaf is a bird's-eye overview of the Small Garden planting plan for 2018.

The cold start to 2018 saw occasional harvests and no gardening until late March, when I spent two hours tidying plants and weeding – I removed yellowing, older leaves as well as slugs. The mesh cover on the chard was to keep birds off, and a fleece cover on spinach was to keep warmth in.

Spring
A first transplanting on 2 April included onions, beetroot, peas, kohlrabi, calabrese, cabbage, turnips, radish, lettuce, fennel, dill and coriander. Mostly they were four-week-old plants.

We sowed carrots with some radish, but the carrot seedlings were eaten by slugs when tiny, because it was a damp and cool April. I don't regret attempting the early sowing: we lost only a few seeds and a little time. In other years it would have worked, with warmer weather.

From top December solstice 2017 – some harvests in early winter

February 2018 – unfleeced spinach, winter leeks, and salads

7 April – raking new compost in the Small Garden, before spring plantings

29 April – Steph with slow new growth of spring plantings, after a cold April

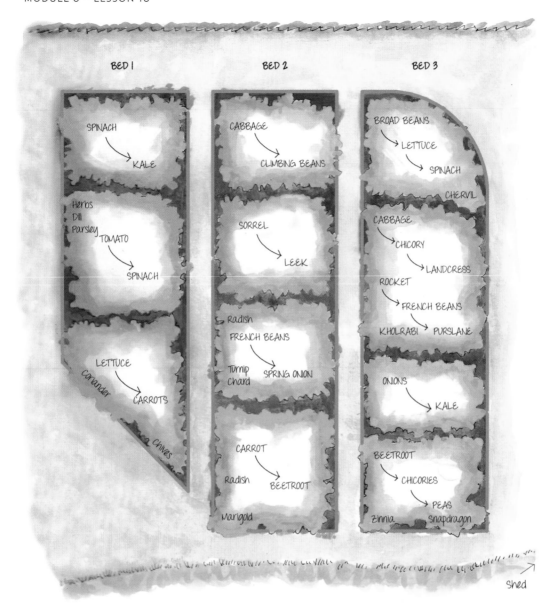

Subsequently a resowing of carrots on 16 April was successful, in rows very close to the young radish.

Harvests were of spinach, salad leaves and leeks, in small amounts because of cool weather. This period of lean harvests continued as normal (the hungry gap) until the middle of May.

From mid-May, harvests become more exciting. The first few picks of lettuce taste especially sweet, and they suddenly become abundant here at this time. Wild rocket grew from some self-sown plants, and the radish went quickly from being small and tender to large and firm, even tough if left too long.

Early summer

Late May through June is my favourite harvest time. Growth changes from hesitant to exuberant, and there are new flavours every week. We picked cabbage hearts, baby beetroot and tender broad beans in early June, carrots from mid-June, and calabrese by the end of June. Cherry tomatoes then followed in early July.

Summer keeps you busy

Harvests increase in July, as plantings of early spring give a final flourish, combined with first pickings from beans, new salads and tomatoes. This month of high summer in 2018 had the biggest weight of harvests.

At different times throughout summer, you take a final harvest from each planting. Then twist out any remaining plants, level the surface and replant. Only the carrots were direct sown.

- 6 June – we intersowed carrot seeds in drills between lettuce.

- 7 June – we cleared sorrel and planted 20 leeks, from modules multi-sown on 5 April.

- 7 June – we cleared chard and planted eight French beans, from modules sown on 14 May.

- 7 June – we cleared over-wintered spinach, spread compost, and planted six kale, from modules sown on 9 May.

- 7 June – we twisted out kohlrabi and planted eight French beans, from modules sown on 14 May.

- 10 June – after we had twisted out cabbage, we planted eight Czar runner/pole bean for dry seeds, from modules sown on 14 May.

- 16 June – we pulled the last carrots and planted 13 beetroot, from multi-sown modules sown in late May.

- 27 June – we cut off broad bean plants after their last harvest, then planted 24 lettuce from a sowing on 4 June.

Left, from top Harvest of 26 March – a leek and some leaves

13 May – still mostly spring leaves, with the first lettuce and a radish too

17 May – a mix of lettuce, just before their first pick of 0.75 kg / 1.7 lb of leaves

After a harvest on 17 May of lettuce, spinach, chard, wild rocket, radish, turnip, sorrel and herbs

Right, from top 25 May – everything looks better after rain, and there are no weeds

21 June 2018 – Small Garden harvests of carrots, broad beans, spring onion and lettuce

You can see how many May to June sowings and plantings are possible. All through summer and early autumn there is a progression of possible sowings – as late as September for lamb's lettuce.

A look at each bed in autumn

The photos, right, from 20 November are to give you a closer look at each bed, and the varied plantings as winter approaches. Carrots and beetroot could be harvested to store, any time from now. I had already pulled 3.3 kg / 7.3 lb of leeks; see how many are still there.

I pulled the last carrots on 14 December, and there was some damage from root fly maggots – laying a mesh cover over from August would have reduced this problem. Beetroot stayed in the ground until needed, all through the winter, and withstood a frost of −6°C / 21°F. There were another 1.53 kg / 3.37 lb of leeks in January.

DECIDING WHAT TO PLANT AND WHERE

It works better to be flexible with areas that are planted with different kinds of vegetables, rather than delimiting, say, a precise quarter of each bed. Partly because some vegetables need more space, but also because you want to eat more or less of each one.Linked to this approach is the understanding that rotation need not be over four years, nor precise (*see the crop rotation myths in Lesson 6*). There is no requirement for a fixed length of time between plants of the same family, but some time is good, when practical for your needs. The first column in my table shows what preceded each planting of spring 2018.

2018 PLANTINGS AND HARVESTS

In this temperate climate of Zone 8, I can grow two crops a year of many vegetables. The table opposite shows examples of first and second & third crops in 2018. It's a quick job to twist out the remains of the first vegetable and pop in the second, without adding compost or other amendments throughout the summer.

From top 15 September – a view of the Small Garden from the drone

29 September – all second plantings since May

7 November – autumn closes in, but there are still many harvests

From top Bed 1 – carrots, coriander, parsley, spinach and kale

Bed 2 – beetroot, spring onions and leeks

Bed 3 – peas, kale, salads and spinach

Apart from the direct sown carrots, I sow seeds in trays or modules in the greenhouse.

The table overleaf shows which harvests arrived when, and in what quantity. For example, the 24 lettuce we transplanted in early April gave large amounts of leaves for over two months. Ease of managing the growth comes from regular picking, whether you need the leaves or not – you may need to give some away.

Left, from top
20 December – a range of vegetables for winter

A January pick of kale, 0.22 kg / 0.49 lb; spinach, 0.21 kg / 0.46 lb; beetroot, 1.51 kg / 3.33 lb; salads, 0.5 kg / 1.1 lb; and purslane is growing

Right, from top With a Small Garden harvest in late February

A Small Garden harvest on 13 May

2018 PLANTING PLAN		
Bed **Sept 2017**	**1st planting 2018**	**2nd & 3rd plantings 2018**
1 Tomatoes, mizuna	Lettuce plants (24)	Carrots Oxhella
1 Kale, peppers	Coriander, dill, fennel, parsley	Tomatoes (7), basil, parsley
1 Spinach	Spinach	Cavolo Nero (6), TD kale
2 Chicory	Carrots Nantaise, radish Poloneza	Beetroot Boltardy
2 Chard	Chard, turnips (6), radish (5), spinach (5)	French beans, Spring Onion
2 Sorrel	Sorrel, spring leaves	Peppers (2), leeks Oarsman
2 Leeks, parsley	Cabbage Greyhound (6)	Climbing beans Czar
3 Bulb fennel, corn salad	Beetroot Avon Early	Chicory 506TT, radicchios, peas to overwinter (small)
3 Mustards	Onion Sturon, multi-sown (18 × 3)	Kale Red Devil
3 Rocket	Azur Star kohlrabi (6), calabrese Parthenon (2)	Kohlrabi, French bean (8), land cress, chervil, claytonia
3 Kaibroc	Broad beans	Lettuce, fennel, spinach

From top 8 August – pinching out tomato tops and more side shoots

With a harvest in mid-October

2018 SMALL GARDEN HARVESTS			
Vegetable	Harvest period	kg	lb
Leeks, planted July 2017	to April	1.92	4.23
Rocket, planted Sept 2017	to May	0.34	0.75
Spinach (1), planted Aug 2017	to May	1.23	2.71
Sorrel, planted May 2015	to May	0.44	0.97
Chard, planted July 2017	to May	0.89	1.96
Herbs	April–May	0.26	0.27
Radish, turnip	May	1.92	4.23
Lettuce (1)	May–July	6.06	13.36
Kohlrabi	June	0.91	2.01
Cabbage hearts	June	1.12	2.47
Broad beans (inc. pods), planted Nov 2017	June	1.30	2.87
Carrots (1)	June–July	4.30	9.48
Beetroot (1)	June–July	2.41	5.31
Calabrese	June–July	1.48	3.26
French beans	Jul–Sep	5.94	13.10
Peppers	Jul–Sept	2.93	6.46
Tomatoes	Aug–Oct	12.71	28.02
Onions	early Aug	5.30	11.68
Kale	Aug–Dec	8.76	19.41
Lettuce (2)	Jul–Oct	6.10	13.45
Leek	Sep–Dec	4.76	10.49
Beetroot (2)	Sep–Dec	1.81	3.99
Dry beans Czar	Oct	2.21	4.87
Radicchio	Sep–Nov	6.88	15.17
Spinach (2)	Oct–Dec	0.83	1.83
Fennel	Nov	1.95	4.30
Chervil etc	Nov–Dec	0.33	0.73
Carrots (2)	Dec	7.45	16.42
Claytonia	Dec	0.98	2.16
TOTAL		**94 kg**	**206 lb**

This highlights an aspect of growing which is so different to shopping: the garden keeps giving! And it links to a saying I hear from old farmers: 'To have enough, you need to have too much.' The changing pattern of weather and pests, every year, means that harvests cannot be predicted, so plant a little more than you expect to need.

RR on YouTube – *Small Garden* video, 9 September 2018:

I have learned a lot from you and now my neighbours also get free vegetables during the growing season.

One thing we can be sure of is the amazing variety of seasonal produce, and how harvests vary through each season in a way that matches the conditions. For example, tomatoes taste better in August than they do in February.

Left, from top Early March sees the first new planting of 2019 – multi-sown radish between overwintered garlic

Here, equinox is the average time for making many new plantings of four-week-old seedlings

Fleece covers were on all plantings until 28 April, when it warmed up – we have just removed them

5 May was 2019's final frost – there was no damage to these lettuce; the mesh cover is against rabbits

Right, from top
By 8 May spring is in full flow

17 June – 2.1 kg / 4.63 lb of Lilla spring onions; we pulled 1–3 plants from each clump, leaving four onions per clump

25 June – the middle bed has new seedlings, with mesh against damage by rabbits

The potato harvest of Casablanca in early July gave 5.1 kg / 11.2 lb from the five remaining plants

2019 PLANTING PLAN
The plan for three beds, showing what will be in each section over the coming months
(Veg in bold means it's ready for cropping)

BLOCK	JAN/FEB	MARCH	APRIL	MAY	JUNE	JULY	AUGUST	SEPTEMBER	OCTOBER	NOVEMBER	DECEMBER
BED ONE											
1	Kale	**Kale** Potatoes	Potatoes	Potatoes	**Potatoes** Beetroot	Beetroot	Beetroot	**Beetroot**	**Beetroot**	**Beetroot**	**Beetroot**
2	Spinach	**Spinach**	**Spinach**	**Spinach**	Leeks	Leeks	Leeks	**Leeks**	**Leeks**	**Leeks**	**Leeks**
3		Spring onions	Spring onions	**Spring onions**	**Spring onions**	Spring onions	Chicory	**Chicory**	**Chicory**	**Chicory**	
4	Herbs	**Herbs**	**Herbs**	**Herbs**	**Herbs**	**Herbs**	**Herbs**	**Herbs**	**Herbs**	**Herbs**	**Herbs**
BED TWO											
1	Garlic	Garlic	Garlic	Garlic French beans	French beans	**French beans**	**French beans**	Spinach	**Spinach**	**Spinach**	**Spinach**
2	**Leeks**	Carrots Radish	Carrots **Radish**	Carrots	**Carrots** Kale	Kale	Kale	**Kale**	**Kale**	**Kale**	**Kale**
3	Spring onions	**Spring onions**	**Spring onions**	**Spring onions**	Endive	Endive	Dill Coriander **Endive**	**Dill** Coriander **Endive**	Dill Coriander **Endive**	Dill Coriander **Endive**	
4		Dill and coriander	**Dill and coriander**	Lettuce	**Lettuce**	**Lettuce** Fennel	Fennel	**Fennel**			
5	**Beetroot**	Lettuce	Lettuce	**Lettuce**	**Lettuce** Carrots	Carrots	Carrots	**Carrots**	**Carrots**	**Carrots**	
BED THREE											
1	**Spinach**	**Spinach**	**Spinach**	**Spinach** Tomatoes	Tomatoes	**Tomatoes**	**Tomatoes**	**Tomatoes** Spring onions	Spring onions	Spring onions	Spring onions
2	**Salads**	**Salads**	**Salads**	Aubergines Sweet peppers	Aubergines Sweet peppers	**Aubergines Sweet peppers**	**Aubergines Sweet peppers** Salad rocket	**Aubergines Sweet peppers** Salad rocket Chervil	Salad rocket Chervil	**Salad rocket Chervil**	**Salad rocket Chervil**
3	Kale	**Kale** Beetroot	Beetroot	**Beetroot**	**Beetroot**	Carrots	Carrots	Carrots	**Carrots**	**Carrots**	**Carrots**
4		Pea shoots	**Pea shoots**	**Pea shoots**	Swede	Swede	Swede	Swede	Swede Lamb's lettuce	**Swede** Lamb's lettuce	**Swede** Lamb's lettuce

2019 PLAN AND HARVESTS

Far left is my plan for 2019, which includes a few overwintered plantings in the first months. Plans like this are a starting point. Weather, pests and seed quality cause alterations.

The total harvests for 2019 were 170 kg / 375 lb, shown in the table overleaf. This compares to the 94 kg / 206 lb total from 2018, and is higher because I grew some more productive vegetables like early potatoes. Also it rained more, and I was intercropping more often.

Further viewing
In September 2017 we made a video to introduce the Small Garden – *Small Garden (1), varied growing & regular harvesting from 3 beds 5 m / 16 ft long*. There are many subsequent Small Garden videos about plantings, harvests, successes and failures!

Left, from top Picking French beans in July with photographer Jason Ingram, for a series of articles in *Which? Gardening* magazine

July 29 – a harvest of the Lilla bulb onions; behind are multi-sown leeks which followed spinach

29 August – the mesh over the carrots is against both rabbits and root flies; the chicories to the left are also under mesh

Right, from top With the covers removed you can see all the growth; since January there have already been harvests of 103 kg / 227 lb

Drone view – the garden of 25 m² / 269 ft² needs three minutes per week of weeding the paths and beds

16 September – with tomatoes now cropping at their peak; I am about to plant spring onions beneath them

6 October – by now the swedes are swelling, the leeks and chicories are cropping, and there are a few carrots too

2019 SMALL GARDEN BY HARVESTS, BY MONTH			
Month	Vegetable	Total weight kg	Total weight lb
January	Beetroot, leeks, spinach, kale	6.7 kg	14.77 lb
February	Spinach, kale, leek	1.7 kg	3.75 lb
March	Beetroot, spinach, leek	7.99 kg	17.61 lb
April	Spinach, Claytonia, radish spring onion, kale, herbs	5.87 kg	12.94 lb
May	Spinach, lettuce, spring onion, radish, Claytonia, kale, beets, herbs	24.73 kg	54.52 lb
June	Spring onion, lettuce, carrots, beets, potatoes, kale, pea shoots, spinach, garlic	20.93 kg	46.14 lb
July	Potatoes, salad leaves, beetroot, carrot, kale, a few first beans, tomatoes	19.32 kg	42.59 lb
August	Salad (mostly endive), beans, tomato, kale, onion	16.05 kg	35.38 lb
September	Tomatoes, kale, salads, leek	14.73 kg	32.47 lb
October	Tomatoes, leeks, 2 each of kale and chicory, salad (mostly endive)	17.63 kg	38.87 lb
November	Carrot, leeks, radicchio, beets, spinach	15.94 kg	35.14 lb
December	Carrots, beets, swede, chicory, leeks	18.41 kg	40.59 lb
	TOTAL	170 kg	375 lb

Half harvest 26 May, Small Garden

Quiz Lesson 18

	Question	Multiple choice
1	You need direct sunlight throughout the day to grow vegetables.	True or false?
2	If there are large slabs of stone or concrete in soil, that still have soil around them, is it vital to get them out before planting?	A No, except for ones protruding above surface level. B Yes, they will be a problem in the future.
3	How should you work out what to plant where?	A It's always best to divide the plot into equal quarters / halves / thirds. B Work clockwise and alphabetically around the plot, so you know what's where. C Don't limit yourself to planning the plot in precise and non-varying sections.
4	Complete the old farmers' saying as given in the lesson: 'To have enough, you need to have . . .'	A Too much. B The right seed. C Little waste. D Plenty of space. E Love.
5	In 2018, which of these needed more time?	A Weeding the beds and paths. B Keeping the edges tidy.
6	Which time of year saw the most first harvests, from vegetables planted in 2018?	A April to early May. B From mid-May, and through June. C July.
7	During 2018, which were the two highest-yielding vegetables per area?	A Lettuce and tomatoes. B Carrots and broad / fava beans. C Beetroot and czar dry beans.
8	How many new plantings of vegetables were there, between June and September?	A Four. B More than twelve. C Nine.
9	In 2018, how many lettuce plantings gave the five months of harvests?	A Two. B One. C Three. D Four.

Module 7

A summary and the final quiz

Lesson 19
No dig distilled

No dig is a simple and easy method. You are now equipped to profit from it. Along with your soil and plants.

A SUMMARY

1 Soil is undisturbed, its organisms can work and multiply. With no dig you build on the existing network of life.

2 Organisms are fed with organic matter on the surface, as in nature but faster. This is because decomposition has already happened in compost heaps, together with a multiplication of microbes. Compost enables soil organisms to work their magic more quickly.

3 Plant feeding is about biology (fungi etc.) more than chemistry (nutrients/minerals). No dig increases the ability of plants to find food which is already there.

THE THREE MAIN BENEFITS OF NO DIG

- Speed.
- Ease.
- Productivity.

For example, you can plant into a new bed created on weeds, and on the same day. Even with perennial weeds still alive underneath.

Problems diminish and gardening becomes easier, in particular because weeds appear less, since their healing properties are not needed by healthy soil.

No dig uses less compost than an equivalent dug area, because no carbon is lost from cultivation, and active soil life increases fertility.

From top Charles' no dig market garden in September 2019 – 1000 m^2 / 0.25 acres of beds; use the same approach for one bed or 100 beds

Homeacres' no dig garden 29 October – no compost or feeds have been applied for ten months, showing how nutrients are available all the time without using fertilisers

From top Feeding soil organisms by mulching with old cow manure (compost) on newly planted garlic in October

New summer planting of lettuce after clearing onions, with no bed preparation or compost added

Other benefits of no dig are:

- Soil is lively, structured and does not stick to your boots.
- You can walk on your beds, thanks to soil's firm but open structure.
- Absence of digging means no compaction layers, and therefore no fermentations due to anaerobic conditions, which otherwise produce alcohol. This results in fewer slugs – no 'slug pubs'!

TENETS

1 Feed the soil not the plants.

2 Straightforward, easy methods are not lazy but clever.

3 Do your homework on the best sowing and harvest times for each plant.

FIRST STEPS

- Practise. Start with a pot or a box, on or in a window, and sow a few salad leaves (they are fast to harvest). Perhaps buy a few plants as well, for rapid results.
- Plant a first early potato in spring in a small bag or bucket of compost, it's fun and fast to harvest. Remember the leaves need space to grow!
- Make one small bed, say 1.2 m² / 12.9 ft², and pack it full of multi-purpose compost. Sow or plant in that, and keep replanting as soon as gaps appear.

FINAL THOUGHTS

- Don't use synthetic fertilisers or chemicals – they are bad for soil life.
- Buy some mesh to keep pests off, perhaps also some fleece (30 gsm thickness) to warm early plantings in spring.
- No dig is great for flowers and ornamental plants: fewer weeds, and gorgeous blooms.

May your garden glow with health.

Left, from top One of Charles' no dig flower borders at Homeacres in July

A bed of 1.2 x 2.3 m / 3.9 x 7.5 ft in May, with first plantings of beetroot, carrots and peas for shoots

The same bed in October, with harvests of second and third plantings: radish, celery, leek, radicchio, beetroot and chard

Right, from top The west side of Homeacres in a January frost, with chard, lettuce, spinach, broad beans and kale

The west side of Homeacres in September, with dew on the asparagus ferns in the foreground

The west side of Homeacres on 20 December

Course quiz Lesson 19

	Question	Multiple choice
1	With no dig, why might year one be different from subsequent years? Choose the answer which covers most aspects.	A Perennial weeds often regrow through mulches of organic matter, and the regrowth needs regular pulling. B Your need for compost and other organic matter is higher, to build fertility and suppress weeds. C Any or all of these. D There may be a residual and high population of slugs, as well as other soil pests.
2	Why do you think that water drains more quickly through undisturbed, no dig soil with a mulch of organic matter? Choose the answer which covers the most aspects.	A The structure is intact, with soil aggregated into crumbs and air passages between. B All of these. C Surface organic matter absorbs water more quickly than surface soil. D There is no interruption in downward flow, from a capillary line forming between dug / tilled soil and undug / untilled soil.
3	With no dig, how is it possible to achieve 100% clearance of most perennial weeds?	A Because you dig them out first. B Because undisturbed soil does not need to recover with weeds. C Because perennial weed roots get burned by compost mulches.
4	Which answer best describes a soil type which is no good for no dig?	A Sand. B Clay. C Any soil is fine. D Stony.
5	Choose the only one of these statements that does not define the difference between soil (topsoil) and compost, as described in Lesson 15.	A Soil is more dense and maintains the same volume for many years, whereas compost reduces in volume. B Weeds pull out of compost more cleanly and easily than out of soil. C Wet soil is more likely to squash into a compacted, airless state than wet compost. D Compost contains fewer nutrients than the same volume of soil.
6	How long would you wait before sowing or planting, after you had laid cardboard and then spread 4–6 in / 10–15 cm of compost on top of a thick mat of weeds?	A One week for the compost to settle. B Two months for the cardboard to decompose. C No time. D Four months for the weeds to die.
7	In the preceding question, when would the correct answer have been incorrect? Choose the answer which covers most aspects.	A If the compost was loose and fluffy. B If the compost was still warm and steaming. C Any or all of these. D If the time of year was not correct for the intended sowings and plantings.
8	Which answer describes the difference(s) between annual and perennial weeds? Choose the answer which covers the most aspects.	A The roots of perennial weeds survive winter and regrow the following year. B Most annual weeds drop seeds before winter and then die, although a few continue as small plants, or even germinate in winter. C All of these. D Perennial weeds mostly propagate by spreading their roots; annual weeds mostly by dropping seeds. E Year one mulches need to exclude light for longer where there are many perennial weeds.
9	Second plantings in summer need extra compost before they go in the ground.	True or false?

	Question	Multiple choice
10	Soil fertility and successful growth – what determines how plants grow? Choose the incorrect statement.	A Successful growth is enabled by and needs a high level of biological activity. B Roots need air, moisture and space, as much as nutrients being available. C Soil fertility is exclusively about nutrients in soil.
11	Why do compost heaps need slatted sides?	A To allow entry of air. B To let weed roots out. C They don't. D To allow moisture to pass in and out.
12	Which is the most important factor to consider when deciding how to orientate your beds and paths? Choose the answer which covers the most aspects.	A Slope. B North–south alignment. C Point of access. D A combination and balance of all these. E Making the best use of your site.
13	Why might the four-year rotation be less relevant in no dig gardening as described in this course, compared to gardening in dug or tilled soil? Choose the answer which covers the most aspects.	A The soil becomes and stays healthy with a balance of many organisms, resulting in strong growth and healthy plants. B The lack of weeds makes it easy and viable to space closely, and to interplant. C All of these. D There is no need for soil preparation specific for different plantings, therefore the same bed can grow many kinds of vegetables.
14	Which timing is recommended for spreading compost, for successful growth all year and every year?	A Spread some every time you put in new plants and seeds, to feed that planting. B Spread some once a year to maintain and increase biological activity in soil. C Spread some every three years before growing heavy feeders.
15	Which are the best widths for paths and beds respectively? Choose the answer which covers the most aspects.	A 30 cm and 1 m / 12 in and 3.2 ft. B 40 cm and 1.2 m / 16 in and 3.9 ft. C All of these or others, depending how you like to garden. D 50 cm and 1.5 m / 20 in and 4.9 ft.
16	Which approach to weeding is recommended in this course?	A A big hit every spring is the main job needed. B Weed every month or two, after a big mulching when you start. C Keep beds weed-free at all times and don't worry about path weeds. D Little and often weeding all the time – of paths too if there are no sides – after a thorough initial mulch.
17	You can make fine compost without the heap temperature rising above 40°C / 104°F.	True or false?
18	Which of these are important for decomposing organic matter? Choose the answer which covers the most aspects.	A Bacteria. B Fungi. C Brandling red worms. D All of these.

Quiz
answers

Lesson 1

	Answer	Feedback
1	False.	As observed by myself *(see Lesson 4)*, F.C. King and Arthur Guest, among others.
2	A No dig results in fewer pests and diseases.	
3	D Slugs.	Ruth Stout gardened in a climate zone where slugs are not common.
4	C In almost all cases, I don't see the benefit of soil tests for gardeners.	Just noticing that growth of weeds is abundant usually tells you that the soil is working well.
5	A Straight after you stop forking / digging / tilling.	Soil organisms have evolved to feed and breed, if only we leave them alone. We can build their population rapidly, with mulches of organic matter *(See Lesson 2)*.
6	A Mulching and managing weeds, so as to have very few.	Having few weeds is vital for time-efficient success with plantings and harvests.
7	A Soil fertility, as more than measuring nutrients.	In general I suggest allowing your feeling for jobs (does this feel right and good?) to grow alongside your mental analysis of what you are doing.
8	D Jobs you don't need to do.	Discover more yourself, with a careful application of common sense.
9	False.	Actually both were very rare, and even among organic gardeners the use of compost was less common than it is now.

Lesson 2

	Answer	Feedback
1	D Sometimes – if there are many weeds and they are growing strongly.	It depends on how many weeds are there. *We'll cover this in more detail in Lesson 10.*
2	A To feed soil life with mulches, whatever you plan to grow.	Balanced feeding of plants happens indirectly, via feeding of soil life and maintenance of the fungal network.
3	True.	You can also walk on beds.
4	False.	The organisms in undisturbed and well-mulched soil maintain drainage and aeration.
5	D Most nutrients in compost, and nutrients processed by organisms in soil, are not water-soluble.	This is why you can spread compost at any time of year, even before winter.
6	C You can plant on the same day as you mulch the bed, when it's the correct season and the compost is mature.	A rapid return of food helps to pay for the compost!

Answers continue

	Answer	Feedback
7	A No – it's better not to have them, as they provide a haven for slugs and other pests.	There are times when sides make sense. *We'll cover this in more detail in Lesson 17.*
8	C It's entirely your choice, mostly it works well to keep cropping vegetables.	Although do sow them if you wish – the point is they are not obligatory.
9	C Both of these can be a starting point.	
10	A Absolutely not – perhaps only if you have spread very little compost in the preceding winter.	

Lesson 3

	Answer	Feedback
1	False.	The key to success is soil life, which is present and can be encouraged in the same way in all types of soils. Results may vary, but the methodology does not. Mulch materials vary with climate.
2	A On a site which lies very wet, from drainage being slow in that area. C To reduce the amount of bending down (though there is always some bending required).	On most soils, and for most people, I recommend beds with only a slight raise.
3	C All of these.	*See Lesson 8 for more on this.*
4	A It slows the rise of the temperature in spring, and generally keeps soil cooler.	The cooling effect of straw in sunlight is an advantage for hot climates, but mostly not in temperate climates.
5	A It holds more moisture in spring, but can prevent rain reaching the soil in dry conditions, unless the rain is heavy.	In damp climates with potential slug problems, straw and hay mulches are best avoided, so that the surface can sometimes be dry.
6	A By mulching the surface with compost.	Surface organic matter leads to more active soil life and a more open, stable soil structure.
7	False.	This was shown at Sissinghurst! Grow more intensively, all season long, and keep improving soil fertility *(See lesson 14).*

Lesson 4

	Answer	Feedback
1	A All of these.	
2	A Three hours.	This is my experience of many years. Other people might dig more quickly!
3	A Most vegetables grow in half a year, in climates with this level of warmth. B A four-year rotation is less important than usually thought.	In cooler climates – or shorter seasons – fewer, but still a large number of vegetables, mature in half of the growing season *See Lesson 6 for more on rotation.*
4	False.	On the programme, I saw that at first they struggled to explain the success of no dig! I appreciate this trial even more, for how the result was not expected.

Lesson 5

	Answer	Feedback
1	D In this trial there is a four-year rotation for each bed.	
2	A Moisture was retained better in the dug strip. C Weeds grew more in the no dig strip.	
3	A Yields were 50% lower in 2013, from not spreading mulch (compost). D To have more harvests for the same amount of work. E More time would be needed for weeding if no compost was added.	In a funded research station, it would be interesting to compare the difference between mulched and unmulched strips over a period of several years.
4	A All of these.	Then, in 2018, the total yield was lower because of dry conditions, even though we watered some of the time.
5	A A no dig approach, leaving soil life undisturbed.	This question arises from my experience of the Shumei farm at Avebury, which I found both stimulating and difficult!

Lesson 6

	Answer	Feedback
1	False.	The four-year rotation comes from farms with animals.
2	B Occasional stepping on the bed is fine, to walk over or reach the middle. C Any time you need to, but don't dance on them after heavy rain!	
3	A Large enough to accommodate the roots or rootball.	
4	D Any of these, as long as it is free draining.	
5	B Good drainage and air.	
6	C It retains warmth and moisture.	
7	False.	It's fine not to harden off as long as plants are covered with fleece in cold conditions, straight after planting.
8	C In paper sacks, crates or boxes, unwashed.	
9	D You don't need to feed them.	
10	C Yes, it is.	Give a decent amount of water so it soaks in, to minimise the proportion lost to evaporation.

Lesson 7

	Answer	Feedback
1	A Some that is as thick as possible.	The cardboard should be brown not shiny, and with no tape or staples. Overlap the edges by 15 cm / 6 in.
2	A The width which works best for you and your space.	
3	True.	
4	C Because it's assumed that soil is loose after digging and tilling, and therefore will be squashed down again. D Because it's commonly thought that roots need mechanically-loosened soil to grow in.	The statement hides an assumption of prior digging and tilling, which does not apply in no dig.
5	A A slight slope, or holes made in the concrete to ensure drainage, and 20 cm / 8 in of compost.	You need to avoid stagnating water – drainage is vital.
6	False.	North to south alignment is a factor to consider, but is only one of many and may not be the most important, depending on the layout of different sites.

	Answer	Feedback
7	A Access points for paths. D Any general slope of the land.	
8	A No dig soil is firm and stable, so there is little erosion in heavy rain.	
9	A When the compost has settled and won't roll into the path.	

Lesson 8

	Answer	Feedback
1	True.	
2	D All of these.	
3	D Gravel adds nothing for soil life, structure or drainage.	
4	A Any width.	Whatever suits you best – there is no right or wrong (however narrow paths save space).
5	False.	Mulched paths develop good soil structure, and are useful for plant roots; keeping them in the same place saves much time.
6	D All of these.	
7	False.	They may disturb the top layer of compost, but will not damage plants.
8	True.	However this can make path width very narrow, if the plants are large ones like cabbage and courgette. It's mainly a question of access, and my rule of thumb is to keep a planting distance between the bed edge and the plants, of a third to a half of the plants' eventual size.
9	B 6–10 weeks, depending on the thickness of the cardboard.	These are approximate figures, to give you an idea of how soon you may need to re-cover (unless the weeds are already dead).
10	C When on the surface, they do not deprive plants of nitrogen but even add some, once decomposed.	This is as long as they're only on the surface, and not mixed into soil.

Lesson 9

	Answer	Feedback
1	A The soil is left in a state of shock, and weeds help recovery.	
2	False.	Mulching can wither and kill off the majority of perennial weeds.
3	A It makes strong, woody growth, which can push through the mulch.	
4	False.	The roots may last for up to six months – but often for only a few months.
5	A Dock (*Rumex* of either type).	Dock roots can take a long time to expire, so it's best to remove at least the top and fattest part before mulching.
6	A Annual weeds need a year of light exclusion to die.	Annual weeds also die when pulled by hand, or when hoed.
7	A Through seed dispersal.	
8	A From seeds in new mulches. C From seeds blowing in.	
9	True.	As long as the root is cut, it will not regrow.
10	A Weed little and often.	

Lesson 10

	Answer	Feedback
1	A It excludes light.	Excluding light will stop weeds from photosynthesising, so they will die.
2	C No, although it's always an option.	The layer of cardboard is not vital, if you're blessed with few weeds when starting out.
3	C Cardboard prevents weeds from growing upwards in search of light, for about six to ten weeks, until it decomposes.	Slowing the growth means that it's unlikely the weeds will arrive at the surface before having died.
4	A It degrades. C It's free.	
5	True.	
6	C Because it has to be all wool, yet most (but not all) carpets contain plastic threads and synthetic chemicals.	Wool carpets are best as they are a natural product, but they are rare.
7	B Dig out the main stems, and just a few of the larger roots attached to them.	

	Answer	Feedback
8	False.	Planting dates are governed by the best season for whichever vegetables you grow. For example, you can make beds in winter, to plant in the spring.
9	A Any time.	Start today if you have the time and materials!
10	B No – unless the soil life has eaten all the mulch, which is unlikely if you applied 5 cm / 2 in before the season began.	
11	C Either before or after – whichever is easier.	

Lesson 11

	Answer	Feedback
1	A How much light it excludes.	If the material doesn't exclude enough light, you can supplement with cardboard – landscape fabric for example.
2	A That it's moist.	Moisture cannot penetrate the polythene, so make sure the soil is moist before laying.
3	False.	They love it, as long as it doesn't dry out.
4	A Many perennials	Polythene mulch should only be used when there are many perennial weeds to remove.
5	A Lay a plastic mulch with compost on top.	It is horribly difficult to remove buried plastic, and removing it disturbs soil life, breaking its structure in the process.
6	False.	Once the main mass of perennial weeds is dead (year one), there is simply no more need to use them.
7	True.	
8	C Polythene mulches, used for a few months to kill weeds, are bad for soil organisms. D It's quicker to mulch a large area with cardboard, compared to polythene.	

Lesson 12

	Answer	Feedback
1	A Whenever you see weed seedlings.	The habit you need is a willingness to be proactive: to pull weed seedlings when it's still optional, rather than vital.
2	B To cut stems and / or dislodge weed roots, so they die in situ.	This works when weeds are small, unless conditions are very dry.
3	A Skim the surface shallowly, and in a circular motion – this also breaks up surface lumps.	Mostly this is a job from late winter to early spring.

Answers continue

	Answer	Feedback
4	A Because you are mostly removing small weeds, which pull easily without a tool. C Because there won't be many weeds.	The exception to this is if your soil has a lot of bindweed and marestail, which weaken more quickly when a trowel is used to remove longer pieces of root than those you can pull by hand.
5	C It's a relief to see the vegetables again, after having been covered by weeds!	
6	A If they are grasses, and the weather is damp. C If the weeds have more than one true leaf, so are bigger than seedlings, and the weather is damp.	
7	A All of these.	
8	C To make success more likely with subsequent plantings, and to save time yourself.	

Lesson 13

	Answer	Feedback
1	A They give shelter to slugs.	
2	A Compost is organic matter, in a stable, soil-enhancing form.	
3	C Fungi and bacteria, then worms – all or any of these.	The process of decomposition depends on heat in the heap, according to the quantity and quality of materials added.
4	A After bacterial decomposition has happened, and the temperature has fallen. D When only small and occasional additions mean little heat, therefore the heap behaves more like a wormery.	
5	A 50:50.	These are proportions to aim for, but this is not always easy to manage!
6	A Kitchen scraps. D Weed leaves. E Grass cuttings. F Coffee grounds. G Horse poo.	
7	D All of these.	
8	B During spells of hot summer weather, when you are adding few fresh, moist leaves.	
9	B Yes.	As long as the heap is being added to regularly – non-slatted sides help.
10	False.	They will break down in cooler heaps, and would regrow in a heap only if exposed to light before they wither.
11	B Add them to the compost heap.	Two exceptions, for heaps below 55°C / 131°F, are onion white rot and brassica clubroot.

12   A   Temperatures above approx 55°C / 130°F kill
         most weed seeds.
     B   The higher microbial count from cooler heaps
         (less than 50°C / 122°F), especially of fungi, is
         excellent for soil biology.

13   B   In level layers.

14   B   Completely fill a smaller compost bin / bay / heap.

15   C   Turning it once.

Lesson 14

	Answer	Feedback
1	B Soil structure and moisture retention / drainage of excess water are more important for growth than soil chemistry.	
2	C All of these.	
3	C No, not normally.	Perhaps, with an exception of sandy soil, and if you had applied only thin mulches so far.
4	B Nutrients stay in compost when rain droplets run through.	
5	B Yes, if you need to, and the first planting grew healthily.	
6	C It builds structure by helping to aggregate soil into crumbs, when soil is undisturbed.	
7	True.	This is an important benefit of a compost heap, beyond just recycling nutrients.
8	B In late summer and autumn, when there are fewer brassica pests.	
9	True.	It's good to sow them as early as possible, so they have time to make a lot of growth before their flowering season of early summer.
10	C You don't.	You may find it most convenient to apply the compost in late spring, before summer plantings.
11	False.	You are feeding soil organisms around the plants, which will benefit both the plants growing now, and subsequent plantings.

Lesson 15

		Answer	Feedback
1	A	Because the bed was originally filled with soil, which, unlike compost, doesn't condense.	
2	D	All of these.	
3	C	It has changed colour to orange, grey or pale blue, with a smell of putrefaction.	This is because air and moisture cannot enter or leave through any channels.
4	B	No – best results are from using only compost.	Compost ensures maximum fertility and moisture retention; soil is not needed except for in deeper beds, and then only as a base layer.
5	B	Because it helps to retain the volume of the bed.	Make sure that the soil contains no roots of perennial weeds, such as bindweed.
6	C	Because you then have space to add compost to the surface each year.	This is what maintains the high fertility levels, and good structure for growth.
7	C	Wet soil sticks to the weed roots and fingers, while dry soil is often hard.	
8		True.	Bought soil often includes some subsoil, and has been stacked for long enough to kill many soil organisms.
9	B	First plantings (potatoes, shallots, garlic).	Related to the initial aeration – see next question!
10	C	Moving / loosening / digging soil exposes some of it to air (oxygen), which stimulates bacteria, thus decomposing some nutrients and making them available to plants.	This is a reason why crops can grow in cultivated / dug / tilled soil, without adding compost for a number of years. However true fertility is declining, as soil biology and organic matter decrease. Weeds increase, as the soil uses them to improve structure and recover the biology, and diseases tend to increase as well.

Lesson 16

		Answer	Feedback
1		True.	If the bedding was wood, two years old would be better.
2	E	All of these.	
3	B	It then holds most nutrients in a water-insoluble form, and is more crumbly – easier for sowing and planting.	
4		False.	Just make sure you use the strategies I explain, to hoe and rake tiny new weeds from the compost you are spreading.
5	D	That it has been passed through a 15 mm / 0.6 in sieve, or finer.	Even make a visual check, to ensure that it's free of large amounts of plastic and wood.
6	C	That it's usually neutral and fine for all uses (but check with your supplier).	Even if the pH is high, I advise using it, and not worrying about pH.

	Answer	Feedback
7	A On paths yes, in a thin layer. B On beds only if decomposed – and mostly like compost – if sowing carrots, or planting salads and small seedlings.	Preferably only use after stacking for 6–24 months, so they look like compost with woody pieces. Time before use depends on the age and type of wood chip, and also on your climate, because in damp areas larger pieces of wood can be a habitat for slugs.
8	B Fungi. D Millipedes. E Woodlice.	And many others too!
9	B Remove decaying wood from the whole area.	
10	D Test it by sowing some peas, beans, potatoes or tomatoes.	The growing tips will be curled and twisted after 3–4 weeks.

Lesson 17

	Answer	Feedback
1	A You don't need to wait.	As long as you have firmed the compost by treading.
2	C None.	I spread some compost in August 2016, after the first harvests.
3	A Because we walked on the compost to make it firm, before the first plantings in May 2015.	Notice how long the carrots grew in this walked-on, firm compost.
4	C Yes.	
5	A To shelter leaves and stems from cold winds. D To protect plants from birds and rabbits.	The plants may survive without protection, but it increases growth for little expense or time needed.
6	A No, this is a myth.	Undisturbed soil ensures even growth downwards, while a compost mulch increases the harvest.
7	A Late summer and early autumn (August and September at Homeacres).	
8	False.	But people do claim this!

Lesson 18

	Answer	Feedback
1	False.	Half, or even a quarter day of sunlight on plants, can still produce good results. Light is important; sunlight on leaves is a (lovely) bonus.
2	A No, except for ones protruding above surface level.	
3	C Don't limit yourself to planning the plot in precise and non-varying sections.	Be flexible, and above all, grow what you want to eat.
4	A Too much.	Weather, pests and diseases are unpredictable, therefore so is yield.
5	B Keeping the edges tidy.	
6	C July.	This reflects the 'hungry gap' of May, even continuing into June.
7	A Lettuce and tomatoes.	Lettuce yields are usually high, and mostly made up of water, while the tomatoes grew well in a warm summer, with little late blight.
8	B More than twelve.	There are so many possibilities for summer and autumn plantings.
9	A Two.	Picking outer leaves, and not cutting over the top, gives plants a long and productive life.

Lesson 19

	Answer	Feedback
1	C Any or all of these.	
2	B All of these.	
3	B Because undisturbed soil does not need to recover with weeds.	This saves so much time in every subsequent year.
4	C Any soil is fine.	
5	D Compost contains fewer nutrients than the same volume of soil.	
6	C No time.	Make a bed any time, and plant straight away!
7	C Any or all of these.	
8	C All of these.	You need some garden practice to build on these understandings about weed growth, but not too much I hope!
9	False.	This is such a timesaver when one has little spare time.
10	C Soil fertility is exclusively about nutrients in soil.	Learn to ignore the gardening industry's fixation on nutrients being the main requirement for strong growth.
11	C They don't.	Use cardboard to line heaps if yours have slatted sides.
12	D A combination and balance of all these.	
13	C All of these.	
14	B Spread some once a year to maintain and increase biological activity in soil.	Annual mulches also protect the soil surface for a whole year.
15	C All of these or others, depending how you like to garden.	
16	D Little and often weeding all the time – of paths too if there are no sides – after a thorough initial mulch.	An almost weed-free garden is less difficult than imagined by diggers!
17	True.	This will be fungi-dominated compost of great value, perhaps with weed seeds.
18	D All of these.	

Glossary

Annual A plant that completes its life cycle (germination, flowering, seeding, dying) in one growing season

Bed An area of mulched soil for vegetables and flowers, may or may not be raised

Compost Decomposed organic matter, usually dark and crumbly

Compacted soil From damage caused by excessive weight when fully moist: soil remains airless, relatively lifeless, and water can hardly soak in, or drain out

Dibber A wooden, rounded stick used to make holes for planting – I recommend a long one

Digging Soil broken by a spade or fork to c. 25 cm / 10 in depth, with compost incorporated

Drill A channel 2–3 cm / 1 in deep for sowing seeds – made by a rake, hoe or finger

Edging Maintaining the area around any plot so that weeds and bushes don't invade

Fertility The best balance plus combination of soil life, structure and nutrients/ minerals

Firm A natural condition of soil, neither compacted nor loose

Forking Soil loosened and broken by a fork or broadfork, to the depth of the prongs

Humus Organic matter/carbon such as mature compost, with a stable and aerated structure

Manure Animal poo with variable amounts of bedding, decomposed for garden use

Microbes Invisible soil organisms such as bacteria, fungi and protozoa

Mulch Surface material, either to exclude light or feed soil organisms, or both

No dig Soil is not disturbed – its inhabitants are fed with organic matter on the surface

NPK Nitrogen, potassium, phosphorus

Nutrients Food for plants, also called minerals in the USA

Pasture A mix of grasses and other vegetation, as food for grazing animals

Path Access strip between and around beds

Perennial Any plant living for at least 3 years (annual = 1 year, biennial = 2 years)

Permaculture Living / farming efficiently, and according to nature's methods – inspired by Bill Mollison

Plastic Sheets of non-biodegradable mulch, mostly polythene and polypropylene

Rotation Growing plants of the same family in a different place, after any harvest finishes

Sides Optional edging for beds, often made of wood; open, sloping sides also an option

Soil Earth surface that plants root into, the lower levels are subsoil

Sowing Seeds going into drills / holes made in a compost mulch or in propagation trays

Tilth A fine, crumbly surface layer of soil – produced by cultivation

Transplanting Plants going into holes made quickly by a dibber, or more slowly by a trowel

Trials Comparing growth of the same plants in different conditions, not 'scientific'

Vermiculite For aeration of potting composts – made by superheating rock (mica)

Weeds Plants growing where you don't want them

Index

Testimonials

From the online course can be found on this page – https://charlesdowding.co.uk/testimonials/

Trish, May 2020
Thank you so much for your fantastic course, I really enjoyed it. I was attracted to 'no dig' gardening because of the no digging – of course! Who wants to break their back gardening? Also the fact that it mimics nature was appealing, I'd always wondered why we had to faff around with all the digging and adding chemicals when nature gets on perfectly well without us interfering. But the biggest bonus that I wasn't aware of till I did your course was the lack of weeding – that is just the most fantastic thing.

Jerry, May 2020
Despite having grown vegetables (to some degree) for 20 years, I have gained so much new knowledge by studying your Course 1. I am applying this new knowledge to my garden this Spring, gaining new experience and modifying old habits. This has involved improved propagation practices as well as beginning structural changes to my garden, mainly to the paths thus far since I had already prepared the planting beds prior to starting the coursework. But I am also drastically modifying and expanding my composting, expecting to treat the planting beds as you suggest this Fall and Winter. All this has become a primary focus area for me, and I cannot thank you enough for the way you teach and share your knowledge with others. I greatly look forward to learning from Course 2, which I will be beginning very soon.

Sam, Orkney, April 2020
After completing online Course 1, I am growing veg on an exposed site in Orkney. I have gale force winds to keep me plenty sharp! I'd be lost without my max-strength Keder greenhouse. But thanks to your technique of putting very small plants out under fleece and nestling them down into the mulch a bit, I'm already cropping spinach, pea shoots and lettuce OUTSIDE! In April, at 59 degrees North!

Michael, Germany, April 2020
After completing the online Course, I feel the value of the information that I have received is worth much more than the actual cost. Nobody does a better job than Charles of collecting information from experiences and then summarizing and providing this information to the benefit of others. For me, the cost of the online Course was a very small price to pay in order to gain 36 years of experience!

Stewart, May 2020
It's been really useful to work through the course.
I wish I had done it months ago! I already started no dig in January after seeing your YouTube channel but the course content is so much more in depth and the course structure provides a greater understanding. I expect to forget things so I'm grateful I can easily refer back to the lessons. Onward and upwards with the second course now!

Charles Dowding's
No dig gardening Courses

Online Course 2
GROWING SUCCESS

58,000 words, 900 captioned photos and 47 videos. Of these, 33 are exclusive to the course.

Discover how to sow, grow, space, pick and succeed with many different vegetables.
The theme of this course is how to achieve your harvests more easily and quickly.

Charles explains and demonstrates his chosen methods for small and medium scale growing, and how they are time-saving and cost-effective. He gives examples of how you can grow and harvest different vegetables throughout the year.

You learn that a planting plan is advisable, but does not need to be precise. There is advice on propagation, succession and inter-planting, including quick ways to set plants in the ground. Charles describes spacing, picking methods and watering, as well as how to use covers for both warmth and pest protection.

The advice given in Course 2 is based on having a clean and fertile area in which to grow vegetables. The space does not need to be large, and there is a whole lesson about growing in containers.

Lessons are illustrated with tables, diagrams and captioned photos from Charles' highly productive gardens. They all contain 'how to' videos, most of which are exclusive to this course.

Each lesson finishes with a multiple choice quiz, for enjoyment and to consolidate learning. On passing the final quiz, you receive an online certificate, in recognition of your achievement.

Purchase of 'Growing Success' gives you lifetime access. You can refer back to any part of the course at any time.

Online videos, Course 1
NO DIG GARDENING ONLINE

30 videos, 28 of which are exclusive to the course.

The videos are filmed in Charles' gardens at Homeacres, at different times of year. They give you ideas about creating and managing a growing space in all four seasons.

Course 3

Being created through 2020 for publication February 2021. The course contains case studies with videos on how to sow, grow and harvest 17 common vegetables, from seed to harvest.

Charles advises on how to avoid too many problems, including weed growth, and how to reduce insect damage and diseases.

There are lessons about growing under cover, interplanting and companion planting.

For more information on Charles' online courses, please visit his website: charlesdowding.co.uk, and look under the 'Courses' tab.